V. I. Lenin

On Utopian and Scientific Socialism

Articles and Speeches

Fredonia Books
Amsterdam, The Netherlands

On Utopian and Scientific Socialism:
Articles and Speeches

by
Vladimir Ilyich Ulyanov (Lenin)

ISBN: 1-58963-934-0

Reprinted from the 1965 edition

Fredonia Books
Amsterdam, The Netherlands
http://www.fredoniabooks.com

CONTENTS

Page

WHAT THE "FRIENDS OF THE PEOPLE" ARE AND HOW THEY FIGHT THE SOCIAL-DEMOCRATS (*Extract*) 7

OUR PROGRAMME 11

FROM NARODISM TO MARXISM. Article One 16

SOCIALISM AND THE PEASANTRY 23

PETTY-BOURGEOIS AND PROLETARIAN SOCIALISM 32

INSERT TO V. KALININ'S ARTICLE "THE PEASANT CONGRESS" (*Extract*) 41

THE PROLETARIAT AND THE PEASANTRY 42

THE AGRARIAN PROGRAMME OF SOCIAL-DEMOCRACY IN THE FIRST RUSSIAN REVOLUTION, 1905-1907 46

    7. Municipalisation of the Land and Municipal Socialism . . . 46

IN MEMORY OF HERZEN 52

DEMOCRACY AND NARODISM IN CHINA 59

TWO UTOPIAS 66

THE THREE SOURCES AND THREE COMPONENT PARTS OF MARXISM (*Extract*) 71

LEFT-WING NARODISM AND MARXISM 73

KARL MARX. A Brief Biographical Sketch with an Exposition of Marxism (*Extract*) 76

    Socialism 76

    Tactics of the Class Struggle of the Proletariat 79

A CARICATURE OF MARXISM AND IMPERIALIST ECONOMISM (*Extract*) 85

THE IMPENDING CATASTROPHE AND HOW TO COMBAT IT (*Extract*) 87

    Can We Go Forward if We Fear to Advance Towards Socialism? 87

THE STATE AND REVOLUTION. The Marxist Theory of the State and the Tasks of the Proletariat in the Revolution (*Extract*) . 91

Chapter V. The Economic Basis of the Withering Away of the State 91

    1. Presentation of the Question by Marx 91

    2. The Transition from Capitalism to Communism 93

    3. The First Phase of Communist Society 98

    4. The Higher Phase of Communist Society 102

MEETING OF THE ALL-RUSSIA CENTRAL EXECUTIVE COM-
MITTEE, November 4 (17), 1917   110

   2. Reply to a Question from the Left Socialist-Revolutionaries .   110

ALLIANCE BETWEEN THE WORKERS AND THE WORKING AND
EXPLOITED PEASANTS. A Letter to *Pravda*   112

HOW TO ORGANISE COMPETITION?   115

THE IMMEDIATE TASKS OF THE SOVIET GOVERNMENT
(*Extract*)   125

   Raising the Productivity of Labour   125

   The Development of Soviet Organisation   128

SPEECH AT THE FIRST CONGRESS OF ECONOMIC COUNCILS,
May 26, 1918 (*Extract*)   132

DRAFT PROGRAMME OF THE R.C.P.(B.) (*Extract*)   138

   The Basic Tasks of the Dictatorship of the Proletariat in Russia   138

A GREAT BEGINNING. Heroism of the Workers in the Rear.
"Communist Subbotniks" (*Extract*)   151

ECONOMICS AND POLITICS IN THE ERA OF THE DICTATOR-
SHIP OF THE PROLETARIAT   167

   1   167

   2   168

   3   170

   4   171

   5   174

REPORT ON SUBBOTNIKS DELIVERED TO A MOSCOW CITY
CONFERENCE OF THE R.C.P.(B.), December 20, 1919 . . .   178

"LEFT-WING" COMMUNISM, AN INFANTILE DISORDER . . .   184

   VI. Should Revolutionaries Work in Reactionary Trade
Unions? (*Extract*)   184

   X. Certain Conclusions (*Extract*)   185

THE TASKS OF THE YOUTH LEAGUES. Speech Delivered at the
Third All-Russia Congress of the Russian Young Communist
League, October 2, 1920   189

EIGHTH ALL-RUSSIA CONGRESS OF SOVIETS, December 22-29,
1920   206

   1. Report on the Work of the Council of People's Commissars,
December 22 (*Extract*)   206

ON CO-OPERATION   211

OUR REVOLUTION. Apropos of N. Sukhanov's Notes   219

NOTES   223

NAME INDEX   241

WHAT THE "FRIENDS OF THE PEOPLE" ARE AND HOW THEY FIGHT THE SOCIAL-DEMOCRATS

(Extract)

This idea of materialism in sociology was in itself a stroke of genius. Naturally, *for the time being* it was only a hypothesis, but one which first created the possibility of a strictly scientific approach to historical and social problems. Hitherto, not knowing how to get down to the simplest primary relations such as those of production, the sociologists undertook the direct investigation and study of political and legal forms, stumbled on the fact that these forms emerge from certain of mankind's ideas in the period in question—and there they stopped; it appeared as if social relations are consciously established by men. But this conclusion, fully expressed in the idea of *Contrat social*[1] (traces of which are very noticeable in all systems of utopian socialism), was in complete contradiction to all historical observations. It never has been the case, nor is it so now, that the members of society conceive the sum-total of the social relations in which they live as something definite, integral, pervaded by some principle; on the contrary, the mass of people adapt themselves to these relations unconsciously, and have so little conception of them as specific historical social relations that, for instance, an explanation of the exchange relations under which people have lived for centuries was found only in very recent times. Materialism removed this contradiction by carrying the analysis deeper, to the origin of man's social ideas themselves; and its conclusion that the course of ideas depends on the course of things is the only one compatible with scientific psychology. Further, and from yet another aspect, this hypothesis was the first to elevate sociology to the level of a science. Hitherto, sociologists had found it difficult to distin-

guish the important and the unimportant in the complex network of social phenomena (that is the root of subjectivism
in sociology) and had been unable to discover any objective
criterion for such a demarcation. Materialism provided an
absolutely objective criterion by singling out "production
relations" as the structure of society, and by making it possible to apply to these relations that general scientific criterion
of recurrence whose applicability to sociology the subjectivists denied. So long as they confined themselves to ideological
social relations (i.e., those which pass through man's mind
before taking shape*) they could not observe recurrence and
regularity in the social phenomena of the various countries,
and their science was at best only a description of these
phenomena, a collection of raw material. The analysis of
material social relations (i.e., of those that take shape without
passing through man's mind: when exchanging products men
enter into *production relations* without even realising that
there is a social relation of production here)—the analysis of
material social relations at once made it possible to observe
recurrence and regularity and to generalise the systems of
the various countries in the single fundamental concept:
social formation. It was this generalisation alone that made
it possible to proceed from the description of social phenomena (and their evaluation from the standpoint of an ideal)
to their strictly scientific analysis, which isolates, let us say
by way of example, that which distinguishes one capitalist
country from another and investigates that which is common
to all of them.

And, finally, a third reason why this hypothesis for the
first time made a *scientific* sociology possible was that only
the reduction of social relations to production relations and
of the latter to the level of the productive forces, provided a
firm basis for the notion that the development of formations
of society is a process of natural history. And it goes without
saying that without such a view there can be no social science.
(The subjectivists, for instance, although they admitted that
historical phenomena conform to law, were incapable of
regarding their evolution as a process of natural history, pre-

---

* We are, of course, referring all the time to the consciousness of
social relations and no others.

cisely because they came to a halt before man's social ideas and aims and were unable to reduce them to material social relations.)

Then Marx, who had expressed this hypothesis in the forties, set out to study the factual (nota bene) material. He took one of the socio-economic formations—the system of commodity production—and on the basis of a vast mass of data (which he studied for not less than twenty-five years) gave a most detailed analysis of the laws governing the functioning of this formation and its development. This analysis is confined exclusively to production relations between members of society: without ever resorting to features outside the sphere of these production relations for an explanation, Marx makes it possible to discern how the commodity organisation of social economy develops, how it becomes transformed into capitalist organisation, creating antagonistic classes (antagonistic within the bounds of production relations), the bourgeoisie and the proletariat, how it develops the productivity of social labour, and thereby introduces an element that becomes irreconcilably contradictory to the foundations of this capitalist organisation itself.

Such is the *skeleton* of *Capital*. The whole point, however, is that Marx did not content himself with this skeleton, that he did not confine himself to "economic theory" in the ordinary sense of the term, that, while *explaining* the structure and development of the given formation of society *exclusively* through production relations, he nevertheless everywhere and incessantly scrutinised the superstructure corresponding to these production relations and clothed the skeleton in flesh and blood. The reason *Capital* has enjoyed such tremendous success is that this book by a "German economist" showed the whole capitalist social formation to the reader as a living thing—with its everyday aspects, with the actual social manifestation of the class antagonism inherent in production relations, with the bourgeois political superstructure that protects the rule of the capitalist class, with the bourgeois ideas of liberty, equality and so forth, with the bourgeois family relationships. It will now be clear that the comparison with Darwin is perfectly accurate: *Capital* is nothing but "certain closely interconnected generalising ideas crowning a veritable

Mont Blanc of factual material". And if anybody has read *Capital* and contrived not to notice these generalising ideas, it is not the fault of Marx, who, as we have seen, pointed to these ideas even in the preface. And that is not all; such a comparison is correct not only from the external aspect (which for some unknown reason particularly interests Mr. Mikhailovsky), but also from the internal aspect. Just as Darwin put an end to the view of animal and plant species being unconnected, fortuitous, "created by God" and immutable, and was the first to put biology on an absolutely scientific basis by establishing the mutability and the succession of species, so Marx put an end to the view of society being a mechanical aggregation of individuals which allows of all sorts of modification at the will of the authorities (or, if you like, at the will of society and the government) and which emerges and changes casually, and was the first to put sociology on a scientific basis by establishing the concept of the economic formation of society as the sum-total of given production relations, by establishing the fact that the development of such formations is a process of natural history.

Now—since the appearance of *Capital*—the materialist conception of history is no longer a hypothesis, but a scientifically proven proposition. And until we get some other attempt to give a scientific explanation of the functioning and development of some formation of society—formation of society, mind you, and not the way of life of some country or people, or even class, etc.—another attempt just as capable of introducing order into the "pertinent facts" as materialism is, that is just as capable of presenting a living picture of a definite formation, while giving it a strictly scientific explanation—until then the materialist conception of history will be a synonym for social science. Materialism is not "primarily a scientific conception of history", as Mr. Mikhailovsky thinks, but the only scientific conception of it.

Written in the spring
and summer of 1894

First printed in 1894   *Collected Works*, Vol. 1
on a hectograph

OUR PROGRAMME

International Social-Democracy is at present in a state of ideological wavering. Hitherto the doctrines of Marx and Engels were considered to be the firm foundation of revolutionary theory, but voices are now being raised everywhere to proclaim these doctrines inadequate and obsolete. Whoever declares himself to be a Social-Democrat and intends to publish a Social-Democratic organ must define precisely his attitude to a question that is preoccupying the attention of the German Social-Democrats and not of them alone.

We take our stand entirely on Marxist theory: Marxism was the first to transform socialism from a utopia into a science, to lay a firm foundation for this science, and to indicate the path that must be followed in further developing and elaborating it in all its parts. It disclosed the nature of modern capitalist economy by explaining how the hire of the labourer, the purchase of labour-power, conceals the enslavement of millions of propertyless people by a handful of capitalists, the owners of the land, factories, mines, and so forth. It showed that all modern capitalist development displays the tendency of large-scale production to eliminate petty production and creates conditions that make a socialist system of society possible and necessary. It taught us how to discern, beneath the pall of rooted customs, political intrigues, abstruse laws, and intricate doctrines—the *class struggle*, the struggle between the propertied classes in all their variety and the propertyless mass, the *proletariat*, which is at the head of all the propertyless. It made clear the real task of a revolutionary socialist party: not to draw up plans for refashioning society, not to preach to the capitalists and their hangers-on about improving the lot of the workers, not to hatch conspiracies, *but to organise the class struggle of the proletariat and to lead this struggle, the ultimate aim of which is the conquest of political power by the proletariat and the organisation of a socialist society.*

And we now ask: Has anything new been introduced into this theory by its loud-voiced "renovators" who are raising so much noise in our day and have grouped themselves around the German socialist Bernstein? *Absolutely nothing.* Not by a single step have they advanced the science which Marx and Engels enjoined us to develop; they have not taught the proletariat any new methods of struggle; they have only retreated, borrowing fragments of backward theories and preaching to the proletariat, not the theory of struggle, but the theory of concession—concession to the most vicious enemies of the proletariat, the governments and bourgeois parties who never tire of seeking new means of baiting the socialists. Plekhanov, one of the founders and leaders of Russian Social-Democracy, was entirely right in ruthlessly criticising Bernstein's latest "critique"[2]; the views of Bernstein have now been rejected by the representatives of the German workers as well (at the Hannover Congress).[3]

We anticipate a flood of accusations for these words; the shouts will rise that we want to convert the socialist party into an order of "true believers" that persecutes "heretics" for deviations from "dogma", for every independent opinion, and so forth. We know about all these fashionable and trenchant phrases. Only there is not a grain of truth or sense in them. There can be no strong socialist party without a revolutionary theory which unites all socialists, from which they draw all their convictions, and which they apply in their methods of struggle and means of action. To defend such a theory, which to the best of your knowledge you consider to be true, against unfounded attacks and attempts to corrupt it, is not to imply that you are an enemy of *all* criticism. We do not regard Marx's theory as something completed and inviolable; on the contrary, we are convinced that it has only laid the foundation stone of the science which socialists *must* develop in all directions if they wish to keep pace with life. We think that an *independent* elaboration of Marx's theory is especially essential for Russian socialists;

for this theory provides only general *guiding* principles, which, *in particular*, are applied in England differently than in France, in France differently than in Germany, and in Germany differently than in Russia. We shall therefore gladly afford space in our paper[4] for articles on theoretical questions and we invite all comrades openly to discuss controversial points.

What are the main questions that arise in the application to Russia of the programme common to all Social-Democrats? We have stated that the essence of this programme is to organise the class struggle of the proletariat and to lead this struggle, the ultimate aim of which is the conquest of political power by the proletariat and the establishment of a socialist society. The class struggle of the proletariat comprises the economic struggle (struggle against individual capitalists or against individual groups of capitalists for the improvement of the workers' condition) and the political struggle (struggle against the government for the broadening of the people's rights, i.e., for democracy, and for the broadening of the political power of the proletariat). Some Russian Social-Democrats (among them apparently those who direct *Rabochaya Mysl*[5]) regard the economic struggle as incomparably the more important and almost go so far as to relegate the political struggle to the more or less distant future. This standpoint is utterly false. All Social-Democrats are agreed that it is necessary to organise the economic struggle of the working class, that it is necessary to carry on agitation among the workers on this basis, i.e., to help the workers in their day-to-day struggle against the employers, to draw their attention to every form and every case of oppression and in this way to make clear to them the necessity for combination. But to forget the political struggle for the economic would mean to depart from the basic principle of international Social-Democracy, it would mean to forget what the entire history of the labour movement teaches us. The confirmed adherents of the bourgeoisie and of the government which serves it have even made repeated attempts to organise purely economic unions of workers and to divert them in this way from "politics", from socialism. It is quite possible that the Russian Government, too, may undertake something of the kind, as it has always endeavoured to throw some paltry sops or, rather, sham sops, to the people, only to turn their thoughts away from the fact that they are oppressed and without rights. No economic struggle can bring the workers any lasting improvement, or can even be conducted on a large scale, unless the workers have the right freely to organise meetings and unions, to have their own newspapers, and to send their representatives to the national assemblies, as do the workers in Germany and all other European countries (with the exception of Turkey and Russia). But in order to win these rights it is necessary to wage a *political struggle*. In Russia, not only the workers, but all citizens are deprived of political rights. Russia is an absolute and unlimited monarchy. The tsar alone promulgates laws, appoints officials and controls them. For this reason, *it seems* as though in Russia the tsar and the tsarist government are independent of all classes and accord equal treatment to all. But *in reality* all officials are chosen exclusively from the propertied class and all are subject to the influence of the big capitalists, who make the ministers dance to their tune and who achieve whatever they want. The Russian working class is burdened by a double yoke: it is robbed and plundered by the capitalists and the landowners, and to prevent it from fighting them, the police bind it hand and foot, gag it, and every attempt to defend the rights of the people is persecuted. Every strike against a capitalist results in the military and police being let loose on the workers. Every economic struggle necessarily becomes a political struggle, and Social-Democrats must indissolubly combine the one with the other into a *single class struggle of the proletariat*. The first and chief aim of such a struggle must be the conquest of political rights, *the conquest of political liberty*. If the workers of St. Petersburg alone, with a little help from the socialists, have rapidly succeeded in wringing a concession from the government—the adoption of the law on the reduction of the working day[6]—then the Russian working class as a whole, led by a single Russian Social-Democratic Labour Party, will be able, in persistent struggle, to win incomparably more important concessions.

The Russian working class is able to wage its economic and political struggle alone, even if no other class comes to its aid. But in the political struggle the workers do not stand alone. The people's complete lack of rights and the savage lawlessness of the bashi-bazouk officials rouse the indignation of all honest educated people who cannot reconcile themselves to the persecution of free thought and free speech; they rouse the indignation of the persecuted Poles, Finns, Jews, and Russian religious sects; they rouse the indignation of the small merchants, manufacturers, and peasants, who can nowhere find protection from the harassment of officials and police. All these groups of the population are incapable, separately, of carrying on a persistent political struggle. But when the working class raises the banner of this struggle, it will receive support from all sides. Russian Social-Democracy will place itself at the head of all fighters for the rights of the people, of all fighters for democracy, and it will prove invincible!

These are our fundamental views, and we shall develop them systematically and from every aspect in our paper. We are convinced that in this way we shall tread the path which has been indicated by the Russian Social-Democratic Labour Party in its published *Manifesto.*

Written not earlier
than October 1899

First published in 1925   *Collected Works,* Vol. 4
in *Lenin Miscellany III*

FROM NARODISM[7] TO MARXISM

ARTICLE ONE

A legal newspaper recently expressed the opinion that this is no time to dwell on the "antagonism" of interests among the different classes opposing the autocracy. This opinion is not new. We have come across it, of course, with reservations of one sort or other, in the columns of *Osvobozhdeniye*[8] and *Revolutsionnaya Rossiya*.[9] It is natural that such a point of view should prevail among the representatives of the bourgeois democrats. As far as the Social-Democrats are concerned, there can be no two opinions among them on this question. The combined struggle of the proletariat and the bourgeoisie against the autocracy must not and cannot make the proletariat forget the antagonism of interests between it and the propertied classes. To get a clear idea of this antagonism it is necessary to have a clear idea of the profound differences that exist between the points of view of the different trends. This does not imply, of course, that we should reject temporary agreements with the adherents of other trends, both with the Socialist-Revolutionaries[10] and the liberals, such as the Second Congress of our Party[11] declared permissible for Social-Democrats.

The Social-Democrats consider the Socialist-Revolutionaries to be the representatives of the extreme Left group of our bourgeois democracy. The Socialist-Revolutionaries resent this opinion of them and regard it as a mean attempt to humiliate an opponent and to question his sincerity and good faith. Actually, such an opinion has nothing whatever to do with suspicion; it is merely a Marxist definition of the class origin and the class nature of the views of the Socialist-Revolutionaries. The more clearly and definitely the Socialist-

Revolutionaries state their views, the more they confirm the Marxist characterisation of them. Of great interest in this respect is the draft programme of the Party of the Socialist-Revolutionaries published in *Revolutsionnaya Rossiya*, No. 46.

This draft is a considerable step forward, not only in relation to clarity of exposition of principles. The progress is to be noted in the content of the principles themselves, the progress from Narodism to Marxism, from democracy to socialism. Our criticism of the Socialist-Revolutionaries has obviously borne fruit; it has compelled them to lay particular stress on their socialist good intentions and the views which they hold in common with Marxism. All the more glaring, on the other hand, are the features of their old, Narodnik, vaguely democratic views. We would remind those who are prone to accuse us of being contradictory (recognising the socialist good intentions of the Socialist-Revolutionaries, while defining their social nature as bourgeois-democratic) that examples of socialism, not only of the petty-bourgeois but of the bourgeois variety, were long ago analysed in the *Communist Manifesto*.[12] The good intentions of being a socialist do not rule out a bourgeois-democratic essence.

A study of the draft reveals three main features of the Socialist-Revolutionary world outlook. First, theoretical emendations of Marxism. Second, the survivals of Narodism in their views of the labouring peasantry and the agrarian question. Third, the same Narodnik survivals in their view of the impending Russian revolution as non-bourgeois in character.

I said *emendations* of Marxism. Precisely. The whole main trend of thought, the whole framework of the programme, points to the victory of Marxism over Narodism. The latter is still alive (kept so with the aid of injections of revisionism of the latest style), but only as partial "corrections" of Marxism. Let us take the main general theoretical emendation, the theory of the favourable and unfavourable relation between the positive and negative sides of capitalism. This emendation, insofar as it is not completely muddled, introduces the old Russian subjectivism into Marxism. The recognition of the "creative" historical activity of capitalism,

which socialises labour and creates "a social force" capable
of transforming society, the force of the proletariat, denotes
a break with Narodism and a transition to Marxism. The
theory of socialism is founded on the objective development
of economic forces and of class division. The emendation:
"In some branches of industry, especially agriculture, and
in entire countries" the relation between the positive and
negative sides of capitalism "is becoming [how far they have
gone!] less and less favourable". This is a repetition of Hertz
and David, of Nik. —on, and of V.V. with his theory of the
special "destinies of capitalism in Russia". The backwardness
of Russia in general and of Russian agriculture in particular
is no longer regarded as *capitalist* backwardness, but as a
uniqueness justifying backward theories. Alongside the
materialist conception of history we get the time-worn view
according to which the intelligentsia is capable of choosing
more or less favourable paths for the country and of becoming the supraclass judge of capitalism, not the mouthpiece
of the class that is begotten by capitalism's destruction of the
old forms of life. The fact that capitalist exploitation in
Russia takes on particularly repellent forms because of the
survival of pre-capitalist relations is overlooked in typical
Narodnik fashion.

The Narodnik theory stands revealed still more clearly
in the notions on the peasantry. Throughout the draft the following words and phrases are used without discrimination:
the toilers, the exploited, the working class, the labouring
masses, the class of the exploited, the exploited classes. If
the authors stopped to think over the last term ("classes"),
which escaped them unguardedly, they would realise that
the petty bourgeois as well as the proletarians work and are
exploited under capitalism. What has been said of the legal
Narodniks must be said of our Socialist-Revolutionaries: to
them goes the honour of discovering an unheard-of type of
capitalism without a petty bourgeoisie. They speak of the
labouring peasantry, but shut their eyes to a fact which has
been proved, studied, weighed, described, and pondered,
namely, that the peasant bourgeoisie now definitely pre-
dominates among our labouring peasantry, and that the well-
to-do peasantry, although entitled to the designation labouring peasantry, cannot get along without hiring farm-hands

and already controls the better half of the peasantry's productive forces.

Very odd, indeed, from this point of view, is the goal which the Party of the Socialist-Revolutionaries has set itself in its minimum programme: "In the interests of socialism and of the struggle against bourgeois-proprietary principles, to make use of the views, traditions, and modes of life of the Russian peasantry, both as toilers in general and as members of the village communes, particularly its conception of the land as being the common property of all the toiling people." This objective seems, at first blush, to be a quite harmless, purely academic repetition of the village-commune utopias long since refuted both by theory and life. In reality, however, we are dealing with a pressing political issue which the Russian revolution promises to solve in the very near future: Who will take advantage of whom? Will the revolutionary intelligentsia, which believes itself to be socialist, utilise the toiler conceptions of the peasantry in the interests of the struggle against bourgeois-proprietary principles? Or will the bourgeois-proprietary and at the same time toiling peasantry utilise the socialist phraseology of the revolutionary-democratic intelligentsia in the interests of the struggle against socialism?

We are of the view that the second perspective will be realised (despite the will and the consciousness of our opponents). We are convinced that it will be realised because it has already nine-tenths been realised. The "bourgeois-proprietary" (and at the same time labouring) peasantry has already made good use of the socialist phrases of the Narodnik, democratic intelligentsia, which harboured illusions of sustaining "the toiler traditions and modes of life" by means of its artels, co-operatives, fodder grass cultivation, ploughs, Zemstvo warehouses, and banks, but which actually promoted the development of capitalism within the village commune. Russian economic history has thus proved what Russian political history will prove tomorrow. The class-conscious proletariat has the duty to explain to the rural proletarian, without in any way withholding support of the progressive and revolutionary aspirations of the *bourgeois* labouring peasantry, that a struggle against that peasantry is inevitable in the future; it has the duty to explain to him the real aims of socialism, as opposed to the bourgeois-democratic fancies of equalised land tenure. With the bourgeois peasantry against the survivals of serfdom, against the autocracy, the priests, and the landlords; with the urban proletariat against the bourgeoisie in general and against the bourgeois peasantry in particular—this is the only correct slogan for the rural proletarian, this is the only correct agrarian programme for Russian Social-Democracy at the present moment. It was this programme that our Second Congress adopted. With the peasant bourgeoisie for democracy, with the urban proletariat for socialism—this slogan will have a far stronger appeal to the rural poor than the showy but empty slogans of the Socialist-Revolutionary dabblers in Narodism.

We come now to the third of the above-mentioned main points of the draft. Its authors have by now broken with the view of the consistent Narodniks, who were opposed to political freedom on the grounds that it could only result in turning over power to the bourgeoisie. But the survivals of Narodism stand out very clearly in the part of the draft which characterises the autocracy and the attitude of the various classes towards it. Here too, as always, we see that the very first attempts of the petty-bourgeois revolutionary intelligentsia to clarify its conception of *reality* lead inevitably to the complete exposure of its contradictory and superannuated views. (Let us, therefore, remark, parenthetically, that disputes with the Socialist-Revolutionaries should always be reduced to this very question of their conception of reality, since this question alone clearly reveals the causes of our deep-seated political divergence.)

"The class of big manufacturers and tradesmen, who are more reactionary than anywhere else," we read in the draft, "stands more and more in need of the protection of the autocracy against the proletariat".... This is false; for nowhere in Europe is the indifference of the advanced bourgeoisie towards the autocratic form of rule so evident as in our country. Discontent with the autocratic regime is growing among the bourgeoisie, regardless of its fear of the proletariat, in part simply because the police, for all its unlimited powers, cannot crush the working-class movement. In speaking of "a class" of *big* manufacturers, the draft confounds the subdivisions and groups within the bourgeoisie with the

entire bourgeoisie as a class. It is all the more incorrect since
it is the middle and petty bourgeoisie that the autocracy is
least of all capable of satisfying.

"... The landed nobility and the village kulaks stand more
and more in need of such support against the labouring
masses in the villages...." Indeed? Where, then, does
Zemstvo liberalism come from? Whence the attraction for
the enterprising muzhik on the part of the uplift (democratic) intelligentsia and vice versa? Or does the kulak have
nothing in common with the enterprising muzhik?

"... An irreconcilable and growing antagonism is arising
between the existence of the autocracy and the whole economic, socio-political and cultural development of the
country...."

In this they have reduced their own premises *ad absurdum*.
Is it possible to conceive of an "irreconcilable antagonism"
with the entire economic, as well as other, growth of the
country that would not be reflected in the mood of the
classes in economic command? It is one or the other: *Either*
the autocracy is really incompatible with the economic
development of the country; in that case it is incompatible also
with the interests of the *entire class* of manufacturers, trades-
people, landowners, and enterprising muzhiks. That this
class has been controlling "our" economic development since
1861[13] is probably not unknown even to the Socialist-Revolutionaries (although they were taught the contrary by V. V.).
That a government incompatible with the bourgeois class in
general can make capital out of the conflicts between the
groups and strata of the bourgeoisie, that it can make peace
with the protectionists against the free traders, enlist the
support of one stratum against another, and keep up these
equilibristics for years and decades, is borne out by the
whole trend of European history. *Or*, in our country the
manufacturers, the landowners, and the peasant bourgeoisie
"stand more and more in need" of the autocracy. In that
case we should have to assume that they, the economic lords
of the country, even taken as a whole, as a class, do not
understand the interests of the country's economic development, that not even the advanced, educated and intelligent
representatives and leaders of these classes understand these
interests!

But would it not be more natural to assume that it is our Socialist-Revolutionaries who do not understand the situation? Just look: a little further on, they themselves admit "the existence of a liberal-democratic opposition, which embraces chiefly (in point of class) the intermediate elements of the educated society". But is our educated society not a bourgeois society? Is it not bound by a thousand ties to the tradesmen, manufacturers, landowners, and enterprising muzhiks? Can God have possibly ordained for Russia a capitalism in which the liberal-democratic opposition is not a bourgeois-democratic opposition? Do the Socialist-Revolutionaries know of any precedent in history or can they conceive of any case in which the opposition of the bourgeoisie to the autocratic regime *was not* or *would not* be expressed through the liberal, educated "society"?

The muddle in the draft is the inevitable outcome of confounding Narodism with Marxism. Only Marxism has given a scientifically correct analysis, confirmed more and more by reality, of the relation between the struggle for democracy and the struggle for socialism. Like the rest of the world, we have bourgeois democracy and working-class democracy. With us, as with the rest of the world, the Social-Democrats must expose mercilessly the inevitable illusions of the bourgeois democrats and their ignorance of their own nature. With us, as with the rest of the world, the class-conscious proletariat must support the bourgeois democrats in their opposition to the survivals of serfdom and their struggle against them, against the autocracy, without forgetting for an instant that it is a class by itself, and that it has as its class aim the overthrow of the bourgeoisie.

SOCIALISM AND THE PEASANTRY

The revolution Russia is going through is a revolution of the entire people.[14] The interests of the whole people have come into irreconcilable conflict with those of a handful of men constituting the autocratic government or backing it. The very existence of present-day society, which is based on commodity production and wherein the interests of the various classes and groups of population are extremely varied and conflicting, calls for the destruction of the autocracy, the establishment of political liberty, and the open and direct expression of the dominating classes' interests in the organisation and administration of the state. Bourgeois in its social and economic essence, the democratic revolution cannot but express the needs of all bourgeois society.

However, this society, which now seems a united whole in the struggle against the autocracy, is itself irremediably split by the chasm between capital and labour. The people that have risen against the autocracy are not a united people. Employers and wage-workers, the insignificant number of the rich ("the upper ten thousand") and the tens of millions of those who toil and own no property—these are indeed "two nations", as was said by a far-sighted Englishman as long ago as the first half of the nineteenth century.[15] The struggle between the proletariat and the bourgeoisie stands on the order of the day throughout Europe. This struggle has long spread to Russia as well. In present-day Russia it is not two contending forces that form the content of the revolution, but two distinct and different social wars: one waged within the present autocratic-feudal system, the other within the future bourgeois-democratic system, whose birth we are already witnessing. One is the struggle of the entire people for freedom (the freedom of bourgeois society), for democracy, i.e., the sovereignty of the people; the other is the class struggle of the proletariat against the bourgeoisie for a socialist organisation of society.

An arduous and formidable task thus devolves on the socialists—to wage two wars simultaneously, wars that are totally different in their nature, their aims, and the composition of the social forces capable of playing a decisive part in either of them. The Social-Democratic movement has explicitly set itself this difficult task, and has definitely coped with it thanks to its having based its entire programme on scientific socialism, i.e., Marxism, and thanks to its having become one of the contingents of the army of world Social-Democracy, which has verified, confirmed, explained, and developed in detail the principles of Marxism on the basis of the experience of so many democratic and socialist movements in the most diverse countries of Europe.

Revolutionary Social-Democracy has long since indicated and proved the bourgeois nature of Russian democracy, ranging from the liberal-Narodnik to the *Osvobozhdeniye* varieties. It has always pointed out that it is inevitable for bourgeois democracy to be half-hearted, limited, and narrow. For the period of the democratic revolution it has set the socialist proletariat the task of winning the peasant masses over to its side, and, paralysing the bourgeoisie's instability, of smashing and crushing the autocracy. A decisive victory of the democratic revolution is possible only in the form of a revolutionary-democratic dictatorship of the proletariat and the peasantry. But the sooner this victory is achieved, and the fuller it is, the faster and the more profoundly will fresh contradictions and a fresh class develop within the fully democratised bourgeois system. The more complete our democratic revolution, the closer shall we approach the tasks of the socialist revolution, the more acute and incisive will be the proletariat's struggle against the very foundations of bourgeois society.

The Social-Democrats must wage a relentless struggle against any departure from this presentation of the revolutionary-democratic and socialist tasks of the proletariat. It is absurd to ignore the democratic, i.e., essentially bourgeois,

nature of the present revolution, and hence it is absurd to
bring forward such slogans as the one calling for the establishment of revolutionary communes. It it absurd and reactionary to belittle the tasks of the proletariat's participation—
and leading participation at that—in the democratic revolution, by shunning, for instance, the slogan of a revolutionary-
democratic dictatorship of the proletariat and the peasantry.
It is absurd to confuse the tasks and prerequisites of a
democratic revolution with those of a socialist revolution,
which, we repeat, differ both in their nature and in the composition of the social forces taking part in them.

It is on this last mentioned mistake that we propose to
dwell in detail. The undeveloped state of the class contradictions in the people in general, and in the peasantry in particular, is an unavoidable phenomenon in the epoch of a
democratic revolution, which for the first time lays the
foundations for a really extensive development of capitalism.
This lack of economic development results in the survival and revival, in one form or another, of the backward
forms of a socialism which is petty-bourgeois, for it idealises
reforms that do not go beyond the framework of petty-
bourgeois relationships. The mass of the peasants do not and
cannot realise that the fullest "freedom" and the "justest"
distribution even of all the land, far from destroying capitalism, will, on the contrary, create the conditions for a particularly extensive and powerful development of capitalism.
Whereas Social-Democracy singles out and supports only
the revolutionary-democratic substance of these peasant aspirations, petty-bourgeois socialism elevates to a theory this
political backwardness of the peasants, confusing or jumbling
together the prerequisites and the tasks of a genuine democratic revolution with those of an imaginary socialist revolution.

The most striking expression of this vague petty-bourgeois
ideology is the programme, or rather draft programme, of
the "Socialist-Revolutionaries", who made the more haste to
proclaim themselves a party, the less developed among them
were the forms and prerequisites for a party. When analysing
their draft programme (see *Vperyod* No. 3*) we already had

---

* See this book, pp. 16-22.—*Ed.*

occasion to point out that the Socialist-Revolutionaries' views are rooted in the old Russian Narodnik ideas. However, as the entire economic development of Russia, the entire course of the Russian revolution, is remorselessly and ruthlessly cutting the ground from under the foundations of pure Narodism day by day and hour by hour, the views of the Socialist-Revolutionaries inevitably tend to become eclectic. They are trying to patch up the rents in the Narodnik ideas with bits of fashionable opportunist "criticism" of Marxism, but this does not make the tattered garment wear any the better. All in all, their programme is nothing but an absolutely lifeless and self-contradictory document, which is merely an expression of a stage in the history of Russian socialism on the road from the Russia of serfdom to bourgeois Russia, the road "from Narodism to Marxism". This definition, which typifies a number of more or less small streams of contemporary revolutionary thought, is also applicable to the latest draft agrarian programme of the Polish Socialist Party (P.S.P.),[16] published in No. 6-8 of *Przedświt.*[17]

The draft agrarian programme falls into two parts. Part I sets forth "reforms for the realisation of which social conditions have already matured"; Part II—"formulates the consummation and integration of the agrarian reforms set forth in Part I". Part I, in its turn, is subdivided into three sections: A) labour protection—demands for the benefit of the agricultural proletariat; B) agrarian reforms (in the narrow sense, or, so to say, peasant demands), and C) protection of the rural population (self-government, etc.).

This programme takes a step towards Marxism in attempting to single out something in the nature of a minimum from the maximum programme—then in providing a wholly independent formulation of demands of a purely proletarian nature; further, the preamble to the programme recognises that it is altogether inadmissible for socialists to "flatter the proprietary instincts of the peasant masses". As a matter of fact, if the truth contained in this latter proposition had been given sufficient thought and carried to its logical conclusion, that would have inevitably resulted in a strictly Marxist programme. The trouble, however, is that the P.S.P.

which draws its ideas just as willingly from the fount of opportunist criticism of Marxism is not a consistently proletarian party. "Since it has not been proved that landed property tends to concentrate," we read in the preamble to the programme, "it is inconceivable to champion this form of economy with absolute sincerity and assurance, and to convince the peasant that the small farms will inevitably disappear."

This is nothing but an echo of bourgeois political economy. Bourgeois economists are doing their utmost to instil in the small peasant the idea that capitalism is compatible with the well-being of the small independent farmer. That is why they veil the general question of commodity production, the yoke of capital, and the decline and degradation of small peasant farming by stressing the particular question of the concentration of landed property. They shut their eyes to the fact that large-scale production in specialised branches of agriculture producing for the market is also developing on small and medium-sized holdings, and that ownership of this kind is deteriorating because of greater leasing of land, as well as under the burden of mortgages and the pressure of usury. They obscure the indisputable fact of the technical superiority of large-scale production in agriculture and the fall in the peasant's living standards in his struggle against capitalism. There is nothing in the P.S.P. statements but a repetition of these bourgeois prejudices, resurrected by the present-day Davids.

The unsoundness of theoretical views affects the practical programme as well. Take Part I—the agrarian reforms in the narrow sense of the term. On the one hand, you read in Clause 5: "The abolition of all restrictions on the purchase of land allotments," and in 6: "The abolition of *szarwark*[18] and obligatory cartage (compulsory services)." These are purely Marxist minimum demands. By presenting them (especially Clause 5) the P.S.P. is making a step forward in comparison with our Socialist-Revolutionaries, who in company with *Moskovskiye Vedomosti*[19] have a weakness for the vaunted "inalienability of land allotments". By presenting these demands the P.S.P. is verging on the Marxist idea regarding the struggle against remnants of serfdom, as the basis and content of the present-day peasant movement. But although the P.S.P. verges on to this idea, it is far from fully and consciously accepting it.

The main clauses of the minimum programme under consideration read as follows: "(1) nationalisation through confiscation of the crown and state demesnes as well as estates belonging to the clergy; (2) nationalisation of the big landed estates in the absence of direct heirs; (3) nationalisation of forests, rivers, and lakes". These demands have all the defects of a programme whose main demand at present is the nationalisation of the land. So long as full political liberty and sovereignty of the people do not exist, and there is no democratic republic, it is both premature and inexpedient to present the demand for nationalisation, since nationalisation means transference to the state, and the present state is a police and class state; the state of tomorrow will in any case be a class state. As a slogan meant to lead forward towards democratisation, this demand is quite useless, for it does not place the stress on the peasants' relations to the landowners (the peasants take the land of the landowners) but on the landowners' relations to the state. This presentation of the question is totally wrong at a time like the present, when the peasants are fighting in a revolutionary way for the land, against both the landowners and the landowners' state. Revolutionary peasants' committees for confiscation, as instruments of confiscation—this is the only slogan that meets the needs of such a time and promotes the class struggle against the landowners, a struggle indissolubly bound up with the revolutionary destruction of the landowners' state.

The other clauses of the agrarian minimum programme in the draft programme of the P.S.P. are as follows: "(4) limitation of property rights, inasmuch as they become an impediment to all improvements in agriculture, should such improvements be considered necessary by the majority of those concerned; ... (7) nationalisation of insurance of grain crops against fire and hail, and of cattle against epidemics; (8) legislation for state assistance in the formation of agricultural artels and co-operatives; (9) agricultural schools".

These clauses are quite in the spirit of the Socialist-Revolutionaries, or (what amounts to the same thing) of bourgeois reformism. There is nothing revolutionary about them. They are, of course, progressive—no one disputes that—but progressive in the interests of property-owners. For a socialist to advance them means nothing but flattering proprietary instincts. To advance them is the same as demanding state aid to trusts, cartels, syndicates, and manufacturers' associations, which are no less "progressive" than co-operatives, insurance, etc., in agriculture. All this is capitalist progress. To show concern for that is not our affair, but that of the employers, the entrepreneurs. Proletarian socialism, as distinct from petty-bourgeois socialism, leaves it to the Counts de Rocquigny, the landowning Zemstvo members, etc., to take care of the co-operatives of the landowners, big and little— and concerns itself entirely and exclusively with wage-workers' co-operatives for the purpose of *fighting the landowners*.

Let us now consider Part II of the programme. It consists of only one point: "Nationalisation of the big landed estates through confiscation. The arable land and pastures thus acquired by the people must be divided up into allotments and turned over to the landless peasants and those with small holdings, on guaranteed long-term leases."

A fine "consummation", indeed! Under the guise of "consummation and integration of agrarian reforms" a party calling itself socialist proposes what is by no means a socialist organisation of society, but rather an absurd petty-bourgeois utopia. Here we have a most telling example of complete confusion of the democratic and the socialist revolutions, and complete failure to understand the difference in their aims. The transfer of the land from the landowners to the peasants may be—and in fact has in Europe everywhere been—a component part of the democratic revolution, one of the stages in the bourgeois revolution, but only bourgeois radicals can call it consummation or final realisation. The redistribution of land among the various categories of proprietors, among the various classes of farmers, may be advantageous and necessary for the victory of democracy, the complete eradication of all traces of serfdom, for raising the living standards of the masses, accelerating the development of capitalism, etc.; the most resolute support of a measure like that may be incumbent upon the socialist proletariat in the epoch of a democratic revolution, but only *socialist* production and not petty peasant production, can constitute a "consummation and final realisation". "Guaran-

teeing" small-peasant leaseholds whilst commodity production and capitalism are preserved, is nothing but a reactionary
petty-bourgeois utopia.

We see now that the P.S.P.'s fundamental error is not
peculiar to that Party alone, is not an isolated instance or
something fortuitous. It expresses in a clearer and more
distinct form (than the vaunted "socialisation" of the Socialist-Revolutionaries, which they themselves are unable to
understand) the *basic* error of all Russian Narodism, *all*
Russian bourgeois liberalism and radicalism in the agrarian
question, including the bourgeois liberalism and radicalism
that found expression in the discussions at the recent (September) Zemstvo Congress in Moscow.[20]

This basic error may be expressed as follows:

*In the presentation of immediate aims the programme of
the P.S.P. is not revolutionary. In its ultimate aims it is not
socialist.*

In other words: a failure to understand the difference
between a democratic revolution and a socialist revolution
leads to a failure to express the genuinely revolutionary
aspect of the democratic aims, while all the nebulousness of
the bourgeois-democratic world outlook is brought into the
socialist aims. The result is a slogan which is not revolutionary enough for a democrat, and inexcusably confused for
a socialist.

On the other hand, Social-Democracy's programme meets
all requirements both of support for genuinely revolutionary
democracy and the presentation of a clear socialist aim. In
the present-day peasant movement we see a struggle against
serfdom, a struggle against the landowners and the landowners'
state. We give full support to this struggle. The only correct
slogan for such support is confiscation through revolutionary
peasants' committees. What should be done with the confiscated land is a secondary question. It is not we who will settle
this question, but the peasants. When it comes to being settled
a struggle will begin between the proletariat and the bourgeoisie within the peasantry. That is why we either leave this
question open (which is so displeasing to the petty-bourgeois
projectors) or merely indicate the *beginning* of the road to be
taken, by demanding the return of the cut-off lands[21] (in

which unthinking people see an obstacle to the movement, despite the numerous explanations given by the Social-Democrats).

There is only one way to make the agrarian reform, which is unavoidable in present-day Russia, play a revolutionary-democratic role: it must be effected on the revolutionary initiative of the peasants themselves, despite the landowners and the bureaucracy, and despite the state, i.e., it must be effected by revolutionary means. The very worst distribution of land after a reform of *this sort* will be better from all standpoints than what we have at present. And this is the road we indicate when we make the establishment of revolutionary peasants' committees our prime demand.

But at the same time we say to the rural proletariat: "The most radical victory of the peasants, which you must now help with all your force to achieve, will not rid you of poverty. This can be achieved only by one means: the victory of the entire proletariat—both industrial and agricultural—over the entire bourgeoisie and the formation of a socialist society."

Together with the peasant proprietors, against the landowners and the landowners' state; together with the urban proletariat, against the entire bourgeoisie and all the peasant proprietors. Such is the slogan of the class-conscious rural proletariat. And if the petty proprietors do not immediately accept this slogan, or even if they refuse to accept it altogether, it will nevertheless become the workers' slogan, will inevitably be borne out by the entire course of the revolution, will rid us of petty-bourgeois illusions, and will clearly and definitely indicate to us our socialist goal.

Proletary No. 20,   *Collected Works*, Vol. 9
October 10 (September 27), 1905

PETTY-BOURGEOIS AND PROLETARIAN SOCIALISM

Of the various socialist doctrines, Marxism is now predominant in Europe, the struggle for the achievement of a socialist order being almost entirely waged as a struggle of the working class under the guidance of the Social-Democratic parties. This complete predominance of proletarian socialism grounded in the teachings of Marxism was not achieved all at once, but only after a long struggle against all sorts of outworn doctrines, petty-bourgeois socialism, anarchism, and so on. Some thirty years ago, Marxism was not predominant even in Germany, where the prevailing views of the time were in fact transitional, mixed and eclectic, lying between petty-bourgeois and proletarian socialism. The most widespread doctrines among advanced workers in the Romance countries, in France, Spain and Belgium, were Proudhonism,[22] Blanquism[23] and anarchism, which obviously expressed the viewpoint of the petty bourgeois, not of the proletarian.

What has been the cause of this rapid and complete victory of Marxism during the last decades? The correctness of the Marxist views has been confirmed to an ever greater extent by all the development of contemporary societies, both politically and economically, and by the whole experience of the revolutionary movement and of the struggle of the oppressed classes. The decline of the petty bourgeoisie inevitably led, sooner or later, to the extinction of all kinds of petty-bourgeois prejudices, while the growth of capitalism and the intensification of the class struggle within capitalist society were the best agitation for the ideas of proletarian socialism.

Russia's backwardness naturally accounts for the firm footing that various obsolete socialist doctrines gained in our country. The entire history of Russian revolutionary thought during the last quarter of a century is the history of the struggle waged by Marxism against petty-bourgeois Narodnik socialism. While the rapid growth and remarkable successes of the Russian working-class movement have already brought victory to Marxism in Russia too, the development of an indubitably revolutionary peasant movement—especially after the famous peasant revolts in the Ukraine in 1902[24]—has on the other hand caused a certain revival of senile Narodism. The Narodnik theories of old, embellished with modish European opportunism (revisionism, Bernsteinism,[25] and criticism of Marx), make up all the original ideological stock-in-trade of the so-called Socialist-Revolutionaries. That is why the peasant question is focal in the Marxists' controversies with both the pure Narodniks and the Socialist-Revolutionaries.

To a certain extent Narodism was an integral and consistent doctrine. It denied the domination of capitalism in Russia; it denied the factory workers' role as the front-line fighters of the entire proletariat; it denied the importance of a political revolution and bourgeois political liberty; it preached an immediate socialist revolution, stemming from the peasant commune with its petty forms of husbandry. All that now survives of this integral theory is mere shreds, but to understand the controversies of the present day intelligently, and to prevent these controversies from degenerating into mere squabbles, one should always remember the general and basic Narodnik *roots* of the errors of our Socialist-Revolutionaries.

The Narodniks considered the muzhik the man of the future in Russia, this view springing inevitably from their faith in the socialist character of the peasant commune, from their lack of faith in the future of capitalism. The Marxists considered the worker the man of the future in Russia, and the development of Russian capitalism in both agriculture and industry is providing more and more confirmation of their views. The working-class movement in Russia has won recognition for itself, but as for the peasant movement, the gulf separating Narodism and Marxism is to this day revealed in their different *interpretations* of this movement. To the Narodniks the peasant movement provides a refutation of Marxism. It is a movement that stands for a direct socialist revolution; it does not recognise bourgeois political liberty; it stems from small-scale, not large-scale, production. In a word, to the Narodnik, it is the peasant movement that is the genuine, truly socialist and immediately socialist movement. The Narodnik faith in the peasant commune and the Narodnik brand of anarchism fully explain why such conclusions are inevitable.

To the Marxist, the peasant movement is a democratic, not a socialist, movement. In Russia, just as was the case in other countries, it is a necessary concomitant of the democratic revolution, which is bourgeois in its social and economic content. It is not in the least directed against the foundations of the bourgeois order, against commodity production, or against capital. On the contrary, it is directed against the old, feudal, pre-capitalist relationships in the rural districts, and against the landed estates, which are the mainstay of all the survivals of serf-ownership. Consequently, full victory of this peasant movement will not abolish capitalism; on the contrary, it will create a broader foundation for its development, and will hasten and intensify purely capitalist development. Full victory of the peasant uprising can only create a stronghold for a democratic bourgeois republic, within which a proletarian struggle against the bourgeoisie will for the first time develop in its purest form.

These, then, are the two contrasting views which must be clearly understood by anyone who wishes to examine the gulf in principles that lies between the Socialist-Revolutionaries and the Social-Democrats. According to one view, the peasant movement is socialist, while according to the other it is a democratic-bourgeois movement. Hence one can see what ignorance our Socialist-Revolutionaries betray when they repeat for the hundredth time (see, for example, *Revolutsionnaya Rossiya* No. 75) that orthodox Marxists have ignored the peasant question. There is only one way of combating such crass ignorance, and that is by repeating the ABC, by setting forth the old consistently Narodnik views, and by pointing out for the hundredth or the thousandth time that the real distinction between us does not lie in a desire or the non-desire to reckon with the peasant question, in recognition or non-recognition of it, but in our *different appraisals* of the present-day peasant movement and of the present-day peasant question in Russia. He who says that the Marxists "ignore" the peasant question in Russia is, in the first place, an absolute ignoramus since all the principal writings of Russian Marxists, beginning with Plekhanov's *Our Differences* (which appeared over twenty years ago), have in the main been devoted to explaining the erroneousness of the Narodnik views on the Russian peasant question. Secondly, he who says that Marxists "ignore" the peasant question thereby proves his desire to avoid giving a complete appraisal of the actual difference in principles, giving the answer to the question whether or not the present-day peasant movement is bourgeois-democratic, whether or not it is objectively directed against the survivals of serfdom.

The Socialist-Revolutionaries have never given, nor will they ever be able to give, a clear and precise answer to this question, for they are floundering hopelessly between the old Narodnik view and the present-day Marxist view on the peasant question in Russia. The Marxists say that the Socialist-Revolutionaries represent the standpoint of the petty bourgeoisie (are ideologists of the petty bourgeoisie) for the very reason that they cannot rid themselves of petty-bourgeois illusions and of the Narodnik imaginings in appraising the peasant movement.

That is why we have to go over the ABC once again. What is the present-day peasant movement in Russia striving for? For land and liberty. What significance will the complete victory of this movement have? After winning liberty, it will abolish the rule of the landowners and bureaucrats in the administration of the state. After securing the land, it will give the landowners' estates to the peasants. Will the fullest liberty and expropriation of the landowners do away with commodity production? No, it will not. Will the fullest liberty and expropriation of the landowners abolish individual farming by peasant households on communal, or "socialised", land? No, it will not. Will the fullest liberty and expropriation of the landowners bridge the deep gulf that separates the rich peasant, with his numerous horses and cows, from the farm-hand, the day-labourer, i.e., the gulf that separates the peasant bourgeoisie from the rural proletariat? No, it will not. On the contrary, the more completely the highest *social-estate* (the landowners) is routed and annihilated, the more profound will the *class* distinction between the bourgeoisie and the proletariat be. What will be the objective significance of the complete victory of the peasant uprising? This victory will do away with all survivals of serfdom, but it will by no means destroy the bourgeois economic system, it will not eliminate capitalism or the division of society into classes—into rich and poor, the bourgeoisie and the proletariat. Why is the present-day peasant movement a democratic-bourgeois movement? Because, after destroying the power of the bureaucracy and the landowners, it will set up a democratic system of society, without, however, altering the bourgeois foundation of that democratic society, without abolishing the rule of capital. How should the class-conscious worker, the socialist, regard the present-day peasant movement? He must support this movement, help the peasants in the most energetic fashion, help them throw off completely both the rule of the bureaucracy and that of the landowners. At the same time, however, he should* explain to the peasants that it is not enough to overthrow the rule of the bureaucracy and the landowners. When they overthrow that rule, they must at the same time prepare for the abolition of the rule of capital, the rule of the bourgeoisie, and for that purpose a doctrine that is fully socialist, i.e., Marxist, should be immediately disseminated, the rural proletarians should be united, welded together, and organised for the struggle against the peasant bourgeoisie and the entire Russian bourgeoisie. Can a class-conscious worker forget the democratic struggle for the sake of the socialist struggle, or forget the latter for the sake of the former? No, a class-conscious worker calls himself a Social-Democrat for the reason that he understands the relation between the two struggles. He knows that there is no other road to socialism save the road through democracy, through political liberty. He therefore strives gradually to achieve full democracy in order to attain the ultimate goal—socialism. Why are the conditions for the democratic struggle not the same as those for the socialist struggle? Because the workers will certainly have different allies in each of those two struggles. The democratic struggle

---

* In the manuscript the word "should" is followed by "untiringly".—*Ed.*

is waged by the workers together with a section of the bourgeoisie, especially of the petty bourgeoisie. On the other hand, the socialist struggle is waged by the workers against the whole of the bourgeoisie. The struggle against the bureaucrat and the landowner can and must be waged together with all the peasants, even the well-to-do and the middle peasants. On the other hand, it is only together with the rural proletariat that the struggle against the bourgeoisie, and therefore against the well-to-do peasants too, can be properly waged.

If we keep in mind all these elementary Marxist truths, which the Socialist-Revolutionaries always prefer to avoid going into, we shall have no difficulty in appraising the latter's "latest" objections to Marxism, such as the following:

"Why was it necessary," *Revolutsionnaya Rossiya* (No. 75) exclaims, "first to support the peasant in general against the landowner, and then (i.e., at the same time) to support the proletariat against the peasant in general, instead of at once supporting the proletariat against the landowner; and what Marxism has to do with this, heaven alone knows."

This is the standpoint of the most primitive, childishly naïve anarchism. For many centuries and even for thousands of years, mankind has dreamt of doing away "at once" with all and every kind of exploitation. These dreams remained mere dreams until millions of the exploited all over the world began to unite for a consistent, staunch and comprehensive struggle to change capitalist society in the direction the evolution of that society is naturally taking. Socialist dreams turned into the socialist struggle of the millions only when Marx's scientific socialism had linked up the urge for change with the struggle of a definite class. Outside the class struggle, socialism is either a hollow phrase or a naïve dream. In Russia two different struggles of two different social forces are taking place before our very eyes. The proletariat is fighting against the bourgeoisie wherever capitalist relations of production exist (and they exist–be it known to our Socialist-Revolutionaries–even in the peasant commune, i.e., on the land which from their standpoint is one hundred per cent "socialised"). As a stratum of small landowners, of petty bourgeois, the peasantry is fighting against all survivals of serfdom, against the bureaucrats and the landowners. Only those who are completely ignorant of political economy and of the history of revolutions throughout the world can fail to see that these are two distinct and different social wars. To shut one's eyes to the diversity of these wars by demanding "at once", is like hiding one's head under one's wing and refusing to make any analysis of reality.

The Socialist-Revolutionaries, who have lost the integrity of the old Narodnik views, have even forgotten many of the teachings of the Narodniks themselves. The selfsame *Revolutsionnaya Rossiya* writes in the same article: "By helping the peasantry to expropriate the landowners, Mr. Lenin is unconsciously assisting in building up petty-bourgeois economy on the ruins of the more or less developed forms of capitalist agriculture. Is not this a step backward from the standpoint of orthodox Marxism?"

For shame, gentlemen! Why, you have forgotten your own Mr. V. V.! Consult his *Destiny of Capitalism*, the *Sketches* by Mr. Nikolai —on, and other sources of your wisdom. You will then recollect that landowner farming in Russia combines within itself features both of capitalism and of serf-ownership. You will then find out that there is a system of economy based on labour service,[26] which is a direct survival of the corvée system.[27] If, moreover, you take the trouble to consult such an orthodox Marxist book as the third volume of Marx's *Capital*, you will find that nowhere could the corvée system develop, and nowhere did it develop, and turn into capitalist farming except through the medium of petty-bourgeois peasant farming.[28] In your efforts to demolish Marxism, you resort to methods too primitive, methods too long ago exposed; you ascribe to Marxism a grotesquely oversimplified conception of large-scale capitalist farming directly succeeding to large-scale farming based on the corvée system. You argue that since the yield on the landowners' estates is higher than on the peasant farms, the expropriation of the landowners is a step backward. This argument is worthy of a fourth-form schoolboy. Just consider, gentlemen: was it not a "step backward" to separate the low-yielding peasant lands from the high-yielding landowners' estates when serfdom was abolished?

Present-day landowner economy in Russia combines features of both capitalism and serf-ownership. Objectively, the peasants' struggle against the landowners today is a struggle against survivals of serfdom. However, to attempt to enumerate all individual cases, to weigh each individual case, and to determine with the precision of an apothecary's scales exactly where serf-ownership ends and pure capitalism begins, is to ascribe one's own pedantry to the Marxists. We cannot calculate what portion of the price of provisions bought from a petty shopkeeper represents labour-value and what part of it represents swindling, etc. Does that mean, gentlemen, that we must discard the theory of labour-value?

Contemporary landowner economy combines features of both capitalism and serfdom. But only pedants can conclude from this that it is our duty to weigh, count and copy out every minute feature in every particular instance, and pigeon-hole it in this or that social category. Only utopians can hence conclude that "there is no need" for us to draw a distinction between the two different social wars. Indeed, the only actual conclusion that does follow is that both in our programme and in our tactics we must combine the purely proletarian struggle against capitalism with the general democratic (and general peasant) struggle against serfdom.

The more marked the capitalist features in present-day landowner semi-feudal economy, the more imperative is it to get right down to organising the rural proletariat separately, for this will help purely capitalist, or purely proletarian, antagonisms to assert themselves the sooner, whenever confiscation takes place. The more marked the capitalist features in landowner economy, the sooner will democratic confiscation give an impetus to the real struggle for socialism—and, consequently, the more dangerous is false idealisation of the democratic revolution through use of the catchword of "socialisation". Such is the conclusion to be drawn from the fact that landowner economy is a mixture of capitalism and serf-ownership relations.

Thus, we must combine the purely proletarian struggle with the general peasant struggle, but not confuse the two. We must support the general democratic and general peasant struggle, but not become submerged in this non-class struggle; we must never idealise it with false catchwords such as "socialisation", or ever forget the necessity of organising both the urban *and the rural* proletariat in an entirely independent class party of Social-Democracy. While giving the utmost support to the most determined democracy, that party will not allow itself to be diverted from the revolutionary path by reactionary dreams and experiments in "equalisation" under the system of commodity production. The peasants' struggle against the landowners is now a revolutionary struggle; the confiscation of the landowners' estates at the present stage of economic and political evolution is revolutionary in every respect, and we back this revolutionary-democratic measure. However, to call this measure "socialisation", and to deceive oneself and the people concerning the possibility of "equality" in land tenure under the system of commodity production, is a reactionary petty-bourgeois utopia, which we leave to the socialist-reactionaries.

Proletary No. 24,   *Collected Works*, Vol. 9
November 7 (October 25), 1905

INSERT TO V. KALININ'S ARTICLE "THE PEASANT CONGRESS" [29]

(Extract)

1

We see, consequently, that consistent socialists must give unconditional support to the revolutionary struggle of any section of the peasantry, even the well-to-do, against the bureaucracy and the landowners; however, consistent socialists must make it clearly understood that the "general redistribution"[30] desired by the peasants is far from being socialism. Socialism demands the abolition of the power of money, the power of capital, the abolition of all private ownership of the means of production, the abolition of commodity economy. Socialism demands that the land and the factories should pass into the hands of all the working people, who, following an all-over plan, will organise large-scale—and not scattered and small-scale—production.

The peasants' struggle for land and freedom is a big step towards socialism, but one that is very, very far from socialism.

Proletary No. 25,
November 16 (3), 1905

Collected Works, Vol. 9

THE PROLETARIAT AND THE PEASANTRY

The Congress of the Peasant Union[31] now in session in Moscow once again raises the vital question of the attitude of Social-Democrats to the peasant movement. It has always been a vital question for Russian Marxists when determining their programme and tactics. In the very first draft Programme of the Russian Social-Democrats, printed abroad in 1884 by the Emancipation of Labour group,[32] most serious attention was devoted to the peasant question.

Since then there has not been a single major Marxist work dealing with general questions, or a single Social-Democratic periodical, which has not repeated or developed Marxist views and slogans, or applied them to particular cases.

Today the question of the peasant movement has become vital not only in the theoretical but also in the most direct practical sense. We now have to transform our general slogans into direct appeals by the revolutionary proletariat to the revolutionary peasantry. The time has now come when the peasantry is coming forward as a conscious maker of a new way of life in Russia. And the course and outcome of the great Russian revolution depend in tremendous measure on the growth of the peasants' political consciousness.

What does the peasantry expect of the revolution? What can the revolution give the peasantry? Anyone active in the political sphere, and especially every class-conscious worker who goes in for politics, not in the sense vulgarised by bourgeois politicians, but in the best sense of the word, must answer these two questions.

The peasantry wants land and freedom. There can be no two opinions on this score. All class conscious workers support the revolutionary peasantry with all their might. All class-conscious workers want and are fighting for the peasantry to receive all the land and full freedom. "All the land" means not putting up with any partial concessions and hand-outs; it means reckoning, not on a compromise between the peasantry and the landowners, but on abolition of landed estates. And the party of the class-conscious proletariat, the Social-Democrats, have most vigorously proclaimed this view: at its Third Congress held last May, the R.S.D.L.P. adopted a resolution directly declaring for support of the peasants' revolutionary demands, *including confiscation of all* privately owned estates.[33] This resolution clearly shows that the party of the class-conscious workers supports the peasants' demand for all the land. And in *this* respect the content of the resolution adopted at the conference of the other half of our Party fully coincides with that of the resolution passed by the Third Congress of the R.S.D.L.P.

"Full freedom" means election of officials and other office-holders who administer public and state affairs. "Full freedom" means the complete abolition of a state administration that is not wholly and exclusively responsible to the people, that is not elected by, accountable to, and subject to recall by, the people. "Full freedom" means that it is not the people who should be subordinated to officials, but the officials who should be subordinated to the people.

Of course, not all peasants fighting for land and freedom are fully aware of what their struggle implies, and go so far as to demand a republic. But for all that, the democratic trend of the peasants' demands is beyond all doubt. Hence the peasantry can be certain that the proletariat will support these demands. The peasants must know that the red banner which has been raised in the towns is the banner of struggle for the immediate and vital demands, not only of the industrial and agricultural workers, but also of the millions and tens of millions of small tillers of the soil.

Survivals of serfdom in every possible shape and form are to this day a cruel burden on the whole mass of the peasantry, and the proletarians under their red banner have declared war on this burden.

But the red banner means more than proletarian support of the peasants' demands. It also means the independent demands of the proletariat. It means struggle, not only for land and freedom, but also against all exploitation of man by man, struggle against the poverty of the masses of the people, against the rule of capital. And it is here that we are faced with the second question: what can the revolution give the peasantry? Many sincere friends of the peasants (the Socialist-Revolutionaries, for instance, among them) ignore this question, do not realise its importance. They think it is sufficient to raise and settle the question of what the peasants want, to get the answer: land and freedom. This is a great mistake. Full freedom, election of all officials all the way to the head of the state, will not do away with the rule of capital, will not abolish the wealth of the few and the poverty of the masses. Complete abolition of private land-ownership, too, will not do away either with the rule of capital or with the poverty of the masses. Even on land belonging to the whole nation, only those with capital of their own, only those who have the implements, livestock, machines, stocks of seed, money in general, etc., will be able to farm independently. As for those who have nothing but their hands to work with, they will inevitably remain slaves of capital even in a democratic republic, even when the land belongs to the whole nation. The idea that "socialisation" of land can be effected without socialisation of capital, the idea that equalised land tenure is possible while capital and commodity economy exist, is a delusion. In nearly all countries of Europe, socialism has experienced periods when this or some similar delusions have been prevalent. The experience of working-class struggle in all countries has shown in practice how dangerous such an error is, and today the socialist proletarians of Europe and America have completely rid themselves of it.

Thus the red banner of the class-conscious workers means, first, that we support with all our might the peasants' struggle for full freedom and all the land; secondly, it means that we do not stop at this, but go on further. We are waging, besides the struggle for freedom and land, a fight for social-ism. The fight for socialism is a fight against the rule of capital. It is being carried on first and foremost by the wage-workers, who are directly and wholly dependent on capital. As for the small farmers, some of them own capital themselves, and often themselves exploit workers. Hence not all small peasants join the ranks of fighters for socialism; only those do so who resolutely and consciously side with the workers against capital, with public property against private property.

That is why the Social-Democrats say they are fighting together with the entire peasantry against the landowners and officials, besides which they—the town and village proletarians together—are fighting against capital. The struggle for land and freedom is a democratic struggle. The struggle to abolish the rule of capital is a socialist struggle.

Let us, then, send our warm greetings to the Peasant Union, which has decided to stand together and fight staunchly, selflessly and unswervingly for full freedom and for all the land. These peasants are true democrats. We must explain to them patiently and steadily where their views on the tasks of democracy and socialism are wrong, regarding them as allies with whom we are united by the great common struggle. These peasants are truly revolutionary democrats with whom we must and shall carry on the fight for the complete victory of the present revolution. We are fully in sympathy with the plan to call a general strike and the decision to rise together the next time, with the town workers and all the peasant poor acting in unison. All class-conscious workers will make every effort to help carry out this plan. Yet no alliance, even with the most honest and determined revolutionary democrats, will ever make the proletarians forget their still greater and more important goal, the fight for socialism, for the complete abolition of the rule of capital, for the emancipation of all working people from every kind of exploitation. Forward, workers and peasants, in the common struggle for land and freedom! Forward, proletarians, united by international Social-Democracy, in the fight for socialism!

Novaya Zhizn No. 11,   *Collected Works*, Vol. 10
November 12, 1905
Signed: *N. Lenin*

THE AGRARIAN PROGRAMME
OF SOCIAL -DEMOCRACY
IN THE FIRST RUSSIAN REVOLUTION,
1905-1907

7. MUNICIPALISATION OF THE LAND
AND MUNICIPAL SOCIALISM

These two terms were made equivalent by the Mensheviks themselves, who secured the adoption of the agrarian programme at Stockholm. We need only mention the names of two prominent Mensheviks, Kostrov and Larin. "Some comrades," said Kostrov at Stockholm, "seem to be hearing about municipal ownership for the first time. Let me remind them that in Western Europe there is a whole political trend [!precisely!] called 'municipal socialism' [England], which advocates the extension of ownership of urban and rural municipalities, and which is also supported by our comrades. Many municipalities own real estate, and that does not contradict our programme. We now have the possibility of acquiring [!] real estate for the municipalities gratis [!!] and we should take advantage of it. Of course, the confiscated land should be municipalised" (p. 88).

The naïve idea about "the possibility of acquiring property gratis" is magnificently expressed here. But in citing the example of this municipal socialism "trend" as a special trend mainly characteristic of England, the speaker did not stop to think why this is an *extremely opportunist* trend. Why did Engels, in his letters to Sorge describing this extreme intellectual opportunism of the English Fabians,[34] emphasise the petty-bourgeois nature of their "municipalisation" schemes?[35]

Larin, in unison with Kostrov, says in his comments on the Menshevik programme: "Perhaps in some areas the people's local self-governing bodies will themselves be able to run these large estates, as the horse tramways or slaughter-houses are run by municipal councils, and then all [!!] the profits obtained from them will be placed at the disposal of the whole [!] population"*—and not of the local bourgeoisie, my dear Larin?

The philistine illusions of the philistine heroes of West-European municipal socialism are already making themselves felt. The fact that the bourgeoisie is in power is forgotten; so also is the fact that only in towns with a high percentage of *proletarian* population is it possible to obtain for the working people some crumbs of benefit from municipal government! But all this is by the way. The principal fallacy of the "municipal socialism" idea of municipalising the land lies in the following.

The bourgeois intelligentsia of the West, like the English Fabians, elevate municipal socialism to a special "trend" precisely because it dreams of social peace, of class concilia-tion, and seeks to divert public attention away from the fundamental questions of the economic system as a whole, and of the state *structure* as a whole, to minor questions of *local* self-*government*. In the sphere of questions in the first category, the class antagonisms stand out most sharply; that is the sphere which, as we have shown, affects the very foundations of the class rule of the bourgeoisie. Hence it is in that sphere that the philistine, reactionary utopia of bring-ing about socialism piecemeal is particularly hopeless. Atten-tion is diverted to the sphere of minor local questions, being directed not to the question of the class rule of the bour-geoisie, nor to the question of the chief instruments of that rule, but to the question of distributing the *crumbs* thrown by the rich bourgeoisie for the *"needs of the population"*. Naturally, since attention is focused on such questions as the spending of paltry sums (in comparison with the total surplus value and total state expenditure of the bourgeoisie), which the *bourgeoisie itself is willing* to set aside for public health (Engels pointed out in *The Housing Question* that the bour-geoisie itself is afraid of the spread of epidemic diseases in

---

* *The Peasant Question and Social-Democracy*, p. 66.

the towns), or for education (the bourgeoisie must have trained workers able to adapt themselves to a high technical level!), and so on, it is possible, in the sphere of *such minor* questions, to hold forth about "social peace", about the harmfulness of the class struggle, and so on. What class struggle can there be if the bourgeoisie itself is spending money on the "needs of the population", on public health, on education? What need is there for a social revolution if it is possible through the local self-governing bodies, gradually, step by step, to extend "collective ownership", and "socialise" production: the horse tramways, the slaughter-houses referred to so relevantly by the worthy Y. Larin?

The philistine opportunism of that "trend" lies in the fact that people forget the *narrow limits* of so-called "municipal socialism" (in reality, municipal capitalism, as the English Social-Democrats properly point out in their controversies with the Fabians). They forget that so long as the bourgeoisie rules as a class it cannot allow any encroachment, even from the "municipal" point of view, upon the real *foundations* of its rule; that if the bourgeoisie allows, tolerates, "municipal socialism", it is because the latter does not touch the *foundations* of its rule, does not interfere with the *important* sources of its wealth, but extends only to the narrow sphere of local expenditure, which the bourgeoisie itself *allows* the "population" to manage. It does not need more than a slight acquaintance with "municipal socialism" in the West to know that any attempt on the part of *socialist* municipalities to go a little beyond the boundaries of their normal, i.e., minor, petty activities, which give no *substantial* relief to the workers, any attempt to meddle with *capital*, is invariably vetoed in the most emphatic manner by the central authorities of the bourgeois state.

And it is this fundamental mistake, this petty-bourgeois opportunism of the West-European Fabians, Possibilists, and Bernsteinians that is taken over by our advocates of municipalisation.

"Municipal socialism" means socialism in matters of *local government*. Anything that goes beyond the limits of *local* interests, beyond the limits of state *administration*, i.e., anything that affects the main sources of revenue of the ruling classes and the principal means of securing their rule, any-thing that affects not the administration of the state, but the *structure* of the state, *thereby* goes beyond the sphere of "municipal socialism". But our wiseacres evade this acute national issue, this question of the land, which affects the vital interests of the ruling classes in the most direct way, by *relegating* it to the sphere of "local government ques-tions". In the West they municipalise horse trams and slaughter-houses, so why should we not municipalise the best half of all the land?—argues the Russian intellectual. That would serve both in the event of restoration and in the event of incomplete democratisation of the central govern-ment!

And so we get agrarian socialism in a bourgeois revolu-tion, a socialism of the most petty-bourgeois kind, one that counts on *blunting* the class struggle on *vital* issues by *relegating* the latter to the domain of petty questions affecting only local government. In fact, the question of the disposal of one half of the best land in the country is neither a local question nor a question of administration. It is a question that affects the whole state, a question of the structure, not only of the landowner but of the bourgeois state. And to try to entice the people with the idea that "municipal socialism" can be developed in agriculture before the socialist revolution is accomplished is to practise the most inadmissible kind of demagogy. Marxism permits nationalisation to be included in the programme of a bourgeois revolution because national-isation is a bourgeois measure, because absolute rent hinders the development of capitalism; private ownership of the land is a hindrance to capitalism. But to include the municipalisa-tion of the big estates in the programme of the bourgeois revolution, Marxism must be remodelled into Fabian intel-lectualist opportunism.

It is here that we see the difference between petty-bour-geois and proletarian methods in the bourgeois revolution. The petty bourgeoisie, even the most radical—our Party of Socialist-Revolutionaries included—anticipates that *after* the bourgeois revolution there will be no class struggle, but universal prosperity and peace. Therefore, it "builds its nest" in advance, it introduces plans for petty-bourgeois reforms in the bourgeois revolution, talks about various "norms" and

"regulations" with regard to landownership, about strengthening the labour principle and small farming, etc. The petty-
bourgeois method is the method of building up relations
making for the greatest possible degree of social peace. The
proletarian method is *exclusively* that of clearing the path
of all that is medieval, clearing it for the *class struggle*.
Therefore, the proletarian can leave it to the small proprietors to discuss all "norms" of landownership; the proletarian is interested only in the abolition of the landowner
latifundia, the abolition of private ownership of land, that
last barrier to the class struggle in agriculture. In the bourgeois revolution we are interested not in petty-bourgeois
reformism, not in a future "nest" of tranquillised small
farmers, but in the conditions for the proletarian struggle
against all petty-bourgeois tranquillity on a bourgeois basis.

It is this anti-proletarian spirit that municipalisation
introduces into the programme of the *bourgeois* agrarian
revolution; for, despite the deeply fallacious opinion of the
Mensheviks, municipalisation does not extend and sharpen
the class struggle, but, on the contrary, *blunts* it. It blunts
it, too, by assuming that local democracy is possible without
the complete democratisation of the centre. It also blunts it
with the idea of "municipal socialism", because the latter
is *conceivable* in bourgeois society only *away from* the high
road of the struggle, only in minor, local, unimportant questions on which *even* the bourgeoisie may yield, may reconcile itself to without losing the possibility of preserving its
class rule.

The working class must give bourgeois society the purest,
most consistent and most thorough-going programme of
bourgeois revolution, including the bourgeois nationalisation
of the land. The proletariat scornfully rejects petty-bourgeois
reformism in the bourgeois revolution; we are interested
in freedom for the struggle, not in freedom for philistine
bliss.

Naturally, the opportunism of the intelligentsia in the
workers' party takes a different line. Instead of the broad
revolutionary programme of bourgeois revolution, attention
is focused on a petty-bourgeois utopia: to secure local democracy with undemocratic centre, to secure for petty reformism
a little corner of municipal activity away from great "turmoil",

and to evade the extraordinarily acute conflict over the land by following the recipe of the anti-Semites, i.e., by relegating an important national issue to the domain of petty, local questions.

Written in November-December
1907

First published in 1908
(confiscated); published in 1917
in book form by Zhizn i Znaniye
Publishers

Collected Works, Vol. 13

IN MEMORY OF HERZEN

One hundred years have elapsed since Herzen's birth. The whole of liberal Russia is paying homage to him, studiously evading, however, the serious questions of socialism, and taking pains to conceal that which distinguished Herzen the *revolutionary* from a liberal. The Right-wing press, too, is commemorating the Herzen centenary, falsely asserting that in his last years Herzen renounced revolution. And in the orations on Herzen that are made by the liberals and Narodniks abroad, phrase-mongering reigns supreme.

The working-class party should commemorate the Herzen centenary, not for the sake of philistine glorification, but for the purpose of making clear its own tasks and ascertaining the place actually held in history by this writer who played a great part in paving the way for the Russian revolution.

Herzen belonged to the generation of revolutionaries from among the nobility and landowners of the first half of the last century. The nobility gave Russia the Birons and Arakcheyevs, innumerable "drunken officers, bullies, gamblers, heroes of fairs, masters of hounds, roisterers, floggers, pimps", as well as amiable Manilovs.[36] "But," wrote Herzen, "among them developed the men of December 14,[37] a phalanx of heroes reared, like Romulus and Remus, on the milk of a wild beast.... They were veritable titans, hammered out of pure steel from head to foot, comrades-in-arms who deliberately went to certain death in order to awaken the young generation to a new life and to purify the children born in an environment of tyranny and servility."[38]

Herzen was one of those children. The uprising of the Decembrists awakened and "purified" him. In the feudal Russia of the forties of the nineteenth century, he rose to a height which placed him on a level with the greatest thinkers of his time. He assimilated Hegel's dialectics. He realised that it was "the algebra of revolution". He went further than Hegel, following Feuerbach to materialism. The first of his *Letters on the Study of Nature,* "Empiricism and Idealism", written in 1844, reveals to us a thinker who even now stands head and shoulders above the multitude of modern empiricist natural scientists and the host of present-day idealist and semi-idealist philosophers. Herzen came right up to dialectical materialism, and halted—before historical materialism.

It was this "halt" that caused Herzen's spiritual shipwreck after the defeat of the revolution of 1848. Herzen had left Russia, and observed this revolution at close range. He was at that time a democrat, a revolutionary, a socialist. But his "socialism" was one of the countless forms and varieties of bourgeois and petty-bourgeois socialism of the period of 1848, which were dealt their death-blow in the June days of that year. In point of fact, it was not socialism at all, but so many sentimental phrases, benevolent visions, which were the expression *at that time* of the revolutionary character of the bourgeois democrats, as well as of the proletariat, which had not yet freed itself from the influence of those democrats.

Herzen's spiritual shipwreck, his deep scepticism and pessimism after 1848, was a shipwreck of the *bourgeois illusions* of socialism. Herzen's spiritual drama was a product and reflection of that epoch in world history when the revolutionary character of the bourgeois democrats was *already* passing away (in Europe), while the revolutionary character of the socialist proletariat had *not yet* matured. This is something the Russian knights of liberal verbiage, who are now covering up their counter-revolutionary nature by florid phrases about Herzen's scepticism, did not and could not understand. With these knights, who betrayed the Russian revolution of 1905, and have even forgotten to think of the great name of *revolutionary*, scepticism is a form of transition from democracy to liberalism, to that toadying, vile, foul and brutal liberalism which shot down the workers in 1848, restored the shattered thrones and applauded Napoleon III, and which Herzen *cursed*, unable to understand its class nature.

With Herzen, scepticism was a form of transition from the illusion of a bourgeois democracy that is "above classes" to the grim, inexorable and invincible class struggle of the pro-

letariat. The proof: the *Letters to an Old Comrade*–to Bakunin–written by Herzen in 1869, a year before his death.
In them Herzen breaks with the anarchist Bakunin. True,
Herzen still sees this break as a mere disagreement on tactics
and not as a gulf between the world outlook of the proletarian who is confident of the victory of his class and that
of the petty bourgeois who has despaired of his salvation.
True enough, in these letters as well, Herzen repeats the
old bourgeois-democratic phrases to the effect that socialism
must preach "a sermon addressed equally to workman and
master, to farmer and townsman". Nevertheless, in breaking
with Bakunin, Herzen turned his gaze, not to liberalism, but
to the *International*–to the International led by Marx, to the
International which had begun to *"rally the legions"* of the
proletariat, to unite *"the world of labour"*, which is "aban-
doning the world of those who enjoy without working".[39]

_____

Failing as he did to understand the bourgeois-democratic
character of the entire movement of 1848 and of all the forms
of pre-Marxian socialism, Herzen was still less able to understand the bourgeois nature of the Russian revolution. Herzen
is the founder of "Russian" socialism, of "Narodism". He
saw "socialism" in the emancipation of the peasants *with
land*, in communal land tenure and in the peasant idea of
"the right to land". He set forth his pet ideas on this subject
an untold number of times.

Actually, there is *not a grain* of socialism in this doctrine
of Herzen's, as, indeed, in the whole of Russian Narodism,
including the faded Narodism of the present-day Socialist-
Revolutionaries. Like the various forms of "the socialism of
1848" in the West, it is a sort of benevolent vision, of a
collection of sentimental phrases, in which is expressed the
revolutionism of the bourgeois peasant democracy in Russia.
The more land the peasants would have received in 1861
and the less they would have had to pay for it, the more
would the power of the feudal landowners have been undermined and the more rapidly, freely and widely would capitalism have developed in Russia. The idea of the "right to land"
and of "equalised division of the land" is nothing but a
formulation of the revolutionary aspiration for equality

cherished by the peasants who are fighting for the complete overthrow of the power of the landowners, for the complete abolition of landed proprietorship.

This was fully proved by the revolution of 1905: on the one hand, the proletariat came out quite independently at the head of the revolutionary struggle, having founded the Social-Democratic Labour Party; on the other hand, the revolutionary peasants (the Trudoviks[40] and the Peasant Union[41]), who fought for every form of abolition of landed property including even "the abolition of private landownership", fought precisely as proprietors, as small entrepreneurs.

Today, the controversy over the "socialist nature" of the right to land, and so on, serves only to *obscure* and cover up the really important and serious historical question concerning the difference of *interests* of the liberal bourgeoisie and the revolutionary peasantry in the Russian *bourgeois* revolution; in other words, the question of the liberal and the democratic, the "compromising" (monarchist) and the republican trends manifested in that revolution. This is exactly the question posed by Herzen's *Kolokol*,[42] if we turn our attention to the essence of the matter and not to the words, if we investigate the class struggle as the basis of "theories" and doctrines and not vice versa.

Herzen founded a free Russian press abroad, and that is the great service rendered by him. *Polyarnaya Zvezda*[43] took up the tradition of the Decembrists. *Kolokol* (1857-67) championed the emancipation of the peasants with might and main. The slavish silence was broken.

But Herzen came from a landowner, aristocratic milieu. He left Russia in 1847; he had not seen the revolutionary people and could have no faith in it. Hence his liberal appeal to the "upper ranks". Hence his innumerable sugary letters in *Kolokol* addressed to Alexander II the Hangman, which today one cannot read without revulsion. Chernyshevsky, Dobrolyubov and Serno-Solovyevich, who represented the new generation of revolutionary *raznochintsi*, were a thousand times right when they reproached Herzen for these departures from democracy *to* liberalism. However, it must be said in fairness to Herzen that, much as he vacillated between democracy and liberalism, the democrat in him gained the upper hand nonetheless.

When Kavelin, one of the most repulsive exponents of liberal servility—who at one time was enthusiastic about *Kolokol* precisely because of its *liberal* tendencies—rose in arms against a constitution, attacked revolutionary agitation, rose against "violence" and appeals for it, and began to preach tolerance, Herzen *broke* with that liberal sage. Herzen turned upon Kavelin's "meagre, absurd, harmful pamphlet" written "for the private guidance of a government pretending to be liberal"; he denounced Kavelin's "sentimental political maxims" which represented "the Russian people as brutes and the government as an embodiment of intelligence". *Kolokol* printed an article entitled "Epitaph", which lashed out against "professors weaving the rotten cobweb of their superciliously paltry ideas, ex-professors, once open-hearted and subsequently embittered because they saw that the healthy youth could not sympathise with their scrofulous thinking". Kavelin at once recognised himself in this portrait.

When Chernyshevsky was arrested, the vile liberal Kavelin wrote: "I see nothing shocking in the arrests ... the revolutionary party considers all means fair to overthrow the government, and the latter defends itself by its own means." As if in retort to this Cadet, Herzen wrote concerning Chernyshevsky's trial: "And here are wretches, weed-like people, jellyfish, who say that we must not reprove the gang of robbers and scoundrels that is governing us."

When the liberal Turgenev wrote a private letter to Alexander II assuring him of his loyalty, and donated two goldpieces for the soldiers wounded during the suppression of the Polish insurrection, *Kolokol* wrote of "the grey-haired Magdalen (of the masculine gender) who wrote to the tsar to tell him that she knew no sleep because she was tormented by the thought that the tsar was not aware of the repentance that had overcome her". And Turgenev at once recognised himself.

When the whole band of Russian liberals scurried away from Herzen for his defence of Poland, when the whole of "educated society" turned its back on *Kolokol*, Herzen was not dismayed. He went on championing the freedom of Poland and lashing the suppressors, the butchers, the hangmen in the service of Alexander II. Herzen saved the honour of Russian democracy. "We have saved the honour of the

Russian name," he wrote to Turgenev, "and for doing so we have suffered at the hands of the slavish majority."

When it was reported that a serf peasant had killed a landowner for an attempt to dishonour the serf's betrothed, Herzen commented in *Kolokol*: "Well done!" When it was reported that military commanders would be appointed to supervise the "peaceable" progress of "emancipation", Herzen wrote: "The first wise colonel who with his unit joins the peasants instead of crushing them, will ascend the throne of the Romanovs". When Colonel Reitern shot himself in Warsaw (1860) because he did not want to be a helper of hangmen, Herzen wrote: "If there is to be any shooting, the ones to be shot should be the generals who give orders to fire upon unarmed people." When fifty peasants were massacred in Bezdna, and their leader, Anton Petrov, was executed (April 12, 1861), Herzen wrote in *Kolokol*:

"If only my words could reach you, toiler and sufferer of the land of Russia!... How well I would teach you to despise your spiritual shepherds, placed over you by the St. Petersburg Synod and a German tsar.... You hate the landowner, you hate the official, you fear them, and rightly so; but you still believe in the tsar and the bishop ... do not believe them. The tsar is with them, and they are his men. It is him you now see—you, the father of a youth murdered in Bezdna, and you, the son of a father murdered in Penza.... Your shepherds are as ignorant as you, and as poor.... Such was another Anthony (not Bishop Anthony, but Anton of Bezdna) who suffered for you in Kazan.... The dead bodies of your martyrs will not perform forty-eight miracles, and praying to them will not cure a toothache; but their living memory may produce one miracle—your emancipation."

This shows how infamously and vilely Herzen is being slandered by our liberals entrenched in the slavish "legal" press, who magnify Herzen's weak points and say nothing about his strong points. It was not Herzen's fault but his misfortune that he could not see the revolutionary people in Russia itself in the 1840s. When *in the sixties* he came to see the revolutionary people, he sided fearlessly with the revolutionary democracy against liberalism. He fought for a victory of the people over tsarism, not for a deal between the liberal bourgeoisie and the landowners' tsar. He raised aloft the banner of revolution.

In commemorating Herzen, we clearly see the three generations, the three classes, that were active in the Russian revolution. At first it was nobles and landowners, the Decembrists and Herzen. These revolutionaries formed but a narrow group. They were very far removed from the people. But their effort was not in vain. The Decembrists awakened Herzen. Herzen began the work of revolutionary agitation.

This work was taken up, extended, strengthened, and tempered by the revolutionary *raznochintsi*—from Chernyshevsky to the heroes of Narodnaya Volya.[44] The range of fighters widened; their contact with the people became closer. "The young helmsmen of the gathering storm" is what Herzen called them. But it was not yet the storm itself.

The storm is the movement of the masses themselves. The proletariat, the only class that is thoroughly revolutionary, rose at the head of the masses and for the first time aroused millions of peasants to open revolutionary struggle. The first onslaught in this storm took place in 1905. The next is beginning to develop under our very eyes.

In commemorating Herzen, the proletariat is learning from his example to appreciate the great importance of revolutionary theory. It is learning that selfless devotion to the revolution and revolutionary propaganda among the people are not wasted even if long decades divide the sowing from the harvest. It is learning to ascertain the role of the various classes in the Russian and in the international revolution. Enriched by these lessons, the proletariat will fight its way to a free alliance with the socialist workers of all lands, having crushed that loathsome monster, the tsarist monarchy, against which Herzen was the first to raise the great banner of struggle by addressing his *free Russian word* to the masses.

Sotsial-Demokrat No. 26,   *Collected Works*, Vol. 18
May 8 (April 25), 1912

DEMOCRACY AND NARODISM IN CHINA

The article by Sun Yat-sen, provisional President of the Chinese Republic,[45] which we take from the Brussels socialist newspaper, *Le Peuple*, is of exceptional interest to us Russians.

It is said that the onlooker sees most of the game. And Sun Yat-sen is a most interesting "onlooker", for he appears to be wholly uninformed about Russia despite his European education. And now, quite independently of Russia, of Russian experience and Russian literature, this enlightened spokesman of militant and victorious Chinese democracy, which has won a republic, poses purely Russian questions. A progressive Chinese democrat, he argues exactly like a Russian. His similarity to a Russian Narodnik is so great that it goes as far as a complete identity of fundamental ideas and of many individual expressions.

The onlooker sees most of the game. The platform of the great Chinese democracy—for that is what Sun Yat-sen's article represents—impels us, and provides us with a convenient occasion, to examine anew, in the light of recent world events, the relation between democracy and Narodism in modern bourgeois revolutions in Asia. This is one of the most serious questions confronting Russia in the revolutionary epoch which began in 1905. And it confronts not only Russia, but the whole of Asia, as will be seen from the platform of the provisional President of the Chinese Republic, particularly when this platform is compared with the revolutionary developments in Russia, Turkey, Persia and China. In very many and very essential respects, Russia is undoubtedly an

Asian country and, what is more, one of the most benighted, medieval and shamefully backward of Asian countries.

Beginning with its distant and lone forerunner, the noble-man Herzen, and continuing right up to its mass represent-atives, the members of the Peasant Union of 1905 and the Trudovik deputies to the first three Dumas of 1906-12,[46] Russian bourgeois democracy has had a Narodnik colouring. Bourgeois democracy in China, as we now see, has the same Narodnik colouring. Let us now consider, with Sun Yat-sen as an example, the "social significance" of the ideas generated by the deep-going revolutionary movement of the hundreds of millions who are finally being drawn into the stream of world capitalist civilisation.

Every line of Sun Yat-sen's platform breathes a spirit of militant and sincere democracy. It reveals a thorough under-standing of the inadequacy of a "racial" revolution. There is not a trace in it of indifference to political issues, or even of underestimation of political liberty, or of the idea that Chinese "social reform", Chinese constitutional reforms, etc., could be compatible with Chinese autocracy. It stands for complete democracy and demands a republic. It squarely poses the question of the condition of the masses, of the mass struggle. It expresses warm sympathy for the toiling and exploited people, faith in their strength and in the justice of their cause.

Before us is the truly great ideology of a truly great people capable not only of lamenting its age-long slavery and dreaming of liberty and equality, but of *fighting* the age-long oppressors of China.

One is naturally inclined to compare the provisional Presi-dent of the Republic in benighted, inert, Asiatic China with the presidents of various republics in Europe and America, in countries of advanced culture. The presidents in *those* republics are all businessmen, agents or puppets of a bour-geoisie rotten to the core and besmirched from head to foot with mud and blood—not the blood of padishahs and em-perors, but the blood of striking workers shot down in the name of progress and civilisation. In those countries the presidents represent the bourgeoisie, which long ago re-nounced all the ideals of its youth, has thoroughly prostituted itself, sold itself body and soul to the millionaires and multi-millionaires, to the feudal lords turned bourgeois, etc.

In China, the Asiatic provisional President of the Republic is a revolutionary democrat, endowed with the nobility and heroism of a class that is rising, not declining, a class that does not dread the future, but believes in it and fights for it selflessly, a class that does not cling to maintenance and restoration of the past in order to safeguard its privileges, but hates the past and knows how to cast off its dead and stifling decay.

Does that mean, then, that the materialist West has hopelessly decayed and that light shines only from the mystic, religious East? No, quite the opposite. It means that the East has definitely taken the Western path, that new *hundreds of millions* of people will from now on share in the struggle for the ideals which the West has already worked out for itself. What has decayed is the Western bourgeoisie, which is already confronted by its grave-digger, the proletariat. But in Asia there is *still* a bourgeoisie capable of championing sincere, militant, consistent democracy, a worthy comrade of France's great men of Enlightenment and great leaders of the close of the eighteenth century.[47]

The chief representative, or the chief social bulwark, of this Asian bourgeoisie that is still capable of supporting a historically progressive cause, is the peasant. And side by side with him there already exists a liberal bourgeoisie whose leaders, men like Yüan Shih-kai, are above all capable of treachery: yesterday they feared the emperor, and cringed before him; then they betrayed him when they saw the strength, and sensed the victory, of the revolutionary democracy; and tomorrow they will betray the democrats to make a deal with some old or new, "constitutional", emperor.

The real emancipation of the Chinese people from age-long slavery would be impossible without the great, sincerely democratic enthusiasm which is rousing the working masses and making them capable of miracles, and which is evident from every sentence of Sun Yat-sen's platform.

But the Chinese Narodnik combines this ideology of militant democracy, firstly, with socialist dreams, with hopes of China avoiding the capitalist path, of preventing capitalism, and, secondly, with a plan for, and advocacy of, radical agrarian reform. It is these two last ideological and political trends that constitute the element which forms *Narodism*—Narodism in the specific sense of that term, i.e., as distinct from democracy, as a supplement to democracy.

What is the origin and significance of these trends?

Had it not been for the immense spiritual and revolutionary upsurge of the masses, the Chinese democracy would have been unable to overthrow the old order and establish the republic. Such an upsurge presupposes and evokes the most sincere sympathy for the condition of the working masses, and the bitterest hatred for their oppressors and exploiters. And in Europe and America—from which the progressive Chinese, *all* the Chinese who have experienced this upsurge, have borrowed their ideas of liberation—emancipation *from* the bourgeoisie, i.e., socialism, is the immediate task. This is bound to arouse sympathy for socialism among Chinese democrats, and is the source of their *subjective* socialism.

They are subjectively socialists because they are opposed to oppression and exploitation of the masses. But the *objective* conditions of China, a backward, agricultural, semi-feudal country numbering nearly 500 million people, place on the order of the day only one specific, historically distinctive form of this oppression and exploitation, namely, feudalism. Feudalism was based on the predominance of agriculture and natural economy. The source of the feudal exploitation of the Chinese peasant was his *attachment* to the land in some form. The political exponents of this exploitation were the feudal lords, all together and individually, with the emperor as the head of the whole system.

But it appears that out of the subjectively socialist ideas and programmes of the Chinese democrat there emerges in fact a programme for "changing all the juridical foundations" of "real estate" *alone*, a programme for the abolition of feudal exploitation *alone*.

That is the *essence* of Sun Yat-sen's Narodism, of his progressive, militant, revolutionary programme for bourgeois-democratic agrarian reform, and of his quasi-socialist theory.

From the point of view of doctrine, this theory is that of a petty-bourgeois "socialist" reactionary. For the idea that capitalism can be "prevented" in China and that "social revolution" there will be made easier by the country's backwardness, and so on, is altogether reactionary. And Sun Yat-sen himself, with inimitable, one might say virginal, naïveté, smashes his reactionary Narodnik theory by admitting what reality forces him to admit, namely, that "China is on the eve of a gigantic industrial [i.e., capitalist] development", that in China "trade [i.e., capitalism] will develop to an enormous extent", that "in fifty years we shall have many Shanghais", i.e., huge centres of capitalist wealth and proletarian need and poverty.

But the question arises: does Sun Yat-sen, on the basis of his reactionary economic theory, uphold an actually reactionary agrarian programme? That is the crux of the matter, its most interesting point, and one *on* which curtailed and emasculated liberal quasi-Marxism is often at a loss.

The fact of the matter is that he does not. The dialectics of the social relations in China reveals itself precisely in the fact that, while sincerely sympathising with socialism in Europe, the Chinese democrats have transformed it into a reactionary theory, and *on the basis* of this reactionary theory of "preventing" capitalism are championing a *purely capitalist*, a maximum capitalist, agrarian programme!

Indeed, what does the "economic revolution", of which Sun Yat-sen talks so pompously and obscurely at the beginning of his article, amount to?

It amounts to the transfer of rent to the state, i.e., land nationalisation, by some sort of single tax along Henry George lines. There is absolutely nothing else that is *real* in the "economic revolution" proposed and advocated by Sun Yat-sen.

The difference between the value of land in some remote peasant area and in Shanghai is the difference in the rate of rent. The value of land is capitalised rent. To make the "enhanced value" of land the "property of the people" means transferring the rent, i.e., land ownership, to the state, or, in other words, nationalising the land.

Is such a reform possible within the framework of capitalism? It is not only possible but it represents the purest, most consistent, and ideally perfect capitalism. Marx pointed this out in *The Poverty of Philosophy*, he proved it in detail in Volume III of *Capital*, and developed it with particular clarity in his controversy with Rodbertus in *Theories of Surplus Value.*[48]

Land nationalisation makes it possible to abolish absolute rent, leaving only differential rent. According to Marx's theory, land nationalisation means a maximum elimination of medieval monopolies and medieval relations in agriculture, maximum freedom in buying and selling land, and maximum facilities for agriculture to adapt itself to the market. The irony of history is that Narodism, under the guise of "combating capitalism" in agriculture, champions an agrarian programme that, if fully carried out, would mean the *most* rapid development of capitalism in agriculture.

What economic necessity is behind the spread of the most progressive bourgeois-democratic agrarian programmes in one of the most backward peasant countries of Asia? It is the necessity of destroying feudalism in all its forms and manifestations.

The more China lagged behind Europe and Japan, the more it was threatened with fragmentation and national disintegration. It could be "renovated" only by the heroism of the revolutionary masses, a heroism capable of creating a Chinese republic in the sphere of politics, and of ensuring, through land nationalisation, the most rapid capitalist progress in the sphere of agriculture.

Whether and to what extent this will succeed is another question. In their bourgeois revolutions, various countries achieved various degrees of political and agrarian democracy, and in the most diverse combinations. The decisive factors will be the international situation and the alignment of the social forces in China. The emperor will certainly try to unite the feudal lords, the bureaucracy and the clergy in an attempt at restoration. Yüan Shih-kai, who represents a bourgeoisie that has only just changed from liberal-monarchist to liberal-republican (for how long?), will pursue a policy of manoeuvring between monarchy and revolution. The revolutionary bourgeois democracy, represented by Sun Yatsen, is correct in seeking ways and means of "renovating" China through maximum development of the initiative, determination and boldness of the peasant masses in the matter of political and agrarian reforms.

Lastly, the Chinese proletariat will increase as the number of Shanghais increases. It will probably form some kind of Chinese Social-Democratic labour party which, while criticising the petty-bourgeois utopias and reactionary views of Sun Yat-sen, will certainly take care to single out, defend and develop the revolutionary-democratic core of his political and agrarian programme.

Nevskaya Zvezda No. 17, July 15, 1912

Signed: *Vl. Ilyin*

Collected Works, Vol. 18

TWO UTOPIAS

Utopia is a Greek word, composed of *ou*, not, and *topos*, a place. It means a place which does not exist, a fantasy, invention or fairy-tale.

In politics utopia is a wish that can never come true—neither now nor afterwards, a wish that is not based on social forces and is not supported by the growth and development of political, class forces.

The less freedom there is in a country, the scantier the manifestations of open class struggle and the lower the educational level of the *masses*, the more easily political utopias usually arise and the longer they persist.

In modern Russia, two kinds of political utopia have been most persistent and they exert a certain influence on the masses owing to their appeal. They are the liberal utopia and the Narodnik utopia.

The liberal utopia alleges that one could bring about appreciable improvements in Russia, in her political liberty, and in the condition of the mass of her working people, peacefully and harmoniously, without hurting anyone's feelings, without removing the Purishkeviches, without a ruthless class struggle fought to a finish. It is the utopia of *peace* between a free Russia and the Purishkeviches.

The Narodnik utopia is a dream of the Narodnik intellectuals and Trudovik peasants who imagine that a new and just division of the land could *abolish* the power and rule of capital and do away with wage slavery, or that a "just", "equalised" division of the land could be *maintained* under the domination of capital, under the rule of money, under commodity production.

What is it that gives rise to these utopias? Why do they persist rather strongly in present-day Russia?

They are engendered by the interests of the classes which are waging a struggle against the old order, serfdom, lack of rights—in a word, "against the Purishkeviches", and which do not occupy an independent position in this struggle. Utopia, or day-dreaming, is a product of this lack of independence, this *weakness*. Day-dreaming is the lot of the *weak.*

The liberal bourgeoisie in general, and the liberal-bourgeois intelligentsia in particular, cannot but strive for liberty and legality, since without these the domination of the bourgeoisie is incomplete, is neither undivided nor guaranteed. But the bourgeoisie is *more* afraid of the movement of the masses than of reaction. Hence the striking, incredible *weakness* of the liberals in politics, their absolute impotence. Hence the endless series of equivocations, falsehoods, hypocrisies and cowardly evasions in the entire policy of the liberals, who *have* to play at democracy to win the support of the masses but at the same time are deeply anti-democratic, deeply hostile to the movement of the masses, to their initiative, their way of "storming heaven", as Marx once described one of the mass movements in Europe in the last century.[49]

The utopia of liberalism is a utopia of impotence in the matter of the political emancipation of Russia, a utopia of the self-interested moneybags who want "peacefully" to share privileges with the Purishkeviches and pass off this noble desire as the theory of "peaceful" victory for Russian democracy. The liberal utopia means day-dreaming about how to best the Purishkeviches without defeating them, how to break them without hurting them. Clearly, *this* utopia is harmful not only because it is a utopia, but also because it *corrupts* the democratic consciousness of the masses. If they believe in *this* utopia, the masses will never win freedom; they are not worthy of freedom; they fully deserve to be maltreated by the Purishkeviches.

The utopia of the Narodniks and Trudoviks is the day-dreaming of the petty proprietor, who stands midway between the capitalist and the wage-worker, about abolishing wage slavery without a class struggle. When the issue of economic emancipation becomes as close, immediate and *burning* for Russia as the issue of political emancipation is today, the

5*

utopia of the Narodniks will prove *no less* harmful than that
of the liberals.

But Russia is still in the period of her bourgeois and not
proletarian transformation; it is not the question of the
economic emancipation of the proletariat that has *most
completely* matured, but the question of political liberty,
i.e., (in effect), of complete bourgeois liberty.

And in this latter question, the Narodnik utopia plays a
peculiar historical role. Being a utopia in regard to the
economic consequences that a new division of the land should
(and would) have, it is an accompaniment *and symptom* of
the great, mass *democratic* upsurge of the peasant masses,
i.e., the masses that constitute the *majority* of the population
in bourgeois-feudal, modern, Russia. (In a purely bourgeois
Russia, as in purely bourgeois Europe, the peasantry will
not form the majority of the population.)

The liberal utopia corrupts the democratic consciousness
of the masses. The Narodnik utopia, which corrupts their
socialist consciousness, is an accompaniment, a symptom, and
in part even an expression of their democratic upsurge.

The dialectics of history is such that the Narodniks and
the Trudoviks propose and promote, as an anti-capitalist
remedy, a highly consistent and thoroughgoing capitalist
measure with regard to the agrarian question in Russia. An
"equalised" new division of the land is utopian, yet a most
complete rupture—a rupture indispensable for a *new* division—with the whole of the old landownership, whether land-
lord, allotment or "state", is the most necessary, economically
progressive and, for a state like Russia, most urgent measure
towards bourgeois democracy.

We should remember Engels's notable dictum:

"What formally may be economically incorrect, may all
the same be correct from the point of view of world history."[50]

Engels advanced this profound thesis in connection with
utopian socialism: that socialism was "fallacious" in the
formal economic sense. That socialism was "fallacious" when
it declared surplus value an *injustice* from the point of view
of the laws of exchange. The theoreticians of bourgeois political economy were right, in objecting to *that* socialism, in
the formal economic sense, for surplus value results from
the laws of exchange quite "naturally", quite "justly".

But utopian socialism was *right* from the point of view of world history, for it was a symptom, an expression, a harbinger of the class which, born of capitalism, has by now, in the beginning of the twentieth century, become a mass force which can put an end to capitalism and is irresistibly advancing to this goal.

Engels's profound thesis must be borne in mind when appraising the present-day Narodnik or Trudovik utopia in Russia (perhaps not only in Russia but in a number of Asiatic countries going through bourgeois revolutions in the twentieth century).

Narodnik *democracy*, while fallacious from the formal economic point of view, is correct from the *historical* point of view; *this* democracy, while fallacious as a socialist utopia, is *correct* in terms of the peculiar, historically conditioned democratic struggle of the peasant masses which is an inseparable element of the bourgeois transformation and a condition for its complete victory.

The liberal utopia discourages the peasant masses from fighting. The Narodnik utopia expresses their aspiration to fight, and promises them a million blessings in the event of victory, while this victory will in fact yield them only a hundred blessings. But is it not natural that the millions who are marching to battle, who for ages have lived in unheard-of ignorance, want, poverty, squalor, abandonment and down-troddenness, should magnify tenfold the fruits of an eventual victory?

The liberal utopia is a veil for the self-seeking desire of the new exploiters to share in the privileges of the old exploiters. The Narodnik utopia is an expression of the aspiration of the toiling millions of the petty bourgeoisie to put an end *altogether* to the old, feudal exploiters, but it also expresses the false hope that the new, capitalist exploiters can be abolished along with them.

———

Clearly, the Marxists, who are hostile to *all and every* utopia, must uphold the independence of the class which can fight feudalism *with supreme devotion* precisely because it is not even one-hundredth part involved in property ownership which makes the bourgeoisie a half-hearted opponent, and often an ally, of the feudal lords. The peasants are involved in small commodity production; given a favourable conjuncture of historical circumstances, they *can* achieve the most complete abolition of feudalism, but they will *always*—inevitably and not accidentally—show a certain vacillation between the bourgeoisie and the proletariat, between liberalism and Marxism.

Clearly, the Marxists must carefully extract the sound and valuable kernel of the sincere, resolute, militant democracy of the peasant masses from the husk of Narodnik utopias.

In the old Marxist literature of the eighties one can discover systematic effort to extract this valuable democratic kernel. Some day historians will study this effort systematically and trace its connection with what in the first decade of the twentieth century came to be called "Bolshevism".

Written before October 5 (18), 1912

First published in *Zhizn* No. 1, 1924

Signed: *V. I.*

Collected Works, Vol. 18

THE THREE SOURCES AND THREE COMPONENT PARTS OF MARXISM

(Extract)

III

When feudalism was overthrown, the *"free"* capitalist society appeared in the world, it at once became apparent that this freedom meant a new system of oppression and exploitation of the working people. Various socialist doctrines immediately emerged as a reflection of and protest against this oppression. Early socialism, however, was *utopian* socialism. It criticised capitalist society, it condemned and damned it, it dreamed of its destruction, it had visions of a better order and endeavoured to convince the rich of the immorality of exploitation.

But utopian socialism could not indicate the real solution. It could not explain the real nature of wage-slavery under capitalism, it could not reveal the laws of capitalist development, or show what *social force* is capable of becoming the creator of a new society.

Meanwhile, the stormy revolutions which everywhere in Europe, and especially in France, accompanied the fall of feudalism, of serfdom, more and more clearly revealed the *struggle of classes* as the basis and the driving force of all development.

Not a single victory of political freedom over the class of feudal lords was won except against desperate resistance. Not a single capitalist country evolved on a more or less free and democratic basis except by a life-and-death struggle between the various classes of capitalist society.

The genius of Marx lies in his having been the first to deduce from this the lesson world history teaches and to apply that lesson consistently. The deduction he made is the doctrine of the *class struggle*.

People always have been the foolish victims of deception and self-deception in politics, and they always will be until they have learnt to seek out the *interests* of some class or other behind all moral, religious, political and social phrases, declarations and promises. Champions of reforms and improvements will always be fooled by the defenders of the old order until they realise that every old institution, however barbarous and rotten it may appear to be, is kept going by the forces of certain ruling classes. And there is *only one* way of smashing the resistance of those classes, and that is to find, in the very society which surrounds us, the forces which can—and, owing to their social position, *must*—constitute the power capable of sweeping away the old and creating the new, and to enlighten and organise those forces for the struggle.

Marx's philosophical materialism alone has shown the proletariat the way out of the spiritual slavery in which all oppressed classes have hitherto languished. Marx's economic theory alone has explained the true position of the proletariat in the general system of capitalism.

Independent organisations of the proletariat are multiplying all over the world, from America to Japan and from Sweden to South Africa. The proletariat is becoming enlightened and educated by waging its class struggle; it is ridding itself of the prejudices of bourgeois society; it is rallying its ranks ever more closely and is learning to gauge the measure of its successes; it is steeling its forces and is growing irresistibly.

Prosveshcheniye No. 3,   *Collected Works*, Vol. 19
March 1913
Signed: *V. I.*

LEFT-WING NARODISM AND MARXISM

Marxists have repeatedly spoken about the importance of the free mobilisation (i.e., the buying, selling and mortgaging) of peasant land. This real and practical problem affords a striking illustration of the petty-bourgeois and even *positively reactionary* character of our Narodniks.

All Narodniks, from the semi-Cadets of *Russkoye Bogatstvo*[51] ("Social-Cadets" as Chernov, Vikhlyaev and similar people once rightly called them) to the ultra-"Left" Narodniks of *Stoikaya Mysl*,[52] are opposed to the complete freedom to mobilise peasant land in general, and allotment land in particular.

The Marxists, however, openly state in their *Programme* that they will *"always and invariably oppose any attempt to check the course of economic progress"*.

The economic development of Russia, as of the whole world, proceeds from feudalism to capitalism, and through large-scale, machine, capitalist production to socialism.

Pipe-dreaming about a "different" way to socialism other than that which leads through the *further* development of capitalism, through large-scale, machine, *capitalist* production, is, in Russia, characteristic either of the liberal gentlemen, or of the backward, petty proprietors (the petty bourgeoisie). These dreams, which still clog the brains of the Left Narodniks, merely reflect the backwardness (reactionary nature) and feebleness of the petty bourgeoisie.

Class-conscious workers all over the world, Russia included, are becoming more and more convinced of the correctness of Marxism, for life itself is proving to them that only large-scale, machine production rouses the workers, enlightens and organises them, and creates the *objective* conditions for a *mass* movement.

When *Put Pravdy*[53] reaffirmed the well-known Marxist axiom that capitalism is *progressive* as compared with feudalism, and that the idea of checking the development of capitalism is a utopia, most absurd, reactionary, and harmful to the working people, Mr. N. Rakitnikov, the Left Narodnik (in *Smelaya Mysl* No. 7), accused *Put Pravdy* of having undertaken the "not very honourable task of putting a gloss upon the capitalist noose".

Anyone interested in Marxism and in the experience of the international working-class movement would do well to ponder over this! One rarely meets with such amazing ignorance of Marxism as that displayed by Mr. N. Rakitnikov and the Left Narodniks, except perhaps among bourgeois economists.

Can it be that Mr. Rakitnikov has not read *Capital*, or *The Poverty of Philosophy*, or the *Communist Manifesto*? If he has not, then it is pointless to talk about socialism. That will be a ridiculous waste of time.

If he has read them, then he ought to know that the *fundamental* idea running through *all* Marx's works, an idea which since Marx has been confirmed in all countries, is that capitalism is *progressive* as compared with feudalism. It is in this sense that Marx and all Marxists "put a gloss" (to use Rakitnikov's clumsy and stupid expression) "upon the capitalist noose"!

Only anarchists or petty-bourgeois, who do not understand the conditions of historical development, can say: a feudal noose or a capitalist one—it makes no difference, for both are nooses! That means confining oneself to *condemnation*, and failing to understand the *objective* course of economic development.

Condemnation means our subjective dissatisfaction. The objective course of feudalism's evolution into capitalism enables *millions* of working people—thanks to the growth of cities, railways, large factories and the migration of workers—to *escape* from a condition of feudal torpor. Capitalism itself rouses and organises them.

Both feudalism and capitalism oppress the workers and strive to keep them in ignorance. But feudalism *can* keep, and *for centuries* has kept, millions of peasants in a downtrodden state (for example, in Russia from the ninth to the nineteenth century, in China for even more centuries). But capitalism *cannot* keep the workers in a state of immobility, torpor, downtroddenness and ignorance.

The centuries of feudalism were centuries of torpor for the working people.

The decades of capitalism have roused millions of wage-workers.

Your failure to understand this, gentlemen of the Left-Narodnik fraternity, shows that you do not understand a thing about socialism, or that you are converting socialism from a struggle of millions engendered by objective conditions into a benevolent old gentleman's fairy-tale!

To advocate the slightest *restriction of the freedom* to mobilise allotment land *actually* amounts to becoming a reactionary, an abettor of the feudalists.

Restriction of the freedom to mobilise allotment land *retards* economic development, *hinders* the formation, growth, awakening and organisation of the wage-worker class, *worsens* the conditions of the workers and peasants, and *increases* the influence of the feudalists.

The Peshekhonovs and Rakitnikovs are *in fact* abettors of precisely these "categories", when they advocate restriction of the freedom to mobilise peasant land.

Trudovaya Pravda No. 19,   *Collected Works*, Vol. 20
June 19, 1914

KARL MARX

A BRIEF BIOGRAPHICAL SKETCH
WITH AN EXPOSITION OF MARXISM

(Extract)

SOCIALISM

From the foregoing it is evident that Marx deduces the
inevitability of the transformation of capitalist society into
socialist society wholly and exclusively from the economic
law of the development of contemporary society. The socialisation of labour, which is advancing ever more rapidly in
thousands of forms and has manifested itself very strikingly,
during the half-century since the death of Marx, in the growth
of large-scale production, capitalist cartels, syndicates and
trusts, as well as in the gigantic increase in the dimensions
and power of finance capital, provides the principal material
foundation for the inevitable advent of socialism. The intellectual and moral motive force and the physical executor of
this transformation is the proletariat, which has been trained
by capitalism itself. The proletariat's struggle against the
bourgeoisie, which finds expression in a variety of forms
ever richer in content, inevitably becomes a political struggle
directed towards the conquest of political power by the
proletariat ("the dictatorship of the proletariat"). The socialisation of production cannot but lead to the means of production becoming the property of society, to the "expropriation
of the expropriators". A tremendous rise in labour productivity, a shorter working day, and the replacement of the
remnants, the ruins, of small-scale, primitive and disunited
production by collective and improved labour—such are the
direct consequences of this transformation. Capitalism breaks
for all time the ties between agriculture and industry, but
at the same time, through its highest development, it prepares
new elements of those ties, a union between industry and
agriculture based on the conscious application of science and

the concentration of collective labour, and on a redistribution of the human population (thus putting an end both to rural backwardness, isolation and barbarism, and to the unnatural concentration of vast masses of people in big cities). A new form of family, new conditions in the status of women and in the upbringing of the younger generation are prepared by the highest forms of present-day capitalism: the labour of women and children and the break-up of the patriarchal family by capitalism inevitably assume the most terrible, disastrous, and repulsive forms in modern society. Nevertheless, "modern industry, by assigning as it does, an important part in the socially organised process of production, outside the domestic sphere, to women, to young persons, and to children of both sexes, creates a new economic foundation for a higher form of the family and of the relations between the sexes. It is, of course, just as absurd to hold the Teutonic-Christian form of the family to be absolute and final as it would be to apply that character to the ancient Roman, the ancient Greek or the Eastern forms which, moreover, taken together form a series in historic development. It is obvious that the fact of the collective working group being composed of individuals of both sexes and all ages, must necessarily, under suitable conditions, become a source of humane development; although in its spontaneously developed, brutal, capitalistic form, where the labourer exists for the process of production, and not the process of production for the labourer, that fact is a pestiferous source of corruption and slavery" (*Capital*, Vol. I, end of Chap. 13). The factory system contains "the germ of the education of the future, an education that will, in the case of every child over a given age, combine productive labour with instruction and gymnastics, not only as one of the methods of adding to the efficiency of social production, but as the only method of producing fully developed human beings" (*ibid*.).[54] Marx's socialism places the problems of nationality and of the state on the same historical footing, not only in the sense of explaining the past but also in the sense of a bold forecast of the future and of bold practical action for its achievement. Nations are an inevitable product, an inevitable form, in the bourgeois epoch of social development. The working class could not grow strong, become mature and take shape without "constituting itself within the nation", without being "national" ("though not in the bourgeois sense of the word"). The development of capitalism, however, breaks down national barriers more and more, does away with national seclusion, and substitutes class antagonisms for national antagonisms. It is, therefore, perfectly true of the developed capitalist countries that "the workingmen have no country" and that "united action" by the workers, of the civilised countries at least, "is one of the first conditions for the emancipation of the proletariat" (*Communist Manifesto*).[55] The state, which is organised coercion, inevitably came into being at a definite stage in the development of society, when the latter had split into irreconcilable classes, and could not exist without an "authority" ostensibly standing above society, and to a certain degree separate from society. Arising out of class contradictions, the state becomes "... the state of the most powerful, economically dominant class, which, through the medium of the state, becomes also the politically dominant class, and thus acquires new means of holding down and exploiting the oppressed class. Thus, the state of antiquity was above all the state of the slave-owners for the purpose of holding down the slaves, as the feudal state was the organ of the nobility for holding down the peasant serfs and bondsmen, and the modern representative state is an instrument of exploitation of wage labour by capital" (Engels, *The Origin of the Family, Private Property and the State*, a work in which the writer expounds his own views and Marx's).[56] Even the democratic republic, the freest and most progressive form of the bourgeois state, does not eliminate this fact in any way, but merely modifies its form (the links between the government and the stock exchange, the corruption—direct and indirect—of officialdom and the press, etc.). By leading to the abolition of classes, socialism will thereby lead to the abolition of the state as well. "The first act," Engels writes in *Anti-Dühring*, "by virtue of which the state really constitutes itself the representative of society as a whole—the taking possession of the means of production in the name of society—is, at the same time, its last independent act as a state. The state interference in social relations becomes superfluous in one sphere after another, and then ceases of itself. The government of persons is replaced by the administration of things and by the direction of the processes of production. The state is not 'abolished', it withers away."[57] "The society that will organise production on the basis of a free and equal association of the producers will put the whole machinery of state where it will then belong: into the Museum of Antiquities, by the side of the spinning wheel and the bronze axe" (Engels, *The Origin of the Family, Private Property and the State*).[58]

Finally, as regards the attitude of Marx's socialism towards the small peasantry, which will continue to exist in the period of the expropriation of the expropriators, we must refer to a declaration made by Engels, which expresses Marx's views: "...when we are in possession of state power we shall not even think of forcibly expropriating the small peasants (regardless of whether with or without compensation), as we shall have to do in the case of the big landowners. Our task relative to the small peasant consists, in the first place, in effecting a transition of his private enterprise and private possession to co-operative ones, not forcibly but by dint of example and the proffer of social assistance for this purpose. And then of course we shall have ample means of showing to the small peasant prospective advantages that must be obvious to him even today" (Engels, *The Peasant Question in France and Germany*,[59] p. 17, published by Alexeyeva; there are errors in the Russian translation. Original in *Die Neue Zeit*).

TACTICS OF THE CLASS STRUGGLE
OF THE PROLETARIAT

After examining, as early as 1844-45, one of the main shortcomings in the earlier materialism, namely, its inability to understand the conditions or appreciate the importance of practical revolutionary activity, Marx, along with his theoretical work, devoted unremitting attention, throughout his lifetime, to the tactical problems of the proletariat's class struggle. An immense amount of material bearing on this is contained in *all* the works of Marx, particularly in the four volumes of his correspondence with Engels, published in 1913. This material is still far from having been brought

together, collected, examined and studied. We shall therefore
have to confine ourselves here to the most general and brief
remarks, emphasising that Marx justly considered that,
without *this* aspect, materialism is incomplete, one-sided, and
lifeless. The fundamental task of proletarian tactics was defined by Marx in strict conformity with all the postulates
of his materialist-dialectical *Weltanschauung*. Only an
objective consideration of the sum total of the relations
between absolutely all the classes in a given society, and
consequently a consideration of the objective stage of development reached by that society and of the relations
between it and other societies, can serve as a basis for the
correct tactics of an advanced class. At the same time, all
classes and all countries are regarded, not statically, but
dynamically, i.e., not in a state of immobility, but in motion
(whose laws are determined by the economic conditions of
existence of each class). Motion, in its turn, is regarded from
the standpoint, not only of the past, but also of the future,
and that not in the vulgar sense it is understood by the
"evolutionists", who see only slow changes, but dialectically:
"...in developments of such magnitude twenty years are no
more than a day," Marx wrote to Engels, "though later on
there may come days in which twenty years are embodied"
(*Briefwechsel*, Vol. 3, p. 127).[60] At each stage of development,
at each moment, proletarian tactics must take account of this
objectively inevitable dialectics of human history, on the one
hand, utilising the periods of political stagnation or of
sluggish, so-called "peaceful" development in order to develop the class-consciousness, strength and militancy of the
advanced class, and, on the other hand, directing all the work
of this utilisation towards the "ultimate aim" of that class's
advance, towards creating in it the ability to find practical
solutions for great tasks in the great days, in which "twenty
years are embodied". Two of Marx's arguments are of special
importance in this connection: one of these is contained in
The Poverty of Philosophy and concerns the economic struggle
and economic organisations of the proletariat; the other is
contained in the *Communist Manifesto* and concerns the
political tasks of the proletariat. The former runs as follows:
"Large-scale industry concentrates in one place a crowd of
people unknown to one another. Competition divides their

interests. But the maintenance of wages, this common interest which they have against their boss, unites them in a common thought of resistance—combination.... Combinations, at first isolated, constitute themselves into groups ... and in face of always united capital, the maintenance of the association becomes more necessary to them [i.e., the workers] than that of wages.... In this struggle—a veritable civil war—all the elements necessary for a coming battle unite and develop. Once it has reached this point, association takes on a political character."[61] Here we have the programme and tactics of the economic struggle and of the trade union movement for several decades to come, for all the lengthy period in which the proletariat will muster its forces for the "coming battle". All this should be compared with numerous references by Marx and Engels to the example of the British labour movement, which shows how industrial "prosperity" leads to attempts "to buy the proletariat" (*Briefwechsel*, Vol. 1, p. 136),[62] to divert them from the struggle; how this prosperity in general "demoralises the workers" (Vol. 2, p. 218); how the British proletariat becomes "bourgeoisified"—"this most bourgeois of all nations is apparently aiming ultimately at the possession of a bourgeois aristocracy and a bourgeois proletariat alongside the bourgeoisie" (Vol. 2, p. 290)[63]; how its "revolutionary energy" oozes away (Vol. 3, p. 124); how it will be necessary to wait a more or less lengthy space of time before "the British workers will free themselves from their apparent bourgeois infection" (Vol. 3, p. 127); how the British labour movement "lacks the mettle of the Chartists[64]" (1866; Vol. 3, p. 305)[65]; how the British workers' leaders are becoming a type midway between "a radical bourgeois and a worker" (in reference to Holyoak, Vol. 4, p. 209); how, owing to Britain's monopoly, and as long as that monopoly lasts, "the British workingman will not budge" (Vol. 4, p. 433).[66] The tactics of the economic struggle, in connection with the general course (*and outcome*) of the working-class movement, are considered here from a remarkably broad, comprehensive, dialectical, and genuinely revolutionary standpoint.

The *Communist Manifesto* advanced a fundamental Marxist principle on the tactics of the political struggle: "The Communists fight for the attainment of the immediate aims, for

6—99

the enforcement of the momentary interests of the working class; but in the movement of the present, they also represent and take care of the future of that movement".[67] That was why, in 1848, Marx supported the party of the "agrarian revolution" in Poland, "that party which brought about the Cracow insurrection in 1846".[68] In Germany, Marx, in 1848 and 1849, supported the extreme revolutionary democrats, and subsequently never retracted what he had then said about tactics. He regarded the German bourgeoisie as an element which was "inclined from the very beginning to betray the people" (only an alliance with the peasantry could have enabled the bourgeoisie to completely achieve its aims) "and compromise with the crowned representatives of the old society". Here is Marx's summing-up of the German bourgeoisie's class position in the period of the bourgeois-democratic revolution—an analysis which, incidentally, is a sample of a materialism that examines society in motion, and, moreover, not only from the aspect of a motion that is *backward*: "Without faith in itself, without faith in the people, grumbling at those above, trembling before those below ... intimidated by the world storm ... no energy in any respect, plagiarism in every respect ... without initiative ... an execrable old man who saw himself doomed to guide and deflect the first youthful impulses of a robust people in his own senile interests..." (*Neue Rheinische Zeitung*, 1848; see *Literarischer Nachlass*, Vol. 3, p. 212).[69] About twenty years later, Marx declared, in a letter to Engels (*Briefwechsel*, Vol. 3, p. 224), that the Revolution of 1848 had failed because the bourgeoisie had preferred peace with slavery to the mere prospect of a fight for freedom. When the revolutionary period of 1848-49 ended, Marx opposed any attempt to play at revolution (his struggle against Schapper and Willich), and insisted on the ability to work in the new phase, which in a quasi-"peaceful" way was preparing new revolutions. The spirit in which Marx wanted this work to be conducted is to be seen in his appraisal of the situation in Germany in 1856, the darkest period of reaction: "The whole thing in Germany will depend on the possibility of backing the proletarian revolution by some second edition of the Peasant War" (*Briefwechsel*, Vol. 2, p. 108).[70] While the democratic (bourgeois) revolution in Germany was uncompleted, Marx focussed every attention, in the tactics of the socialist proletariat, on developing the democratic energy of the peasantry. He held that Lassalle's attitude was "objectively ... a betrayal of the whole workers' movement to Prussia" (Vol. 3, p. 210), incidentally because Lassalle was tolerant of the Junkers and Prussian nationalism. "In a predominantly agricultural country," Engels wrote in 1865, in exchanging views with Marx on their forthcoming joint declaration in the press, "... it is dastardly to make an exclusive attack on the bourgeoisie in the name of the industrial proletariat but never to devote a word to the patriarchal exploitation of the rural proletariat under the lash of the great feudal aristocracy" (Vol. 3, p. 217).[71] From 1864 to 1870, when the period of the consummation of the bourgeois-democratic revolution in Germany was coming to an end, a period in which the Prussian and Austrian exploiting classes were struggling to complete that revolution in one way or another *from above,* Marx not only rebuked Lassalle, who was coquetting with Bismarck, but also corrected Liebknecht, who had lapsed into "Austrophilism" and a defence of particularism; Marx demanded revolutionary tactics which would combat with equal ruthlessness both Bismarck and the Austrophiles, tactics which would not be adapted to the "victor"—the Prussian Junker—but would immediately renew the revolutionary struggle against him *also in the conditions* created by the Prussian military victories (*Briefwechsel,* Vol. 3, pp. 134, 136, 147, 179, 204, 210, 215, 418, 437, 440-41).[72] In the celebrated Address of the International of September 9, 1870, Marx warned the French proletariat against an untimely uprising, but when an uprising nevertheless took place (1871), Marx enthusiastically hailed the revolutionary initiative of the masses, who were "storming heaven" (Marx's letter to Kugelmann).[73] From the standpoint of Marx's dialectical materialism, the defeat of revolutionary action in that situation, as in many others, was a lesser evil, in the general course *and outcome* of the proletarian struggle, than the abandonment of a position already occupied, than surrender without battle. Such a surrender would have demoralised the proletariat and weakened its militancy. While fully appreciating the use of legal means of struggle during periods of political stagnation and the domination of bourgeois legality, Marx,

6*

in 1877 and 1878, following the passage of the Anti-Socialist Law,[74] sharply condemned Most's "revolutionary phrases"; but no less sharply, if not more so, did he attack the opportunism that had for a time come over the official Social-Democratic Party, which did not at once display resoluteness, firmness, revolutionary spirit and a readiness to resort to an illegal struggle in response to the Anti-Socialist Law (*Briefwechsel*, Vol. 4, pp. 397, 404, 418, 422, 424[75]; cf. also letters to Sorge).

Written in July-November 1914

First published in 1915 in the Granat Encyclopaedia, Seventh Edition, Vol. 28, over the signature of V. *Ilyin*

Collected Works, Vol. 21

A CARICATURE OF MARXISM
AND IMPERIALIST ECONOMISM

(Extract)

All nations will arrive at socialism–this is inevitable, but all will do so in not exactly the same way, each will contribute something of its own to some form of democracy, to some variety of the dictatorship of the proletariat,[76] to the varying rate of socialist transformations in the different aspects of social life. There is nothing more primitive from the viewpoint of theory, or more ridiculous from that of practice, than to paint, "in the name of historical materialism", *this* aspect of the future in a monotonous grey. The result will be nothing more than Suzdal daubing.[77] And even if reality were to show that *prior* to the first victory of the socialist proletariat only 1/500 of the nations now oppressed will win emancipation and secede, that *prior* to the final victory of the socialist proletariat the world over (i.e., during all the vicissitudes of the socialist revolution) also only 1/500 of the oppressed nations will secede for a very short time–*even* in that event we would be correct, both from the theoretical and practical political standpoint, in advising the workers, already now, not to permit into their Social-Democratic parties those socialists of the oppressor nations who do not recognise and do not advocate freedom of secession for *all* oppressed nations. For the fact is that we do not know, and cannot know, how many of the oppressed nations will in practice require secession in order to contribute something of their own to the different *forms* of democracy, the different *forms* of transition to socialism. And that the negation of freedom of secession now is theoretically false from beginning to end and in practice amounts to servility to the chauvinists of the oppressing nations—this we know, see and feel daily.

Written August-October 1916

First published in the magazine   *Collected Works*, Vol. 23
Zvezda Nos. 1 and 2, 1924

Signed: *V. Lenin*

THE IMPENDING CATASTROPHE
AND HOW TO COMBAT IT

(Extract)

CAN WE GO FORWARD IF WE FEAR
TO ADVANCE TOWARDS SOCIALISM?

What has been said so far may easily arouse the following objection on the part of a reader who has been brought up on the current opportunist ideas of the Socialist-Revolutionaries and Mensheviks. Most measures described here, he may say, are *already* in effect socialist and not democratic measures!

This current objection, one that is usually raised (in one form or another) in the bourgeois, Socialist-Revolutionary and Menshevik press, is a reactionary defence of backward capitalism, a defence decked out in a Struvean garb. It seems to say that we are not ripe for socialism, that it is too early to "introduce" socialism, that our revolution is a bourgeois revolution and therefore we must be the menials of the bourgeoisie (although the great bourgeois revolutionaries in France 125 years ago made their revolution a great revolution by exercising *terror* against all oppressors, landowners and capitalists alike!).

The pseudo-Marxist lackeys of the bourgeoisie, who have been joined by the Socialist-Revolutionaries and who argue in this way, do not understand (as an examination of the theoretical basis of their opinion shows) what imperialism is, what capitalist monopoly is, what the state is, and what revolutionary democracy is. For anyone who understands this is bound to admit that there can be no advance except towards socialism.

Everybody talks about imperialism. But imperialism is merely monopoly capitalism.

That capitalism in Russia has also become monopoly capitalism is sufficiently attested by the examples of the Produgol, the Prodamet, the Sugar Syndicate, etc. This Sugar

Syndicate is an object-lesson in the way monopoly capitalism develops into state-monopoly capitalism.

And what is the state? It is an organisation of the ruling class—in Germany, for instance, of the Junkers and capitalists. And therefore what the German Plekhanovs (Scheidemann, Lensch, and others) call "war-time socialism" is in fact war-time state-monopoly capitalism, or, to put it more simply and clearly, war-time penal servitude for the workers and war-time protection for capitalist profits.

Now try to *substitute* for the Junker-capitalist state, for the landowner-capitalist state, a *revolutionary-democratic* state, i.e., a state which in a revolutionary way abolishes *all* privileges and does not fear to introduce the fullest democracy in a revolutionary way. You will find that, given a really revolutionary-democratic state, state-monopoly capitalism inevitably and unavoidably implies a step, and more than one step, towards socialism!

For if a huge capitalist undertaking becomes a monopoly, it means that it serves the whole nation. If it has become a state monopoly, it means that the state (i.e., the armed organisation of the population, the workers and peasants above all, provided there is *revolutionary* democracy) directs the whole undertaking. In whose interest?

Either in the interest of the landowners and capitalists, in which case we have not a revolutionary-democratic, but a reactionary-bureaucratic state, an imperialist republic.

Or in the interest of revolutionary democracy—and then *it is a step towards socialism.*

For socialism is merely the next step forward from state-capitalist monopoly. Or, in other words, socialism is merely state-capitalist monopoly *which is made to serve the interests of the whole people* and has to that extent *ceased* to be capitalist monopoly.

There is no middle course here. The objective process of development is such that it is *impossible* to advance from *monopolies* (and the war has magnified their number, role and importance tenfold) without advancing towards socialism.

Either we have to be revolutionary democrats in fact, in which case we must not fear to take steps towards socialism.

Or we fear to take steps towards socialism, condemn them in the Plekhanov, Dan or Chernov way, by arguing that our revolution is a bourgeois revolution, that socialism cannot be "introduced", etc., in which case we inevitably sink to the level of Kerensky, Milyukov and Kornilov, i. e., we in a *reactionary-bureaucratic* way suppress the "revolutionary-democratic" aspirations of the workers and peasants.

There is no middle course.

And therein lies the fundamental contradiction of our revolution.

It is impossible to stand still in history in general, and in war-time in particular. We must either advance or retreat. It is *impossible* in twentieth-century Russia, which has won a republic and democracy in a revolutionary way, to go forward without *advancing* towards socialism, without taking *steps* towards it (steps conditioned and determined by the level of technology and culture: large-scale machine production cannot be "introduced" in peasant farming nor abolished in the sugar industry).

But to fear to advance *means* retreating—which the Kerenskys, to the delight of the Milyukovs and Plekhanovs, and with the foolish assistance of the Tseretelis and Chernovs, are actually doing.

The dialectics of history is such that the war, by extraordinarily expediting the transformation of monopoly capitalism into state-monopoly capitalism, has *thereby* extraordinarily advanced mankind towards socialism.

Imperialist war is the eve of socialist revolution. And this not only because the horrors of the war give rise to proletarian revolt—no revolt can bring about socialism unless the economic conditions for socialism are ripe—but because state-monopoly capitalism is a complete *material* preparation for socialism, the *threshold* of socialism, a rung of the ladder of history between which and the rung called socialism *there are no intermediate rungs.*

* * *

Our Socialist-Revolutionaries and Mensheviks approach the question of socialism in a doctrinaire way, from the standpoint of a doctrine learnt by heart but poorly understood. They picture socialism as some remote, unknown and dim future.

But socialism is now gazing at us from all the windows of modern capitalism; socialism is outlined directly, *practically*, by every important measure that constitutes a forward step on the basis of this modern capitalism.

What is universal labour service?

It is a step forward on the basis of modern monopoly capitalism, a step towards the regulation of economic life as a whole, in accordance with a certain general plan, a step towards the economy of national labour and towards the prevention of its senseless wastage by capitalism.

In Germany it is the Junkers (landowners) and capitalists who are introducing universal labour service, and therefore it inevitably becomes war-time penal servitude for the workers.

But take the same institution and think over its significance in a revolutionary-democratic state. Universal labour service, introduced, regulated and directed by the Soviets of Workers', Soldiers' and Peasants' Deputies, will *still not* be socialism, but it will *no longer* be capitalism. It will be a tremendous *step towards* socialism, a step from which, if complete democracy is preserved, there can no longer be any retreat back to capitalism, without unparalleled violence being committed against the masses.

Written September 10-14 (23-27),
1917

Published in pamphlet form by   *Collected Works*, Vol. 25
Priboi Publishers in Petrograd
at the end of October 1917

THE STATE AND REVOLUTION
THE MARXIST THEORY OF THE STATE AND THE TASKS OF THE PROLETARIAT IN THE REVOLUTION

(Extract)

CHAPTER V

THE ECONOMIC BASIS OF THE WITHERING AWAY OF THE STATE

Marx explains this question most thoroughly in his *Critique of the Gotha Programme* (letter to Bracke, May 5, 1875, which was not published until 1891 when it was printed in *Neue Zeit*, Vol. IX, 1, and which has appeared in Russian in a special edition).[78] The polemical part of this remarkable work, which contains a criticism of Lassalleanism, has, so to speak, overshadowed its positive part, namely, the analysis of the connection between the development of communism and the withering away of the state.

1. Presentation of the Question by Marx

From a superficial comparison of Marx's letter to Bracke of May 5, 1875, with Engels's letter to Bebel of March 28, 1875,[79] which we examined above, it might appear that Marx was much more of a "champion of the state" than Engels, and that the difference of opinion between the two writers on the question of the state was very considerable.

Engels suggested to Bebel that all chatter about the state be dropped altogether, that the word "state" be eliminated from the programme altogether and the word "community" substituted for it. Engels even declared that the Commune was no longer a state in the proper sense of the word.[80] Yet Marx even spoke of the "future state in communist society", i.e., he would seem to recognise the need for the state even under communism.

But such a view would be fundamentally wrong. A closer examination shows that Marx's and Engels's views on the state and its withering away were completely identical, and that Marx's expression quoted above refers to the state in the process of *withering away*.

Clearly there can be no question of specifying the moment of the *future* "withering away", the more so since it will obviously be a lengthy process. The apparent difference between Marx and Engels is due to the fact that they dealt with different subjects and pursued different aims. Engels set out to show Bebel graphically, sharply and in broad outline the utter absurdity of the current prejudices concerning the state (shared to no small degree by Lassalle). Marx only touched upon *this* question in passing, being interested in another subject, namely, the *development* of communist society.

The whole theory of Marx is the application of the theory of development—in its most consistent, complete, considered and pithy form—to modern capitalism. Naturally, Marx was faced with the problem of applying this theory both to the *forthcoming* collapse of capitalism and to the *future* development of *future* communism.

On the basis of what *facts*, then, can the question of the future development of future communism be dealt with?

On the basis of the fact that it *has its origin* in capitalism, that it develops historically from capitalism, that it is the result of the action of a social force to which capitalism *gave birth*. There is no trace of an attempt on Marx's part to make up a utopia, to indulge in idle guess-work about what cannot be known. Marx treated the question of communism in the same way as a naturalist would treat the question of the development of, say, a new biological variety, once he knew that it had originated in such and such a way and was changing in such and such a definite direction.

To begin with, Marx brushed aside the confusion the Gotha Programme brought into the question of the relationship between state and society. He wrote:

> " 'Present-day society' is capitalist society, which
> exists in all civilised countries, being more or less free
> from medieval admixture, more or less modified by
> the particular historical development of each country,

more or less developed. On the other hand, the 'present-day state' changes with a country's frontier. It is different in the Prusso-German Empire from what it is in Switzerland, and different in England from what it is in the United States. 'The present-day state' is, therefore, a fiction.

"Nevertheless, the different states of the different civilised countries, in spite of their motley diversity of form, all have this in common, that they are based on modern bourgeois society, only one more or less capitalistically developed. They have, therefore, also certain essential characteristics in common. In this sense it is possible to speak of the 'present-day state', in contrast with the future, in which its present root, bourgeois society, will have died off.

"The question then arises: what transformation will the state undergo in communist society? In other words, what social functions will remain in existence there that are analogous to present state functions? This question can only be answered scientifically, and one does not get a flea-hop nearer the solution by a thousandfold combination of the word people with the word state."[81]

After thus ridiculing all talk about a "people's state", Marx formulated the question and gave warning, as it were, that those seeking a scientific answer to it should use only firmly established scientific data.

The first fact that has been established most accurately by the whole theory of development, by science as a whole—a fact that was ignored by the utopians, and is ignored by the present-day opportunists, who are afraid of the socialist revolution—is that, historically, there must undoubtedly be a special stage, or a special phase, of *transition* from capitalism to communism.

2. The Transition from Capitalism to Communism

Marx continued:

"Between capitalist and communist society lies the period of the revolutionary transformation of the one into the other. Corresponding to this is also a political

transition period in which the state can be nothing but
the revolutionary dictatorship of the proletariat."[82]

Marx bases this conclusion on an analysis of the role played
by the proletariat in modern capitalist society, on the data
concerning the development of this society, and on the irre-
concilability of the antagonistic interests of the proletariat
and the bourgeoisie.

Previously the question was put as follows: to achieve its
emancipation, the proletariat must overthrow the bourgeoisie,
win political power and establish its revolutionary dictatorship.

Now the question is put somewhat differently: the transition from capitalist society—which is developing towards
communism—to communist society is impossible without a
"political transition period", and the state in this period can
only be the revolutionary dictatorship of the proletariat.

What, then, is the relation of this dictatorship to democracy?

We have seen that the *Communist Manifesto* simply places
side by side the two concepts: "to raise the proletariat to the
position of the ruling class" and "to win the battle of democracy".[83] On the basis of all that has been said above, it is
possible to determine more precisely how democracy changes
in the transition from capitalism to communism.

In capitalist society, providing it develops under the most
favourable conditions, we have a more or less complete democracy in the democratic republic. But this democracy is always
hemmed in by the narrow limits set by capitalist exploitation,
and consequently always remains, in effect, a democracy for
the minority, only for the propertied classes, only for the
rich. Freedom in capitalist society always remains about the
same as it was in the ancient Greek republics: freedom for the
slave-owners. Owing to the conditions of capitalist exploitation, the modern wage slaves are so crushed by want and
poverty that "they cannot be bothered with democracy",
"cannot be bothered with politics"; in the ordinary, peaceful
course of events, the majority of the population is debarred
from participation in public and political life.

The correctness of this statement is perhaps most clearly
confirmed by Germany, because constitutional legality steadily
endured there for a remarkably long time—nearly half a
century (1871-1914)—and during this period the Social-

Democrats were able to achieve far more than in other countries in the way of "utilising legality", and organised a larger proportion of the workers into a political party than anywhere else in the world.

What is this largest proportion of politically conscious and active wage slaves that has so far been recorded in capitalist society? One million members of the Social-Democratic Party—out of fifteen million wage-workers! Three million organised in trade unions—out of fifteen million!

Democracy for an insignificant minority, democracy for the rich—that is the democracy of capitalist society. If we look more closely into the machinery of capitalist democracy, we see everywhere, in the "petty"—supposedly petty—details of the suffrage (residential qualification, exclusion of women, etc.), in the technique of the representative institutions, in the actual obstacles to the right of assembly (public buildings are not for "paupers"!), in the purely capitalist organisation of the daily press, etc., etc.—we see restriction after restriction imposed upon democracy. These restrictions, exceptions, exclusions, obstacles for the poor seem slight, especially in the eyes of one who has never known want himself and has never been in close contact with the oppressed classes in their mass life (and nine out of ten, if not ninety-nine out of a hundred, bourgeois publicists and politicians come under this category); but in their sum total these restrictions exclude and squeeze out the poor from politics, from active participation in democracy.

Marx grasped this *essence* of capitalist democracy splendidly when, in analysing the experience of the Commune, he said that the oppressed are allowed once every few years to decide which particular representatives of the oppressing class will represent and repress them in parliament![84]

But from this capitalist democracy—that is inevitably narrow and stealthily pushes aside the poor, and is therefore hypocritical and false through and through—forward development does not proceed simply, directly and smoothly, towards "greater and greater democracy", as the liberal professors and petty-bourgeois opportunists would have us believe. No, forward development, i.e., development towards communism, proceeds through the dictatorship of the proletariat, and cannot do otherwise, for the *resistance* of the capitalist exploiters cannot be *broken* by anyone else or in any other way.

And the dictatorship of the proletariat, i.e., the organisation of the vanguard of the oppressed as the ruling class for the purpose of suppressing the oppressors, cannot result merely in an expansion of democracy. *Simultaneously* with an immense expansion of democracy, which *for the first time* becomes democracy for the poor, democracy for the people, and not democracy for the money-bags, the dictatorship of the proletariat imposes a series of restrictions on the freedom of the oppressors, the exploiters, the capitalists. We must suppress them in order to free humanity from wage slavery, their resistance must be crushed by force; it is clear that there is no freedom and no democracy where there is suppression and coercion.

Engels expressed this splendidly in his letter to Bebel when he said, as the reader will remember, that "the proletariat needs the state, not in the interests of freedom but in order to hold down its adversaries, and as soon as it becomes possible to speak of freedom the state as such ceases to exist".[85]

Democracy for the vast majority of the people, and suppression by force, i.e., exclusion from democracy, of the exploiters and oppressors of the people—this is the change democracy undergoes during the *transition* from capitalism to communism.

Only in communist society, when the resistance of the capitalists has been completely crushed, when the capitalists have disappeared, when there are no classes (i.e., when there is no distinction between the members of society as regards their relation to the social means of production), *only* then "the state ... ceases to exist", and "*it becomes possible to speak of freedom*". Only then will a truly complete democracy become possible and be realised, a democracy without any exceptions whatever. And only then will democracy begin to *wither away*, owing to the simple fact that, freed from capitalist slavery, from the untold horrors, savagery, absurdities and infamies of capitalist exploitation, people will gradually *become accustomed* to observing the elementary rules of social intercourse that have been known for centuries and repeated for thousands of years in all copy-book maxims.

They will become accustomed to observing them without force, without coercion, without subordination, *without the special apparatus* for coercion called the state.

The expression "the state *withers away*" is very well chosen, for it indicates both the gradual and the spontaneous nature of the process. Only habit can, and undoubtedly will, have such an effect; for we see around us on millions of occasions how readily people become accustomed to observing the necessary rules of social intercourse when there is no exploitation, when there is nothing that arouses indignation, evokes protest and revolt, and creates the need for *suppression*.

And so in capitalist society we have a democracy that is curtailed, wretched, false, a democracy only for the rich, for the minority. The dictatorship of the proletariat, the period of transition to communism, will for the first time create democracy for the people, for the majority, along with the necessary suppression of the exploiters, of the minority. Communism alone is capable of providing really complete democracy, and the more complete it is, the sooner it will become unnecessary and wither away of its own accord.

In other words, under capitalism we have the state in the proper sense of the word, that is, a special machine for the suppression of one class by another, and, what is more, of the majority by the minority. Naturally, to be successful, such an undertaking as the systematic suppression of the exploited majority by the exploiting minority calls for the utmost ferocity and savagery in the matter of suppressing, it calls for seas of blood, through which mankind is actually wading its way in slavery, serfdom and wage labour.

Furthermore, during the *transition* from capitalism to communism suppression is *still* necessary, but it is now the suppression of the exploiting minority by the exploited majority. A special apparatus, a special machine for suppression, the "state", is *still* necessary, but this is now a transitional state. It is no longer a state in the proper sense of the word; for the suppression of the minority of exploiters by the majority of the wage slaves of *yesterday* is comparatively so easy, simple and natural a task that it will entail far less bloodshed than the suppression of the risings of slaves, serfs or wage-labourers, and it will cost mankind far less. And it is com-

patible with the extension of democracy to such an overwhelming majority of the population that the need for a
special machine of suppression will begin to disappear.
Naturally, the exploiters are unable to suppress the people
without a highly complex machine for performing this task,
but *the people* can suppress the exploiters even with a very
simple "machine", almost without a "machine", without a
special apparatus, by the simple *organisation of the armed
people* (such as the Soviets of Workers' and Soldiers' Deputies,
we would remark, running ahead).

Lastly, only communism makes the state absolutely
unnecessary, for there is *nobody* to be suppressed—"nobody"
in the sense of a *class*, of a systematic struggle against a
definite section of the population. We are not utopians, and
do not in the least deny the possibility and inevitability of
excesses on the part of *individual persons*, or the need to
stop *such* excesses. In the first place, however, no special
machine, no special apparatus of suppression, is needed for
this; this will be done by the armed people themselves, as
simply and as readily as any crowd of civilised people, even
in modern society, interferes to put a stop to a scuffle or to
prevent a woman from being assaulted. And, secondly, we
know that the fundamental social cause of excesses, which
consist in the violation of the rules of social intercourse, is
the exploitation of the people, their want and their poverty.
With the removal of this chief cause, excesses will inevitably
begin to "*wither away*". We do not know how quickly and
in what succession, but we do know they will wither away.
With their withering away the state will also *wither away*.

Without building utopias, Marx defined more fully what
can be defined *now* regarding this future, namely, the difference between the lower and higher phases (levels, stages)
of communist society.

3. The First Phase of Communist Society

In the *Critique of the Gotha Programme*, Marx goes into
detail to disprove Lassalle's idea that under socialism the
worker will receive the "undiminished" or "full product of
his labour". Marx shows that from the whole of the social

labour of society there must be deducted a reserve fund, a fund for the expansion of production, a fund for the replacement of the "wear and tear" of machinery, and so on. Then, from the means of consumption must be deducted a fund for administrative expenses, for schools, hospitals, old people's homes, and so on.

Instead of Lassalle's hazy, obscure, general phrase ("the full product of his labour to the worker"), Marx makes a sober estimate of exactly how socialist society will have to manage its affairs. Marx proceeds to make a *concrete* analysis of the conditions of life of a society in which there will be no capitalism, and says:

> "What we have to deal with here [in analysing the programme of the workers' Party] is a communist society, not as it has *developed* on its own foundations, but, on the contrary, just as it *emerges* from capitalist society; in every respect, economically, morally and intellectually, it is, therefore, still stamped with the marks of the old society from whose womb it comes."[86]

It is this communist society, which has just emerged into the light of day out of the womb of capitalism and which is in every respect stamped with the birthmarks of the old society, that Marx terms the "first", or lower, phase of communist society.

The means of production are no longer the private property of individuals. The means of production belong to the whole of society. Every member of society, performing a certain part of the socially necessary work, receives a certificate from society to the effect that he has done a certain amount of work. And with this certificate he receives from the public store of consumer goods a corresponding quantity of products. After a deduction is made of the amount of labour which goes to the public fund, every worker, therefore, receives from society as much as he has given to it.

"Equality" apparently reigns supreme.

But when Lassalle, having in view such a social order (usually called socialism, but termed by Marx the first phase of communism), says that this is "equitable distribution", that this is "the equal right of all to an equal product of labour", Lassalle is mistaken and Marx exposes the mistake.

"Equal right," says Marx, we certainly do have here; but it is *still* a "bourgeois right", which, like every right, *implies inequality*. Every right is an application of an *equal* measure to *different* people who in fact are not alike, are not equal to one another. That is why "equal right" is a violation of equality and an injustice. In fact, everyone, having performed as much social labour as another, receives an equal share of the social product (after the above-mentioned deductions).

But people are not alike: one is strong, another is weak; one is married, another is not; one has more children, another has less, and so on. And the conclusion Marx draws is:

> "With an equal performance of labour, and hence an equal share in the social consumption fund, one will in fact receive more than another, one will be richer than another, and so on. To avoid all these defects, right would have to be unequal rather than equal."[87]

The first phase of communism, therefore, cannot yet provide justice and equality: differences, and unjust differences, in wealth will still persist, but the *exploitation* of man by man will have become impossible because it will be impossible to seize the *means of production*—the factories, machines, land, etc.—and make them private property. In smashing Lassalle's petty-bourgeois, vague phrases about "equality" and "justice" *in general*, Marx shows the *course of development* of communist society, which is *compelled* to abolish at first *only* the "injustice" of the means of production seized by individuals, and which is *unable* at once to eliminate the other injustice, which consists in the distribution of consumer goods "according to the amount of labour performed" (and not according to needs).

The vulgar economists, including the bourgeois professors and "our" Tugan, constantly reproach the socialists with forgetting the inequality of people and with "dreaming" of eliminating this inequality. Such a reproach, as we see, only proves the extreme ignorance of the bourgeois ideologists.

Marx not only most scrupulously takes account of the inevitable inequality of men, but he also takes into account the fact that the mere conversion of the means of production into the common property of the whole of society (commonly called "socialism") *does not remove* the defects of distribution and the inequality of "bourgeois right", which *continues to prevail* so long as products are divided "according to the amount of labour performed". Continuing, Marx says:

> "But these defects are inevitable in the first phase of communist society as it is when it has just emerged, after prolonged birth pangs, from capitalist society. Right can never be higher than the economic structure of society and its cultural development conditioned thereby."[88]

And so, in the first phase of communist society (usually called socialism) "bourgeois right" is *not* abolished in its entirety, but only in part, only in proportion to the economic revolution so far attained, i.e., only in respect of the means of production. "Bourgeois right" recognises them as the private property of individuals. Socialism converts them into *common* property. *To that extent*—and to that extent alone— "bourgeois right" disappears.

However, it persists as far as its other part is concerned; it persists in the capacity of regulator (determining factor) in the distribution of products and the allotment of labour among the members of society. The socialist principle, "He who does not work shall not eat", is *already* realised; the other socialist principle, "An equal amount of products for an equal amount of labour", is also *already* realised. But this is not yet communism, and it does not yet abolish "bourgeois right", which gives unequal individuals, in return for unequal (really unequal) amounts of labour, equal amounts of products.

This is a "defect", says Marx, but it is unavoidable in the first phase of communism; for if we are not to indulge in utopianism, we must not think that having overthrown capitalism people will at once learn to work for society *without any standard of right*. Besides, the abolition of capitalism *does not immediately create* the economic prerequisites for *such* a change.

Now, there is no other standard than that of "bourgeois right". To this extent, therefore, there still remains the need for a state, which, while safeguarding the common ownership of the means of production, would safeguard equality in labour and in the distribution of products.

The state withers away insofar as there are no longer any capitalists, any classes, and, consequently, no *class* can be *suppressed*.

But the state has not yet completely withered away, since there still remains the safeguarding of "bourgeois right", which sanctifies actual inequality. For the state to wither away completely, complete communism is necessary.

4. The Higher Phase of Communist Society

Marx continues:

> "In a higher phase of communist society, after the enslaving subordination of the individual to the division of labour and with it also the antithesis between mental and manual labour has vanished, after labour has become not only a livelihood but life's prime want, after the productive forces have increased with the all-round development of the individual, and all the springs of co-operative wealth flow more abundantly—only then can the narrow horizon of bourgeois right be crossed in its entirety and society inscribe on its banners: From each according to his ability, to each according to his needs!"[89]

Only now can we fully appreciate the correctness of Engels's remarks mercilessly ridiculing the absurdity of combining the words "freedom" and "state". So long as the state exists there is no freedom. When there is freedom, there will be no state.

The economic basis for the complete withering away of the state is such a high stage of development of communism at which the antithesis between mental and manual labour disappears, at which there consequently disappears one of the principal sources of modern *social* inequality—a source, moreover, which cannot on any account be removed immediately by the mere conversion of the means of production into public property, by the mere expropriation of the capitalists.

This expropriation will make it *possible* for the productive forces to develop to a tremendous extent. And when we see how incredibly capitalism is already *retarding* this development, when we see how much progress could be achieved on the basis of the level of technique already attained, we are entitled to say with the fullest confidence that the expropriation of the capitalists will inevitably result in an enormous development of the productive forces of human society. But how rapidly this development will proceed, how soon it will reach the point of breaking away from the division of labour, of doing away with the antithesis between mental and manual labour, of transforming labour into "life's prime want"—we do not and *cannot* know.

That is why we are entitled to speak only of the inevitable withering away of the state, emphasising the protracted nature of this process and its dependence upon the rapidity of development of the *higher phase* of communism, and leaving the question of the time required for, or the concrete forms of, the withering away quite open, because there is *no* material for answering these questions.

The state will be able to wither away completely when society adopts the rule: "From each according to his ability, to each according to his needs", i.e., when people have become so accustomed to observing the fundamental rules of social intercourse and when their labour has become so productive that they will voluntarily work *according to their ability*. "The narrow horizon of bourgeois right", which compels one to calculate with the heartlessness of a Shylock whether one has not worked half an hour more than somebody else, whether one is not getting less pay than somebody else—this narrow horizon will then be crossed. There will then be no need for society, in distributing products, to regulate the quantity to be received by each; each will take freely "according to his needs".

From the bourgeois point of view, it is easy to declare that such a social order is "sheer utopia" and to sneer at the socialists for promising everyone the right to receive from society, without any control over the labour of the individual citizen, any quantity of truffles, cars, pianos, etc. Even to this day, most bourgeois "savants" confine themselves to sneering in this way, thereby betraying both their ignorance and their selfish defence of capitalism.

Ignorance—for it has never entered the head of any socialist to "promise" that the higher phase of the development of communism will arrive; as for the great socialists' *forecast* that it will arrive, it presupposes not the present productivity of labour and *not the present* ordinary run of people who, like the seminary students in Pomyalovsky's stories,[90] are capable of damaging the stocks of public wealth "just for fun", and of demanding the impossible.

Until the "higher" phase of communism arrives, the socialists demand the *strictest* control by society *and by the state* over the measure of labour and the measure of consumption; but this control must *start* with the expropriation of the capitalists, with the establishment of workers' control over the capitalists, and must be exercised not by a state of bureaucrats, but by a state of *armed workers*.

The selfish defence of capitalism by the bourgeois ideologists (and their hangers-on, like the Tseretelis, Chernovs and Co.) consists in that they *substitute* arguing and talk about the distant future for the vital and burning question of *present-day* politics, namely, the expropriation of the capitalists, the conversion of *all* citizens into workers and other employees of *one* huge "syndicate"—the whole state—and the complete subordination of the entire work of this syndicate to a genuinely democratic state, *the state of the Soviets of Workers' and Soldiers' Deputies*.

In fact, when a learned professor, followed by the philistine, followed in turn by the Tseretelis and Chernovs, talks of wild utopias, of the demagogic promises of the Bolsheviks, of the impossibility of "introducing" socialism, it is the higher stage, or phase, of communism he has in mind, which no one has ever promised or even thought to "introduce", because, generally speaking, it cannot be "introduced".

And this brings us to the question of the scientific distinction between socialism and communism which Engels touched on in his above-quoted argument about the incorrectness of the name "Social-Democrat". Politically, the distinction between the first, or lower, and the higher phase of communism will with time, probably, be tremendous. But it would be ridiculous to recognise this distinction now, under capitalism, and only individual anarchists, perhaps, could invest it with primary importance (if there still are people among the anarchists who have learned nothing from the "Plekhanov" conversion of the Kropotkins, of Grave, Cornelissen and other "stars" of anarchism into social-chauvinists or "anarcho-trenchists", as Ghe, one of the few anarchists who have still preserved a sense of honour and a conscience, has put it).

But the scientific distinction between socialism and communism is clear. What is usually called socialism was termed by Marx the "first", or lower, phase of communist society. Insofar as the means of production become *common* property, the word "communism" is also applicable here, providing we do not forget that this is *not* complete communism. The great significance of Marx's explanations is that here, too, he consistently applies materialist dialectics, the theory of development, and regards communism as something which develops *out of* capitalism. Instead of scholastically invented, "concocted" definitions and fruitless disputes over words (What is socialism? What is communism?), Marx gives an analysis of what might be called the stages of the economic maturity of communism.

In its first phase, or first stage, communism *cannot* as yet be fully mature economically and entirely free from traditions or vestiges of capitalism. Hence the interesting phenomenon that communism in its first phase retains "the narrow horizon of *bourgeois* right". Of course, bourgeois right in regard to the distribution of *consumer* goods inevitably presupposes the existence of the *bourgeois state*, for right is nothing without an apparatus capable of *enforcing* the observance of the standards of right.

It follows that under communism there remains for a time not only bourgeois right, but even the bourgeois state, without the bourgeoisie!

This may sound like a paradox or simply a dialectical conundrum, of which Marxism is often accused by people who have not taken the slightest trouble to study its extraordinarily profound content.

But in fact, remnants of the old, surviving in the new, confront us in life at every step, both in nature and in society. And Marx did not arbitrarily insert a scrap of "bourgeois" right into communism, but indicated what is economically and politically inevitable in a society emerging *out of the womb* of capitalism.

Democracy is of enormous importance to the working class in its struggle against the capitalists for its emancipation. But democracy is by no means a boundary not to be overstepped; it is only one of the stages on the road from feudalism to capitalism, and from capitalism to communism.

Democracy means equality. The great significance of the proletariat's struggle for equality and of equality as a slogan will be clear if we correctly interpret it as meaning the abolition of *classes*. But democracy means only *formal* equality. And as soon as equality is achieved for all members of society *in relation* to ownership of the means of production, that is, equality of labour and wages, humanity will inevitably be confronted with the question of advancing farther, from formal equality to actual equality, i.e., to the operation of the rule "from each according to his ability, to each according to his needs". By what stages, by means of what practical measures humanity will proceed to this supreme aim we do not and cannot know. But it is important to realise how infinitely mendacious is the ordinary bourgeois conception of socialism as something lifeless, rigid, fixed once and for all, whereas in reality *only* socialism will be the beginning of a rapid, genuine, truly mass forward movement, embracing first the *majority* and then the whole of the population, in all spheres of public and private life.

Democracy is a form of the state, one of its varieties. Consequently, it, like every state, represents, on the one hand, the organised, systematic use of force against persons; but, on the other hand, it signifies the formal recognition of equality of citizens, the equal right of all to determine the structure of, and to administer, the state. This, in turn, results in the fact that, at a certain stage in the development of democracy, it first welds together the class that wages a revolutionary struggle against capitalism—the proletariat, and enables it to crush, smash to atoms, wipe off the face of the earth the bourgeois, even if it is republican-bourgeois, state machine, the standing army, the police and the bureaucracy and to substitute for them a *more* democratic state machine, but a state machine nevertheless, in the shape of armed workers who proceed to form a militia involving the entire population.

Here "quantity turns into quality": *such* a degree of democracy implies overstepping the boundaries of bourgeois society and beginning its socialist reorganisation. If really *all* take part in the administration of the state, capitalism cannot retain its hold. The development of capitalism, in turn, creates the *preconditions* that *enable* really "all" to take part in the administration of the state. Some of these preconditions are: universal literacy, which has already been achieved in a number of the most advanced capitalist countries, then the "training and disciplining" of millions of workers by the huge, complex, socialised apparatus of the postal service, railways, big factories, large-scale commerce, banking, etc., etc.

Given these *economic* preconditions, it is quite possible, after the overthrow of the capitalists and the bureaucrats, to proceed immediately, overnight, to replace them in the *control* over production and distribution, in the work of *keeping account* of labour and products, by the armed workers, by the whole of the armed population. (The question of control and accounting should not be confused with the question of the scientifically trained staff of engineers, agronomists and so on. These gentlemen are working today in obedience to the wishes of the capitalists, and will work even better to-morrow in obedience to the wishes of the armed workers.)

Accounting and control—that is *mainly* what is needed for the "smooth working", for the proper functioning, of the *first phase* of communist society. *All* citizens are transformed into hired employees of the state which consists of the armed workers. *All* citizens become employees and workers of a *single* country-wide state "syndicate". All that is required is that they should work equally, do their proper share of work, and get equal pay. The accounting and control necessary for this have been *simplified* by capitalism to the utmost and reduced to the extraordinarily simple operations—which any literate person can perform—of supervising and recording, knowledge of the four rules of arithmetic, and issuing appropriate receipts.*

---

* When the more important functions of the state are reduced to such accounting and control by the workers themselves, it will cease to be a "political state" and "public functions will lose their political character and become mere administrative functions" (cf. above, Chapter IV, 2, Engels's controversy with the anarchists).

When the *majority* of the people begin independently and everywhere to keep such accounts and exercise such control over the capitalists (now converted into employees) and over the intellectual gentry who preserve their capitalist habits, this control will really become universal, general and popular; and there will be no getting away from it, there will be "nowhere to go".

The whole of society will have become a single office and a single factory, with equality of labour and pay.

But this "factory" discipline, which the proletariat, after defeating the capitalists, after overthrowing the exploiters, will extend to the whole of society, is by no means our ideal, or our ultimate goal. It is only a necessary *step* for thoroughly cleaning society of all the infamies and abominations of capitalist exploitation, *and for further* progress.

From the moment all members of society, or at least the vast majority, have learned to administer the state *themselves*, have taken this work into their own hands, have organised control over the insignificant capitalist minority, over the gentry who wish to preserve their capitalist habits and over the workers who have been thoroughly corrupted by capitalism—from this moment the need for government of any kind begins to disappear altogether. The more complete the democracy, the nearer the moment when it becomes unnecessary. The more democratic the "state" which consists of the armed workers, and which is "no longer a state in the proper sense of the word", the more rapidly *every form* of state begins to wither away.

For when *all* have learned to administer and actually do independently administer social production, independently keep accounts and exercise control over the parasites, the rich idlers, the swindlers and other "guardians of capitalist traditions", the escape from this popular accounting and control will inevitably become so incredibly difficult, such a rare exception, and will probably be accompanied by such swift and severe punishment (for the armed workers are practical men and not sentimental intellectuals, and they will scarcely allow anyone to trifle with them), that the *necessity* of observing the simple, fundamental rules of the community will very soon become a *habit*.

Then the door will be thrown wide open for the transition from the first phase of communist society to its higher phase, and with it to the complete withering away of the state.

Written August-September 1917

Published in pamphlet form   *Collected Works*, Vol. 25
by Zhizn i Znaniye Publishers,
Petrograd, 1918

MEETING OF THE ALL-RUSSIA
CENTRAL EXECUTIVE COMMITTEE
November 4 (17), 1917

2

REPLY TO A QUESTION
FROM THE LEFT SOCIALIST-REVOLUTIONARIES

The Left Socialist-Revolutionaries' question was answered by Lenin. He recalled that in the first days of the revolution the Bolsheviks invited the Left Socialist-Revolutionaries to join the new government, but the group of Left Socialist-Revolutionaries, who refused to share responsibility in those difficult, critical days with their neighbours on the Left, declined to collaborate with the Bolsheviks.

In its activity the new regime could not afford to reckon with all the obstacles which could arise in its way if it scrupulously observed all formalities. The situation was much too grave and allowed of no procrastination. There was no time to waste on smoothing off rough corners that merely changed outward appearances without altering the essence of the new measures. After all, the Second All-Russia Congress of Soviets itself, brushing aside all difficulties of a formal nature, adopted two laws of world importance at one long sitting.[91] These laws may have formal defects from the standpoint of bourgeois society, but power is, after all, in the hands of the Soviets, which can always make the necessary amendments. The Kerensky government's criminal failure to act brought the country and the revolution to the brink of disaster: delay may indeed prove to be fatal, and the new regime is setting up milestones in the development of new forms of life by issuing laws to meet the aspirations and hopes of the broad masses. The local Soviets, depending on time and place, can amend, enlarge and add to the basic provisions worked out by the government. Creative activity at the grass roots is the basic factor of the new public life. Let the workers set about organising workers' control at their factories. Let them supply the villages with manufactures in exchange for grain. Account must be taken of every single article, every pound of grain, because what socialism implies above all is keeping account of everything. Socialism cannot be decreed from above. Its spirit rejects the mechanical bureaucratic approach; living, creative socialism is the product of the masses themselves.

Pravda No. 182 and
Izvestia No. 218,
November 7, 1917

Collected Works, Vol. 26

ALLIANCE BETWEEN THE WORKERS
AND THE WORKING AND EXPLOITED PEASANTS

A LETTER TO *PRAVDA*

Today, Saturday, November 18, in the course of a speech
I made at the Peasants' Congress, I was publicly asked a
question to which I forthwith replied. It is essential that this
question and my reply should immediately be made known
to all the reading public, for while formally speaking only
in my own name, I was actually speaking in the name of the
whole Bolshevik Party.

The matter was the following.

Touching on the question of an alliance between the
Bolshevik workers and the Left Socialist-Revolutionaries,
whom many peasants at present trust, I argued in my speech
that this alliance *can* be an "honest coalition", an honest
alliance, for there is *no* radical divergence of interests between the wage-workers and the working and exploited
peasants. Socialism is *fully* able to meet the interests of both.
Only socialism can meet their interests. Hence the possibility
and necessity for an "honest coalition" between the proletarians and the working and exploited peasantry. On the
contrary, a "coalition" (alliance) between the working and
exploited classes, on the one hand, and the bourgeoisie, on
the other, *cannot* be an "honest coalition" because of the
radical divergence of interests between these classes.

Imagine, I said, that there is a majority of Bolsheviks and
a minority of Left Socialist-Revolutionaries in the government, or even, let us assume, only one Left Socialist-Revolutionary—the Commissar of Agriculture. Could the Bolsheviks
practise an honest coalition under such circumstances?

They could; for, while they are irreconcilable in their fight
against the counter-revolutionary elements (including the

Right Socialist-Revolutionary and the defencist elements), the Bolsheviks would be obliged to *abstain* from voting on questions which concern purely Socialist-Revolutionary points in the land programme approved by the Second All-Russia Congress of Soviets. Such, for instance, is the point on equalised land tenure and the redistribution of land among the small holders.

By abstaining from voting on such a point the Bolsheviks would not be changing their programme in the slightest. For, given the victory of socialism (workers' control over the factories, to be followed by their expropriation, the nationalisation of the banks, and the creation of a Supreme Economic Council for the regulation of the entire economic life of the country)—given that the workers *would be obliged to agree* to the transitional measures proposed by the small working and exploited peasants, provided such measures were *not detrimental* to the cause of socialism. Even Kautsky, when he was still a Marxist (1899-1909), frequently admitted—I said—that the measures of transition to socialism cannot be identical in countries with large-scale and those with small-scale farming.

We Bolsheviks would be obliged to abstain from voting when such a point was being decided in the Council of People's Commissars or in the Central Executive Committee, for if the Left Socialist-Revolutionaries (as well as the peasants who support them) agreed to workers' control, to the nationalisation of the banks, etc., equalised land tenure would be only one of the measures of *transition* to full socialism. For the proletariat to *impose* such transitional measures would be absurd; it is obliged, in the interests of the victory of socialism, to *yield* to the small working and exploited peasants in the choice of these transitional measures, for they could do *no harm* to the cause of socialism.

Thereupon, a Left Socialist-Revolutionary (it was Comrade Feofilaktov, if I am not mistaken) asked me the following question:

"How would the Bolsheviks act if in the Constituent Assembly[92] the peasants wanted to pass a law on equalised land tenure, while the bourgeoisie were opposed to the peasants and the decision depended on the Bolsheviks?"

I replied: under such circumstances, provided the cause

of socialism is ensured by the introduction of workers' control, the nationalisation of the banks, etc., the alliance, between the workers and the working and exploited peasants would make it obligatory for the party of the proletariat to vote for the peasants and against the bourgeoisie. The Bolsheviks, in my opinion, would be entitled when the vote was being taken to make a declaration of dissent, to place on record their non-agreement, etc., but to abstain from voting under such circumstances would be to betray their allies *in the fight for socialism* because of a difference with them on a partial issue. The Bolsheviks would never betray the peasants in such a situation. Equalised land tenure and like measures *cannot* prejudice socialism if the power is in the hands of a workers' and peasants' government, if workers' control has been introduced, the banks nationalised, a workers' and peasants' supreme economic body set up to direct (regulate) the *entire* economic life of the country, and so forth.

Such was my reply.

N. Lenin

Written on November 18
(December 1), 1917

Published in *Pravda* No. 194,   *Collected Works*, Vol. 26
December 2 (November 19),
1917

HOW TO ORGANISE COMPETITION?

Bourgeois authors have been using up reams of paper praising competition, private enterprise, and all the other magnificent virtues and blessings of the capitalists and the capitalist system. Socialists have been accused of refusing to understand the importance of these virtues, and of ignoring "human nature". As a matter of fact, however, capitalism long ago replaced small, independent commodity production, under which competition could develop enterprise, energy and bold initiative to any *considerable* extent, by large- and very large-scale factory production, joint-stock companies, syndicates and other monopolies. Under *such* capitalism, competition means the incredibly brutal suppression of the enterprise, energy and bold initiative of the *mass* of the population, of its overwhelming majority, of ninety-nine out of every hundred toilers; it also means that competition is replaced by financial fraud, nepotism, servility on the upper rungs of the social ladder.

Far from extinguishing competition, socialism, on the contrary, for the first time creates the opportunity for employing it on a really *wide* and on a really *mass* scale, for actually drawing the majority of working people into a field of labour in which they can display their abilities, develop the capacities, and reveal those talents, so abundant among the people whom capitalism crushed, suppressed and strangled in thousands and millions.

Now that a socialist government is in power our task is to organise competition.

The hangers-on and spongers on the bourgeoisie described socialism as a uniform, routine, dreary and drab barrack

8*

system. The lackeys of the money-bags, the lickspittles of the exploiters, the bourgeois intellectual gentlemen used socialism as a bogey to "frighten" the people, who, under capitalism, were doomed to the penal servitude and the barrack-like discipline of arduous, dull toil, to a life of dire poverty and semi-starvation. The first step towards the emancipation of the working people from this penal servitude is the confiscation of the landed estates, the introduction of workers' control and the nationalisation of the banks. The next steps will be the nationalisation of the factories, the compulsory organisation of the whole population in consumers' societies, which are at the same time societies for the sale of products, and the state monopoly of the trade in grain and other necessities.

Only now is the opportunity created for the truly mass display of enterprise, competition and bold initiative. Every factory from which the capitalist has been ejected, or in which he has at least been curbed by genuine workers' control, every village from which the landowning exploiter has been smoked out and his land confiscated has only now become a field in which the working man can reveal his talents, unbend his back a little, rise to his full height, and feel that he is a human being. For the first time after centuries of working for others, of forced labour for the exploiter, it has become possible to *work for oneself* and moreover to employ all the achievements of modern technology and culture in one's work.

Of course, this greatest change in human history from working under compulsion to working for oneself cannot take place without friction, difficulties, conflicts and violence against the inveterate parasites and their hangers-on. No worker has any illusions on that score. The workers and poor peasants, hardened by dire want and by many long years of slave labour for the exploiters, by their countless insults and acts of violence, realise that it will take time to *break* the resistance of those exploiters. The workers and peasants are not in the least infected with the sentimental illusions of the intellectual gentlemen, of the *Novaya Zhizn*[93] crowd and other slush, who "shouted" themselves hoarse "denouncing" the capitalists and "gesticulated" against them, only to burst into tears and to behave like whipped puppies when it came to *deeds*, to putting threats into action, to carrying out in practice the task of *removing* the capitalists.

The great change from working under compulsion to working for oneself, to labour planned and organised on a gigantic, national (and to a certain extent international, world) scale, also requires—in addition to *"military"* measures for the suppression of the exploiters' resistance—tremendous *organisational*, organising effort on the part of the proletariat and the poor peasants. The organisational task is interwoven to form a single whole with the task of ruthlessly suppressing by military methods yesterday's slave-owners (capitalists) and their packs of lackeys—the bourgeois intellectual gentlemen. Yesterday's slave-owners and their "intellectual" stooges say and think, "We have always been organisers and chiefs. We have commanded, and we want to continue doing so. We shall refuse to obey the 'common people', the workers and peasants. We shall not submit to them. We shall convert knowledge into a weapon for the defence of the privileges of the money-bags and of the rule of capital over the people."

That is what the bourgeoisie and the bourgeois intellectuals say, think, and do. From the point of view of *self-interest* their behaviour is comprehensible. The hangers-on and spongers on the feudal landowners—the priests, the scribes, the bureaucrats as Gogol depicted them[94]—and the "intellectuals" who hated Belinsky, also found it "hard" to part with serfdom. But the cause of the exploiters and of their "intellectual" menials is hopeless. The workers and peasants are beginning to break down their resistance—unfortunately, not yet firmly, resolutely and ruthlessly enough—*and break it down they will.*

"They" think that the "common people", the "common" workers and poor peasants, will be unable to cope with the great, truly heroic, in the world-historic sense of the word, organisational task which the socialist revolution has imposed upon the working people. The intellectuals who are accustomed to serving the capitalists and the capitalist state say in order to console themselves: "You cannot do without us." But their insolent assumption has no truth in it; educated men are already making their appearance on the side of the people, on the side of the working people, and are helping to break the resistance of the servants of capital. There are a great many talented organisers among the peasants and the working class, and they are only just beginning to become aware of themselves, to awaken, to stretch out towards great, vital, creative work, to tackle with their own forces the task of building socialist society.

One of the most important tasks today, if not the most important, is to develop this independent initiative of the workers, and of all the working and exploited people generally, develop it as widely as possible in creative *organisational* work. At all costs we must break the old, *absurd*, savage, despicable and disgusting prejudice that only the so-called "upper classes", only the rich, and those who have gone through the school of the rich, are capable of administering the state and directing the organisational development of socialist society.

This is a prejudice fostered by rotten routine, by petrified views, slavish habits, and still more by the sordid selfishness of the capitalists, in whose interest it is to administer while plundering and to plunder while administering. The workers will never forget that they need the power of knowledge. The extraordinary striving after knowledge which the workers reveal, particularly now, shows that mistaken ideas about this do not and cannot exist among the proletariat. But every *rank-and-file* worker and peasant who can read and write, who can judge people and has practical experience, is capable of *organisational* work. Among the "common people", of whom the bourgeois intellectuals speak with such haughtiness and contempt, there are *many* such men and women. This sort of talent among the working class and the peasants is a rich and still untapped source.

The workers and peasants are still "timid", they have not yet become accustomed to the idea that *they* are now the *ruling* class; they are not yet resolute enough. The revolution could not *at one stroke* instil these qualities into millions and millions of people who all their lives had been compelled by want and hunger to work under the threat of the stick. But the Revolution of October 1917 is strong, viable and invincible because it *awakens* these qualities, breaks down the old impediments, removes the worn-out shackles, and leads the working people on to the road of the *independent* creation of a new life.

Accounting and control—this is the *main* economic task of every Soviet of Workers', Soldiers' and Peasants' Deputies, of every consumers' society, of every union or committee of supplies, of every factory committee or organ of workers' control in general.

We must fight against the old habit of regarding the measure of labour and the means of production from the point of view of the slave whose sole aim is to lighten the burden of labour or to snatch at least some little bit *from the bourgeoisie*. The advanced, class-conscious workers have already started this fight, and they are offering determined resistance to the newcomers who flocked to the factory world in particularly large numbers during the war and who now would like to treat the *people*'s factory, the factory that has come into the possession of the people, in the old way, with the sole aim of "snatching the biggest possible piece of the pie and clearing out". All the class-conscious, honest and thinking peasants and working people will take their place in this fight by the side of the advanced workers.

Accounting and control, *if* carried on by the Soviets of Workers', Soldiers' and Peasants' Deputies as the supreme state power, or on the instructions, on the authority, of *this* power—widespread, general, universal accounting and control, the accounting and control of the amount of labour performed and of the distribution of products—is the *essence* of socialist transformation, once the political rule of the proletariat has been established and secured.

The accounting and control essential for the transition to socialism can be exercised only by the masses. Only the voluntary and conscientious co-operation of the *mass* of the workers and peasants in accounting and controlling *the rich, the rogues, the idlers and the rowdies*, a co-operation marked by revolutionary enthusiasm, can conquer these survivals of accursed capitalist society, these dregs of humanity, these hopelessly decayed and atrophied limbs, this contagion, this plague, this ulcer that socialism has inherited from capitalism.

Workers and peasants, working and exploited people! The land, the banks and the factories have now become the property of the entire people! You *yourselves* must set to work to take account of and control the production and distribution of products—this, and this *alone* is the road to the victory of socialism, the only guarantee of its victory, the guarantee of victory over all exploitation, over all poverty and want! For there is enough bread, iron, timber, wool, cotton and flax in Russia to satisfy the needs of everyone, if only labour and its products are properly distributed, if only a *business-like, practical* control over this distribution by the entire people is established, provided only we can defeat the enemies of the people: the rich and their hangers-on, and the rogues, the idlers and the rowdies, *not only* in politics, but also in *everyday economic* life.

No mercy for these enemies of the people, the enemies of socialism, the enemies of the working people! War to the death against the rich and their hangers-on, the bourgeois intellectuals; war on the rogues, the idlers and the rowdies! All of them are of the same brood—the spawn of capitalism, the offspring of aristocratic and bourgeois society; the society in which a handful of men robbed and abused the people; the society in which poverty and want forced thousands and thousands on to the path of rowdyism, corruption and roguery, and caused them to lose all human semblance; the society which inevitably cultivated in the working man the desire to escape exploitation even by means of deception, to wriggle out of it, to escape, if only for a moment, from loathsome labour, to procure at least a crust of bread by any possible means, at any cost, so as not to starve, so as to subdue the pangs of hunger suffered by himself and by his near ones.

The rich and the rogues are two sides of the same coin, they are the two principal categories of *parasites* which capitalism fostered; they are the principal enemies of socialism. These enemies must be placed under the special surveillance of the entire people; they must be ruthlessly punished for the slightest violation of the laws and regulations of socialist society. Any display of weakness, hesitation or sentimentality in this respect would be an immense crime against socialism.

In order to render these parasites harmless to socialist society we must organise the accounting and control of the amount of work done and of production and distribution by the entire people, by millions and millions of workers and peasants, participating voluntarily, energetically and with revolutionary enthusiasm. And in order to organise this accounting and control, which is *fully within the ability* of every honest, intelligent and efficient worker and peasant, we must rouse their organising talent, the talent that is to be found in their midst; we must rouse among them—and organise on a national scale—*competition* in the sphere of organisational achievement; the workers and peasants must be brought to see clearly the difference between the necessary advice of an educated man and the necessary control by the "common" worker and peasant of the *slovenliness* that is so usual among the "educated".

This slovenliness, this carelessness, untidiness, unpunctuality, nervous haste, the inclination to substitute discussion for action, talk for work, the inclination to undertake everything under the sun without finishing anything, are characteristics of the "educated"; and this is not due to the fact that they are bad by nature, still less is it due to their evil will; it is due to all their habits of life, the conditions of their work, to fatigue, to the abnormal separation of mental from manual labour, and so on, and so forth.

Among the mistakes, shortcomings and defects of our revolution a by no means unimportant place is occupied by the mistakes, etc., which are due to these deplorable—but at present inevitable—characteristics of the intellectuals in our midst, and to the *lack* of sufficient supervision by the *workers* over the *organisational* work of the intellectuals.

The workers and peasants are still "timid"; they must get rid of this timidity, and they *certainly* will get rid of it. We cannot dispense with the advice, the instruction of educated people, of intellectuals and specialists. Every sensible worker and peasant understands this perfectly well, and the intellectuals in our midst cannot complain of a lack of attention and comradely respect on the part of the workers and peasants. Advice and instruction, however, is one thing, and the organisation of *practical* accounting and control is another. Very often the intellectuals give excellent advice and instruction, but they prove to be ridiculously, *absurdly*, shamefully "unhandy" and incapable of *carrying out* this advice and instruction, of exercising *practical control* over the translation of words into deeds.

In this very respect it is utterly impossible to dispense with the help and the *leading role* of the practical organisers from among the "people", from among the factory workers and working peasants. "It is not the gods who make pots"–this is the truth that the workers and peasants should get well drilled into their minds. They must understand that the whole thing now is *practical work;* that the historical moment has arrived when theory is being transformed into practice, vitalised by practice, corrected by practice, tested by practice; when the truth of Marx's words "Every step of real movement is more important than a dozen programmes",[95] becomes particularly clear–every step in really curbing in practice, restricting, fully registering the rich and the rogues and keeping them under control is worth more than a dozen excellent arguments about socialism. For, "theory, my friend, is grey, but green is the eternal tree of life".[96]

Competition must be arranged between practical organisers from among the workers and peasants. Every attempt to establish stereotyped forms and to impose uniformity from above, as intellectuals are so inclined to do, must be combated. Stereotyped forms and uniformity imposed from above have nothing in common with democratic and socialist centralism. The unity of essentials, of fundamentals, of the substance, is not disturbed but ensured by *variety* in details, in specific local features, in methods of *approach,* in *methods* of exercising control, in *ways* of exterminating and rendering harmless the parasites (the rich and the rogues, slovenly and hysterical intellectuals, etc., etc.).

The Paris Commune gave a great example of how to combine initiative, independence, freedom of action and vigour from below with voluntary centralism free from stereotyped forms. Our Soviets are following the same road. But they are still "timid"; they have not yet got into their stride, have not yet "bitten into" their new, great, creative task of building the socialist system. The Soviets must set to work more boldly and display greater initiative. All "communes"–factories, villages, consumers' societies, and committees of supplies–must *compete* with each other as practical organisers of accounting and control of labour and distribution of products. The programme of this accounting and control is simple, clear and intelligible to all–everyone to have bread; everyone to have sound footwear and good clothing; everyone to have warm dwellings; everyone to work conscientiously; not a single rogue (including those who shirk their work) to be allowed to be at liberty, but kept in prison, or serve his sentence of compulsory labour of the hardest kind; not a single rich man who violates the laws and regulations of socialism to be allowed to escape the fate of the rogue, which should, in justice, be the fate of the rich man. "He who does not work, shall not eat"—this is the *practical* commandment of socialism. This is how things should be organised *practically*. These are the *practical* successes our "communes" and our worker and peasant organisers should be proud of. And this applies particularly to the organisers among the intellectuals (*particularly,* because they are *too much, far too much* in the habit of being proud of their general instructions and resolutions).

Thousands of practical forms and methods of accounting and controlling the rich, the rogues and the idlers must be devised and put to a practical test by the communes themselves, by small units in town and country. Variety is a guarantee of viability here, a pledge of success in achieving the single common aim—to *clean* the land of Russia of all vermin, of fleas—the rogues, of bugs—the rich, and so on, and so forth. In one place half a score of rich, a dozen rogues, half a dozen workers who shirk their work (in the manner of rowdies, the manner in which many compositors in Petrograd, particularly in the Party printing-shops, shirk their work) will be put in prison. In another place they will be put to cleaning latrines. In a third place they will be provided with "yellow tickets" after they have served their time, so that everyone shall keep an eye on them, as *harmful* persons, until they reform. In a fourth place, one out of every ten idlers will be shot on the spot. In a fifth place mixed methods may be adopted, and by probational release, for example, the rich, the bourgeois intellectuals, the rogues and rowdies who are corrigible will be given an opportunity to reform quickly. The more variety there will be, the better and richer will be our common experience, the more certain and rapid will be the success of socialism, and the easier will it be for practice to devise—for only practice can devise—the *best* methods and means of struggle.

In what commune, in what district of a large town, in what factory and in what village are there *no* starving people, *no* unemployed, *no* idle rich, *no* despicable lackeys of the bourgeoisie, saboteurs who call themselves intellectuals? Where has most been done to raise the productivity of labour, to build good new houses for the poor, to put the poor in the houses of the rich, to regularly provide a bottle of milk for every child of every poor family? It is on these points that *competition* should develop between the communes, communities, producers'-and-consumers' societies and associations, and Soviets of Workers', Soldiers' and Peasants' Deputies. This is the work in which *talented organisers* should come to the fore *in practice* and be promoted to work in state administration. There is a great deal of talent among the people. It is merely suppressed. It must be given an opportunity to display itself. It *and it alone*, with the support of the people, can save Russia and save the cause of socialism.

Written December 24-27, 1917
(January 6-9, 1918)

First published in *Pravda* No. 17,   Collected Works, Vol. 26
January 20, 1929

Signed: V. *Lenin*

THE IMMEDIATE TASKS
OF THE SOVIET GOVERNMENT

(Extract)

RAISING THE PRODUCTIVITY OF LABOUR

In every socialist revolution, after the proletariat has solved the problem of capturing power, and to the extent that the task of expropriating the expropriators and suppressing their resistance has been carried out in the main, there necessarily comes to the forefront the fundamental task of creating a social system superior to capitalism, namely, raising the productivity of labour, and in this connection (and for this purpose) securing better organisation of labour. Our Soviet state is precisely in the position where, thanks to the victories over the exploiters—from Kerensky to Kornilov—it is able to approach this task directly, to tackle it in earnest. And here it becomes immediately clear that while it is possible to take state power in the centre in a few days, while it is possible to suppress the military resistance (and sabotage) of the exploiters even in different parts of a big country in a few weeks, the capital solution of the problem of raising the productivity of labour requires, at all events (particularly after a most terrible and devastating war), several years. The protracted nature of the work is certainly dictated by objective circumstances.

The raising of the productivity of labour first of all requires that the material basis of large-scale industry shall be assured, namely, the development of the production of fuel, iron, the engineering and chemical industries. The Russian Soviet Republic enjoys the favourable position of having at its command, even after the Brest peace,[97] enormous reserves of ore (in the Urals), fuel in Western Siberia (coal), in the Caucasus and the South-East (oil), in Central Russia (peat), enormous timber reserves, water power, raw materials for the chemical industry (Karabugaz), etc. The development of these natural resources by methods of modern technology will provide the basis for the unprecedented progress of the productive forces.

Another condition for raising the productivity of labour is, firstly, the raising of the educational and cultural level of the mass of the population. This is now taking place extremely rapidly, a fact which those who are blinded by bourgeois routine are unable to see; they are unable to understand what an urge towards enlightenment and initiative is now developing among the "lower ranks" of the people thanks to the Soviet form of organisation. Secondly, a condition for economic revival is the raising of the working people's discipline, their skill, the effectiveness, the intensity of labour and its better organisation.

In this respect the situation is particularly bad and even hopeless if we are to believe those who have allowed themselves to be intimidated by the bourgeoisie or by those who are serving the bourgeoisie for their own ends. These people do not understand that there has not been, nor could there be, a revolution in which the supporters of the old system did not raise a howl about chaos, anarchy, etc. Naturally, among the people who have only just thrown off an unprecedentedly savage yoke there is deep and widespread seething and ferment; the working out of new principles of labour discipline by the people is a very protracted process, and this process could not even start until complete victory had been achieved over the landowners and the bourgeoisie.

We, however, without in the least yielding to the despair (it is often false despair) which is spread by the bourgeoisie and the bourgeois intellectuals (who have despaired of retaining their old privileges), must under no circumstances conceal an obvious evil. On the contrary, we shall expose it and intensify the Soviet methods of combating it, because the victory of socialism is inconceivable without the victory of proletarian conscious discipline over spontaneous petty-bourgeois anarchy, this real guarantee of a possible return of Kerensky and Kornilov.

The more class-conscious vanguard of the Russian proletariat has already set itself the task of raising labour discipline. For example, both the Central Committee of the Metalworkers' Union and the Central Council of Trade Unions have begun to draft the necessary measures and decrees. This work must be supported and pushed ahead with all speed. We must raise the question of piece-work[98] and apply and test it in practice; we must raise the question of applying much of what is scientific and progressive in the Taylor system; we must make wages correspond to the total amount of goods turned out, or to the result of operations by the railways, the water transport system, etc., etc.

The Russian is a bad worker compared with people in advanced countries. It could not be otherwise under the tsarist regime and in view of the persistence of the hangover from serfdom. The task that the Soviet government must set the people in all its scope is—learn to work. The Taylor system, the last word of capitalism in this respect, like all capitalist progress, is a combination of the refined brutality of bourgeois exploitation and a number of the greatest scientific achievements in the field of analysing mechanical motions during work, the elimination of superfluous and awkward motions, the elaboration of correct methods of work, the introduction of the best system of accounting and control, etc. The Soviet Republic must at all costs adopt all that is valuable in the achievements of science and technology in this field. The possibility of building socialism depends exactly upon our success in combining the Soviet power and the Soviet organisation of administration with the up-to-date achievements of capitalism. We must organise in Russia the study and teaching of the Taylor system and systematically try it out and adapt it to our own ends. At the same time, in working to raise the productivity of labour, we must take into account the specific features of the transition period from capitalism to socialism, which, on the one hand, require that the foundations be laid of the socialist organisation of competition, and, on the other hand, require the use of compulsion, so that the slogan of the dictatorship of the proletariat shall not be desecrated by the practice of a flabby proletarian government.

THE DEVELOPMENT OF SOVIET ORGANISATION

The socialist character of Soviet, i.e., *proletarian*, democracy, as concretely applied today, lies first in the fact that the electors are the working and exploited people; the bourgeoisie is excluded. Secondly, it lies in the fact that all bureaucratic formalities and restrictions of elections are abolished; the people themselves determine the order and time of elections, and are completely free to recall any elected person. Thirdly, it lies in the creation of the best mass organisation of the vanguard of the working people, i.e., the proletariat engaged in large-scale industry, which enables it to lead the vast mass of the exploited, to draw them into independent political life, to educate them politically by their own experience; therefore for the first time a start is made by the *entire* population in learning the art of administration, and in beginning to administer.

These are the principal distinguishing features of the democracy now applied in Russia, which is a higher *type* of democracy, a break with the bourgeois distortion of democracy, transition to socialist democracy and to the conditions in which the state can begin to wither away.

It goes without saying that the element of petty-bourgeois disorganisation (which must *inevitably* be apparent to some extent in *every* proletarian revolution, and which is especially apparent in our revolution, owing to the petty-bourgeois character of our country, its backwardness and the consequences of a reactionary war) cannot but leave its impress upon the Soviets as well.

We must work unremittingly to develop the organisation of the Soviets and of the Soviet government. There is a petty-bourgeois tendency to transform the members of the Soviets into "parliamentarians", or else into bureaucrats. We must combat this by drawing *all* the members of the Soviets into the practical work of administration. In many places the departments of the Soviets are gradually merging with the Commissariats. Our aim is to draw *the whole of the poor* into the practical work of administration, and all steps that are taken in this direction—the more varied they are, the better—should be carefully recorded, studied, systematised, tested by wider experience and embodied in law. Our aim is to ensure that *every* toiler, having finished his eight hours' "task" in productive labour, shall perform state duties *without pay*; the transition to this is particularly difficult, but this transition alone can guarantee the final consolidation of socialism. Naturally, the novelty and difficulty of the change lead to an abundance of steps being taken, as it were, gropingly, to an abundance of mistakes, vacillation—without this, any marked progress is impossible. The reason why the present position seems peculiar to many of those who would like to be regarded as socialists is that they have been accustomed to contrasting capitalism with socialism abstractly, and that they profoundly put between the two the word "leap" (some of them, recalling fragments of what they have read of Engels's writings, still more profoundly add the phrase "leap from the realm of necessity into the realm of freedom"[99]). The majority of these so-called socialists, who have "read in books" about socialism but who have never seriously thought over the matter, are unable to consider that by "leap" the teachers of socialism meant turning-points on a world-historical scale, and that leaps of this kind extend over decades and even longer periods. Naturally, in such times, the notorious "intelligentsia" provides an infinite number of mourners of the dead. Some mourn over the Constituent Assembly, others mourn over bourgeois discipline, others again mourn over the capitalist system, still others mourn over the cultured landowner, and still others again mourn over imperialist Great Power policy, etc., etc.

The real interest of the epoch of great leaps lies in the fact that the abundance of fragments of the old, which sometimes accumulate more rapidly than the rudiments (not always immediately discernible) of the new, calls for the ability to discern what is most important in the line or chain of development. History knows moments when the most important thing for the success of the revolution is to heap up as large a quantity of the fragments as possible, i.e., to blow up as many of the old institutions as possible; moments arise when enough has been blown up and the next task is to perform the "prosaic" (for the petty-bourgeois revolutionary, the "boring") task of clearing away the fragments; and moments arise when the careful nursing of the shoots of the new system, which are growing amidst the wreckage on a soil which as yet has been badly cleared of rubble, is the most important thing.

It is not enough to be a revolutionary and an adherent of socialism or a Communist in general. You must be able at each particular moment to find the particular link in the chain which you must grasp with all your might in order to hold the whole chain and to prepare firmly for the transition to the next link; the order of the links, their form, the manner in which they are linked together, the way they differ from each other in the historical chain of events, are not as simple and not as meaningless as those in an ordinary chain made by a smith.

The fight against the bureaucratic distortion of the Soviet form of organisation is assured by the firmness of the connection between the Soviets and the "people", meaning by that the working and exploited people, and by the flexibility and elasticity of this connection. Even in the most democratic capitalist republics in the world, the poor never regard the bourgeois parliament as "their" institution. But the Soviets are "theirs" and not alien institutions to the mass of workers and peasants. The modern "Social-Democrats" of the Scheidemann or, what is almost the same thing, of the Martov type are repelled by the Soviets, and they are drawn towards the respectable bourgeois parliament, or to the Constituent Assembly, in the same way as Turgenev, sixty years ago, was drawn towards a moderate monarchist and noblemen's Constitution and was repelled by the peasant democracy of Dobrolyubov and Chernyshevsky.

It is the closeness of the Soviets to the "people", to the working people, that creates the special forms of recall and other means of control from below which must be most zealously developed now. For example, the Councils of Public Education, as periodical conferences of Soviet electors and their delegates called to discuss and control the activities of the Soviet authorities in this field, deserve full sympathy and support. Nothing could be sillier than to transform the Soviets into something congealed and self-contained. The more resolutely we now have to stand for a ruthlessly firm government, for the dictatorship of individuals *in definite processes of work*, in definite aspects of *purely executive* functions, the more varied must be the forms and methods of control from below in order to counteract every shadow of a possibility of distorting the principles of Soviet government, in order repeatedly and tirelessly to weed out bureaucracy.

Written between April 13 and 16, 1918

Published in *Pravda* No. 83, and in the Supplement to *Izvestia* No. 85, April 28, 1918

Signed: *N. Lenin*

Collected Works, Vol. 27

SPEECH AT THE FIRST CONGRESS
OF ECONOMIC COUNCILS
May 26, 1918

(Extract)

All that we knew, all that the best experts on capitalist society, the greatest minds who foresaw its development, exactly indicated to us was that transformation was historically inevitable and must proceed along a certain main line, that private ownership of the means of production was doomed by history, that it would burst, that the exploiters would inevitably be expropriated. This was established with scientific precision, and we knew this when we grasped the banner of socialism, when we declared ourselves socialists, when we founded socialist parties, when we transformed society. We knew this when we took power for the purpose of proceeding with socialist reorganisation; but we could not know the forms of transformation, or the rate of development of the concrete reorganisation. Collective experience, the experience of millions can alone give us decisive guidance in this respect, precisely because, for our task, for the task of building socialism, the experience of the hundreds and hundreds of thousands of those upper sections which have made history up to now in feudal society and in capitalist society is insufficient. We cannot proceed in this way precisely because we rely on joint experience, on the experience of millions of working people.

We know, therefore, that organisation, which is the main and fundamental task of the Soviets, will inevitably entail a vast number of experiments, a vast number of steps, a vast number of alterations, a vast number of difficulties, particularly in regard to the question of how to fit every person into his proper place, because we have no experience of this; here we have to devise every step ourselves, and the more serious the mistakes we make on this path, the more the certainty will grow that with every increase in the membership of the trade unions, with every additional thousand, with every additional hundred thousand that come over from the camp of working people, of exploited, who have hitherto lived according to tradition and habit, into the camp of the builders of Soviet organisations, the number of people who should prove suitable and organise the work on proper lines is increasing.

Take one of the secondary tasks that the Economic Council—the Supreme Economic Council—comes up against with particular frequency, the task of utilising bourgeois experts. We all know, at least those who take their stand on the basis of science and socialism, that this task can be fulfilled only when—that this task can be fulfilled only to the extent that international capitalism has developed the material and technical prerequisites of labour, organised on an enormous scale and based on science, and hence on the training of an enormous number of scientifically educated specialists. We know that without this socialism is impossible. If we reread the works of those socialists who have observed the development of capitalism during the last half-century, and who have again and again come to the conclusion that socialism is inevitable, we shall find that all of them without exception have pointed out that socialism alone will liberate science from its bourgeois fetters, from its enslavement to capital, from its slavery to the interests of dirty capitalist greed. Socialism alone will make possible the wide expansion of social production and distribution on scientific lines and their actual subordination to the aim of easing the lives of the working people and of improving their welfare as much as possible. Socialism alone can achieve this. And we know that it must achieve this, and in the understanding of this truth lies the whole complexity and the whole strength of Marxism.

We must achieve this while relying on elements which are opposed to it, because the bigger capital becomes the more the bourgeoisie suppresses the workers. Now that power is in the hands of the proletariat and the poor peasants and the government is setting itself tasks with the support of the people, we have to achieve these socialist changes with

the help of bourgeois experts who have been trained in bourgeois society, who know no other conditions, who cannot
conceive of any other social system. Hence, even in cases
when these experts are absolutely sincere and loyal to their
work they are filled with thousands of bourgeois prejudices,
they are connected by thousands of ties, imperceptible to
themselves, with bourgeois society, which is dying and
decaying and is therefore putting up furious resistance.

We cannot conceal these difficulties of endeavour and
achievement from ourselves. Of all the socialists who have
written about this, I cannot recall the work of a single socialist or the opinion of a single prominent socialist on future
socialist society, which pointed to this concrete, practical
difficulty that would confront the working class when it took
power, when it set itself the task of turning the sum total
of the very rich, historically inevitable and necessary for us
store of culture and knowledge and technique accumulated
by capitalism from an instrument of capitalism into an instrument of socialism. It is easy to do this in a general formula,
in abstract reasoning, but in the struggle against capitalism,
which does not die at once but puts up increasingly furious
resistance the closer death approaches, this task is one that
calls for tremendous effort. If experiments take place in this
field, if we make repeated corrections of partial mistakes, this
is inevitable because we cannot, in this or that sphere of the
national economy, immediately turn specialists from servants
of capitalism into servants of the working people, into their
advisers. If we cannot do this at once it should not give rise
to the slightest pessimism, because the task which we set
ourselves is a task of world-historic difficulty and significance.
We do not shut our eyes to the fact that in a single country,
even if it were a much less backward country than Russia,
even if we were living in better conditions than those prevailing after four years of unprecedented, painful, severe
and ruinous war, we could not carry out the socialist revolution completely, solely by our own efforts. He who turns
away from the socialist revolution now taking place in Russia
and points to the obvious disproportion of forces is like the
conservative "man in a muffler"[100] who cannot see further
than his nose, who forgets that not a single historical change
of any importance takes place without there being several

instances of a disproportion of forces. Forces grow in the process of the struggle, as the revolution grows. When a country has taken the path of profound change, it is to the credit of that country and the party of the working class which achieved victory in that country, that they should take up in a practical manner the tasks that were formerly raised abstractly, theoretically. This experience will never be forgotten. The experience which the workers now united in trade unions and local organisations are acquiring in the practical work of organising the whole of production on a national scale cannot be taken away, no matter how difficult the vicissitudes the Russian revolution and the international socialist revolution may pass through. It has gone down in history as socialism's gain, and on it the future world revolution will erect its socialist edifice.

Permit me to mention another problem, perhaps the most difficult problem, for which the Supreme Economic Council has to find a practical solution. This is the problem of labour discipline. Strictly speaking, in mentioning this problem, we ought to admit and emphasise with satisfaction that it was precisely the trade unions, their largest organisations, namely, the Central Committee of the Metalworkers' Union and the All-Russia Trade Union Council, the supreme trade union organisations uniting millions of working people, that were the first to set to work independently to solve this problem and this problem is of world-historic importance. In order to understand it we must abstract ourselves from those partial, minor failures, from the incredible difficulties which, if taken separately, seem to be insurmountable. We must rise to a higher level and survey the historical change of systems of social economy. Only from this angle will it be possible to appreciate the immensity of the task which we have undertaken. Only then will it be possible to appreciate the enormous significance of the fact that on this occasion, the most advanced representatives of society, the working and exploited people are, on their own initiative, taking on themselves the task which hitherto, in feudal Russia, up to 1861, was solved by a handful of landed proprietors, who regarded it as their own affair. At that time it was their affair to bring about state integration and discipline.

We know how the feudal landowners created this discipline.

It was oppression, humiliation and the incredible torments of penal servitude for the majority of the people. Recall the whole of this transition from serfdom to the bourgeois economy. From all that you have witnessed—although the majority of you could not have witnessed it—and from all that you have learned from the older generations, you know how easy, historically, seemed the transition to the new bourgeois economy after 1861, the transition from the old feudal discipline of the stick, from the discipline of the most senseless, arrogant and brutal humiliation and personal violence, to bourgeois discipline, to the discipline of starvation, to so-called free hire, which in fact was the discipline of capitalist slavery. This was because mankind passed from one exploiter to another; because one minority of plunderers and exploiters of the people's labour gave way to another minority, who were also plunderers and exploiters of the people's labour; because the feudal landowners gave way to the capitalists, one minority gave way to another minority, while the toiling and exploited classes remained oppressed. And even this change from one exploiter's discipline to another exploiter's discipline took years, if not decades, of effort; it extended over a transition period of years, if not decades. During this period the old feudal landowners quite sincerely believed that everything was going to rack and ruin, that it was impossible to manage the country without serfdom, while the new, capitalist boss encountered practical difficulties at every step and gave up his enterprise as a bad job. The material evidence, one of the substantial proofs of the difficulty of this transition was that Russia at that time imported machinery from abroad, in order to have the best machinery to use, and it turned out that no one was available to handle this machinery, and there were no managers. And all over Russia one could see excellent machinery lying around unused, so difficult was the transition from the old feudal discipline to the new, bourgeois, capitalist discipline.

And so, comrades, if you look at the matter from this angle, you will not allow yourselves to be misled by those people, by those classes, by those bourgeoisie and their hangers-on whose sole task is to sow panic, to sow despondency, to cause complete despondency concerning the whole of our work, to make it appear to be hopeless, who point to every single case of indiscipline and corruption, and for that reason give up the revolution as a bad job, as if there has ever been in the world, in history, a single really great revolution in which there was no corruption, no loss of discipline, no painful experimental steps, when the people were creating a new discipline. We must not forget that this is the first time that this preliminary stage in history has been reached, when a new discipline, labour discipline, the discipline of comradely contact, Soviet discipline, is being created in fact by millions of working and exploited people. We do not claim, nor do we expect, quick successes in this field. We know that this task will take an entire historical epoch. We have begun this historical epoch, an epoch in which we are breaking up the discipline of capitalist society in a country which is still bourgeois, and we are proud that all politically conscious workers, absolutely all the toiling peasants are everywhere helping this destruction; an epoch in which the people voluntarily, on their own initiative, are becoming aware that they must—not on instructions from above, but on the instructions of their own living experience—change this discipline based on the exploitation and slavery of the working people into the new discipline of united labour, the discipline of the united, organised workers and working peasants of the whole of Russia, of a country with a population of tens and hundreds of millions. This is a task of enormous difficulty, but it is also a thankful one, because only when we solve it in practice shall we have driven the last nail into the coffin of capitalist society which we are burying. (*Applause.*)

Newspaper report published in *Petrogradskaya Pravda* No. 108, (evening issue), May 27, 1918 and in *Pravda* No. 104 and *Izvestia* No. 106, May 28, 1918

First published in full in 1918 in the book *Proceedings of the First All-Russia Congress of Economic Councils. Verbatim Report.* Moscow

DRAFT PROGRAMME
OF THE R.C.P.(B.)

(Extract)

THE BASIC TASKS OF THE DICTATORSHIP
OF THE PROLETARIAT IN RUSSIA

The basic tasks of the dictatorship of the proletariat in present-day Russia are to complete, to consummate, the expropriation of the landowners and the bourgeoisie which has been begun, and the conversion of all factories, railways, banks, merchant vessels and other means of production and exchange into the property of the Soviet Republic;

to employ the alliance of the urban workers and the poor peasants which has already led to the abolition of private property in land and to the enactment of that form of transition from small-scale peasant farming to socialism called the socialisation of the land by present-day theoreticians of that part of the peasantry, that sides with the workers—to employ this alliance to promote a gradual but steady transition to tilling the land in common and to large-scale socialist farming;

to strengthen and develop the Federative Soviet Republic which is an immeasurably higher and more progressive form of democracy than bourgeois parliamentarism and which— as the experience of the Paris Commune of 1871 and of the Russian Revolutions of 1905 and 1917-18 have shown—is the only type of state suitable for the period of transition from capitalism to socialism, i.e., the period of the dictatorship of the proletariat;

to make use in every way and to the fullest extent of the torch of the world socialist revolution that has been ignited in Russia to carry the revolution to the more advanced countries, and to all countries in general, while at the same time thwarting the attempts of imperialist bourgeois governments to intervene in the internal affairs of Russia and to unite for a direct struggle and a war against the socialist Soviet Republic;

by a number of gradual but undeviating measures to abolish private trading completely and to organise the regular, planned exchange of products between producers'-and-consumers' communes to form the single economic entity the Soviet Republic must become.

The Russian Communist Party, giving more concrete expression to the general tasks of the Soviet government, at present formulates them as follows.

In the Political Sphere

Prior to the capture of political power by the proletariat it was (obligatory) necessary to make use of bourgeois democracy, parliamentarism in particular, for the political education and organisation of the working masses; now that the proletariat has won political power and a higher type of democracy is being put into effect in the Soviet Republic, any step backward to bourgeois parliamentarism and bourgeois democracy would undoubtedly be reactionary service to the interests of the exploiters, the landowners and capitalists. Such catchwords as supposedly popular, national, general, extra-class but actually bourgeois democracy serve the interests of the exploiters alone, and as long as the land and other means of production remain private property the most democratic republic must inevitably remain a bourgeois dictatorship, a machine for the suppression of the overwhelming majority of working people by a handful of capitalists.

The historical task that has fallen to the lot of the Soviet Republic, a new type of state that is transitional until the state disappears altogether, is the following.

(1) The creation and development of universal mass organisations of precisely those classes that are oppressed under capitalism—the proletariat and semi-proletariat. A bourgeois democratic republic at best permits the organisation of the exploited masses to the extent that it declares them free, but actually it has always placed countless actual obstacles in the way of their organisation, obstacles that were connected with the private ownership of the means of produc-

tion in a way that made them irremovable. For the first time in history, Soviet power has not only greatly facilitated the organisation of the masses who were oppressed under capitalism, but has made that organisation the invariable and indispensable basis of the entire state apparatus, local and central, from top to bottom. Only in this way can democracy be put into effect, democracy for the great majority of the nation, the working people, through their actual participation in state administration in contrast to the actual administration of the state mainly by representatives of the bourgeois classes, as is the case in the most democratic bourgeois republics.

(2) The Soviet system of state administration gives a certain actual advantage to that section of the working people that all the capitalist development that preceded socialism has made the most concentrated, united, educated and steeled in the struggle, i.e., to the urban industrial proletariat. This advantage must be used systematically and unswervingly to counteract the narrow guild and narrow trade interests that capitalism fostered among the workers splitting them into competitive groups, by uniting the most backward and disunited masses of rural proletarians and semi-proletarians more closely with the advanced workers, by snatching them away from the influence of the village kulaks and village bourgeoisie, and organising and educating them for communist development.

(3) Bourgeois democracy that solemnly announced the equality of all citizens, in actual fact hypocritically concealed the domination of the capitalist exploiters and deceived the masses with the idea that the equality of exploiters and exploited is possible. The Soviet organisation of the state destroys this deception and this hypocrisy by the implementation of real democracy, i.e., the real equality of all working people, and by excluding the exploiters from the category of members of society possessing full rights. The experience of world history, the experience of all revolts of the exploited classes against their exploiters shows the inevitability of long and desperate resistance of the exploiters in their struggle to retain their privileges. Soviet state organisation is adapted to the suppression of that resistance, for unless it is sup-

pressed there can be no question of a victorious communist revolution.

(4) The more direct influence of the working masses on state structure and administration—i.e., a higher form of democracy—is also effected in the Soviet type of state, first, by the possibility of holding elections more frequently, by making the electoral procedure and also the conditions for reelection and for the recall of deputies simpler and more comprehensible to the urban and rural workers than is the case under the best forms of bourgeois democracy.

(5) Secondly, by making the primary electoral unit and the nucleus of the state structure under Soviet power the economic, production unit (factory) and not a territorial division. This closer contact between the state apparatus and the masses of advanced proletarians that capitalism has united, in addition to effecting a higher level of democracy, also makes profound socialist reforms possible.

(6) Soviet organisation has made possible the creation of armed forces of workers and peasants which are much more closely connected with the working and exploited people than before. If this had not been done it would have been impossible to achieve one of the basic conditions for the victory of socialism—the arming of the workers and the disarming of the bourgeoisie.

(7) Soviet organisation has developed incomparably farther and deeper that feature of bourgeois democracy which marks historically its great progressive nature as compared with medieval times, i.e., the participation of the people in the election of individuals to office. In none of the most democratic bourgeois state have the working masses ever been able to enjoy the electoral rights that the bourgeoisie has formally granted them (but actually hinders their enjoyment) anywhere near as extensively, frequently, universally, easily and simply as they are enjoyed under Soviet power. Soviet power has, at the same time, swept away those negative aspects of bourgeois democracy that the Paris Commune began to abolish, i.e., parliamentarism, or the separation of legislative and executive powers, the narrow, limited nature of which Marxism has long since indicated. By merging the two aspects of government the Soviets bring the state apparatus closer to the working people and remove the fence of

the bourgeois parliament that fooled the masses with hypocritical signboards, that concealed the financial and stock-exchange deals of parliamentary businessmen and ensured the inviolability of the bourgeois apparatus of state administration.

(8) Soviet state organisation alone has enabled the proletarian revolution to smash the old bourgeois state apparatus at one blow and destroy it to the very foundations; had this not been done no start could have been made on socialist development. Those strongholds of the bureaucracy which everywhere, both under monarchies and in the most democratic bourgeois republics, has always kept the state bound to the interests of the landowners and capitalists, have been destroyed in present-day Russia. The struggle against the bureaucracy, however, is certainly not over in our country. The bureaucracy is trying to regain some of its positions by taking advantage, on the one hand, of the unsatisfactory cultural level of the masses of the people and, on the other, of the tremendous, almost superhuman efforts of the most developed section of the urban workers on war work. The continuation of the struggle against the bureaucracy, therefore, is absolutely necessary, is imperative, to ensure the success of future socialist development.

(9) Work in this field is closely connected with the implementation of the chief historical purpose of Soviet power, i.e., to advance towards the final abolition of the state, and should consist of the following. First, every member of a Soviet must, without fail, do a certain job of state administration; secondly, these jobs must be consistently changed so that they embrace all aspects of government, all its branches; and, thirdly, literally all the working population must be drawn into independent participation in state administration by means of a series of measures that are carefully selected and unfailingly implemented.

(10) By and large, the difference between bourgeois democracy and parliamentarism on the one hand and Soviet or proletarian democracy on the other boils down to this: the centre of gravity of the former is in its solemn, pompous declarations of numerous liberties and rights which the majority of the population, the workers and peasants, are actually not allowed to enjoy to the full. Proletarian, or Soviet,

democracy, on the contrary, has transferred the centre of gravity away from the declaration of rights and liberties for the entire people to the actual participation of none but the working people, who were oppressed and exploited by capital, in the administration of the state, the actual use of the best buildings and other premises for meetings and congresses, the best printing works and the biggest warehouses (stocks) of paper for the education of those who were stultified and downtrodden under capitalism, and to providing a real (actual) opportunity for those masses to free themselves little by little from the burden of religious prejudices, etc., etc. It is precisely in making the benefits of culture, civilisation and democracy really available to the working and exploited people that Soviet power sees its most important work, work which it must continue unswervingly in the future.

The policy of the R.C.P. on the national question, unlike the bourgeois-democratic declaration of the equality of nations, which cannot be implemented under imperialism, is that of effecting the drawing together and merging of the proletarians and the working masses of all nations in their revolutionary struggle for the overthrow of the bourgeoisie. Among the working people of the nations that entered into the former Russian Empire the mistrust of the Great Russians inherited from the tsarist and bourgeois epoch of Great-Russian imperialism is rapidly disappearing under the influence of acquaintance with Soviet Russia, but that mistrust has not yet completely disappeared among all nations and among all sections of the working people. It is, therefore, necessary to exercise special caution in respect of national feelings and to ensure the careful pursuance of a policy of actual equality and freedom to secede so as to remove the grounds for this mistrust and achieve the close voluntary union of the Soviet republics of all nations.

Aid to backward and weak nations must be increased by assisting the independent organisation and education of the workers and peasants of all nations in the struggle against medieval and bourgeois oppression and also by means of help in developing the language and literature of nations that have been until now oppressed or have been underprivileged.

In respect of the policy on religion the (R.C.P.) dictatorship of the proletariat must not confine itself to decreeing the separation of the church from the state and the school from the church, that is, measures promised by bourgeois democrats but which have not been put into effect in full anywhere else in the world because of the multifarious factual bonds between capital and religious propaganda. The proletarian dictatorship must completely destroy the connection between the exploiting classes—the landowners and capitalists—and the organisation of religious propaganda as something which keeps the masses in ignorance. The proletarian dictatorship must consistently effect the emancipation of the working people from religious prejudices, doing so by means of propaganda and by raising the political consciousness of the masses but carefully avoiding anything that may insult the feelings of the religious section of the population and serve to increase religious fanaticism.

In the sphere of public education the R.C.P. is faced with the task of completing the conversion of the school from an instrument of the class rule of the bourgeoisie that began with the October Revolution of 1917 into an instrument of the overthrow of that rule and of the complete abolition of the division of society into classes.

In the period of the dictatorship of the proletariat, i.e., in the period in which conditions are being prepared for the full realisation of communism, the school must be the vehicle, not merely of the general principles of communism but also of the ideological, organisational and educational influence of the proletariat on the semi-proletarian and non-proletarian sections of the working people, in order to train a generation that is capable of building full communism.

The immediate tasks in this field are, for the present, the following.

(1) The implementation of free, obligatory general and polytechnical education (acquaintance with all the main branches of production theoretically and in practice) for all children up to the age of 16.

(2) The close connection between schooling and productive social labour.

(3) The provision of food, clothing, books and other teaching aids at the expense of the state.

(4) Greater agitation and propaganda among school-teachers.

(5) The training of new teaching staffs imbued with communist ideas.

(6) The working people must be drawn into active participation in education (the development of the public education councils, mobilisation of the educated, etc.).

(7) All-round help on the part of Soviet power in the matter of the self-education and self-development of workers and working peasants (organisation of libraries, schools for adults, people's universities, courses of lectures, cinemas, studios, etc.).

(8) Development of the most extensive propaganda of communist ideas.

The R.C.P., giving a more concrete expression to the general tasks of Soviet power, defines them as follows.

In the Economic Sphere

The present tasks of Soviet power are:

(1) To continue undeviatingly and complete the expropriation of the bourgeoisie that has been started and has basically, in the main, already been carried out, and the conversion of the means of production and distribution into the property of the Soviet Republic, i.e., into the common property of all working people.

(2) Particularly great attention is to be paid to the development and strengthening of comradely discipline among the working people together with the all-round improvement of their independent activity and sense of responsibility. This is the most important, if not the only, means of completely overcoming capitalism and the habits formed by the rule of private property in the means of production. This aim can only be achieved by means of slow persistent work for the re-education of the masses; this re-education has not only become possible now that the masses have seen in reality that the landowner, capitalist and merchant have been removed, but it is actually being carried out in thousands of ways through the practical experience of the workers and peasants. It is extremely important in this respect to work for the further or-

ganisation of working people in trade unions; never before has this organisation developed as rapidly anywhere in the world as under Soviet power, and it must be developed until literally all working people are organised in effective, centralised, disciplined industrial unions. We must not confine ourselves to the old, stereotyped forms of the trade union movement, but must, on the one hand, systematically convert the trade unions into organs administering the economy, carefully checking every step we take against the results of practical work; there must be greater and stronger bonds between the trade unions and the Supreme Economic Council, the Commissariat of Labour and, later, with all other branches of the state administration; on the other hand, the trade unions must to a greater degree become organs for the labour and socialist education of the working masses as a whole so that the more backward sections of the workers are allowed to gain practical experience of participation in the administration under the control of the vanguard of the workers.

(3) One of the basic tasks is to raise the level of labour productivity, for without this the full transition to communism is impossible. In addition to lengthy work to educate the masses and raise their cultural level, the achievement of this goal requires the immediate, extensive and comprehensive employment of specialists in science and technology that have been left us as our heritage from capitalism and, as a rule, are imbued with the bourgeois world outlook and habits. The Party, jointly with the trade union organisations, must continue its former line—on the one hand there must not be the slightest political concession made to the bourgeois section of the population, and any counter-revolutionary attempts must be ruthlessly suppressed, and, on the other hand, there must be a ruthless struggle against the would-be radical but actually ignorant and conceited opinion that the working people are capable of overcoming capitalism and the bourgeois social system without learning from bourgeois specialists, without making use of them and without going through the lengthy schooling of work side by side with them.

Although we aim at equality of remuneration for all kinds of labour and at full communism, under no circumstances do we set ourselves the task of immediately, at the present moment, effecting that equality since only the first steps in the transition from capitalism to communism are being taken. For a certain time, therefore, specialists must receive a higher remuneration in order to enable them to work better and not worse than before; for the same reason we must not reject the bonus system for the most successful work, especially for organisational work; bonuses would be impermissible under a full communist system but in the period of transition from capitalism to communism bonuses are indispensable, as is borne out by theory and by a year's experience of Soviet power.

We must, furthermore, work consistently to surround the bourgeois specialists with a comradely atmosphere created by working hand in hand with the masses of rank-and-file workers led by politically conscious communists; we must not be dismayed by the inevitable individual failures but must strive to arouse in people possessing scientific knowledge a consciousness of how loathsome it is to use science for personal enrichment and for the exploitation of man by man, a consciousness of the more lofty aim of using science for the purpose of making it known to the working people.

(4) The realisation of communism undoubtedly requires the greatest possible and most strict centralisation of labour on a nation-wide scale, and this presumes overcoming the scattering and disunity of workers, by trades and locally, which was one of the sources of capital's strength and labour's weakness. The struggle against the narrowness and limitations of the guild and against its egoism is closely connected with the struggle to remove the antithesis between town and country; it presents great difficulties and cannot be begun on a broad scale without first achieving a considerable increase in the productivity of the people's labour. A start on this work must, however, be made immediately, if at first only on a small, local scale and by way of experiment for the purpose of comparing the results of various measures that are to be adopted in different trades and in different places. The total mobilisation of the entire able-bodied population by the Soviet government, with the trade unions participating, for certain public works must be much more widely and systematically practised than has heretofore been the case.

(5) In the sphere of distribution the present task of Soviet power is to continue unswervingly replacing trade by the

10*

planned, organised, nation-wide distribution of products. The goal is the organisation of the entire population in producers'-and-consumers' communes that can distribute all essential products with the greatest possible speed, economically, on planned lines and with the least expenditure of labour by centralising the entire distribution machinery. The co-operatives are a transitional means of achieving this aim. The use of them is similar to the use of bourgeois specialists insofar as the co-operative machinery we have inherited from capitalism is in the hands of people whose thinking and business habits are bourgeois. The R.C.P. must pursue its own policy systematically; it must be the duty of all Party members to work in the co-operatives, to give them direction in a communist spirit with the aid of the trade unions, to develop the initiative and discipline of the working population united in the co-operatives and to ensure that the co-operatives embrace the entire population and that all co-operatives, from top to bottom, merge into a single co-operative organisation of the Soviet Republic; lastly, the most important thing is to ensure the constant, decisive influence of the proletariat on the other sections of the working people and that everywhere various measures that facilitate and realise the transition from the petty-bourgeois co-operatives of the old, capitalist type to the producers'-and-consumers' communes led by proletarians and semi-proletarians should be tested in practice.

(6) It is impossible to abolish money immediately, in the first period of the transition from capitalism to communism. As a result of this the bourgeois elements of the population are continuing to use the currency that still remains their private property, currency that certifies to the right of the exploiters to obtain public wealth for the purpose of speculation, profit and the plundering of the working people. The nationalisation of the banks alone is insufficient to combat this survival of bourgeois robbery. The R.C.P. will strive for the most rapid implementation of the most radical measures preparing the way for the abolition of money, the first among them being the exchange of cash for savings-bank books, cheques, short-term bills entitling the owner to receive products from public funds, etc., the introduction of the obligatory deposit of money in banks, etc. The practical experience

of preparing and implementing these and similar measures will show which of them are the most suitable.

(7) In the sphere of finances the R.C.P. will implement a progressive income and property tax wherever it is possible; cases where it is possible will not be very numerous after the abolition of private property in land, and in most factories and other enterprises. In the period of the dictatorship of the proletariat and the state ownership of the most important means of production, state finances must be based on the direct appropriation of a certain part of the revenues of the various state monopolies for the needs of the state. It is possible to balance expenditure against revenue only if the exchange of commodities is properly organised; the organisation of producers'-and-consumers' communes and the rehabilitation of transport (one of the most important immediate aims of the Soviet government) will lead to this.

In the Sphere of Agriculture

After the abolition of private property in land and the [almost] complete expropriation of the landowners and the promulgation of a law on the socialisation of the land which regards as preferable the large-scale farming of commonly-owned estates, the chief task of Soviet power is to discover and test in practice the most expedient and practicable transitional measures to effect this.

The main line and the guiding principle of the R.C.P. agrarian policy under these circumstances still remains the effort to rely on the proletarian and semi-proletarian elements of the countryside. They must first and foremost be organised into an independent force, they must be brought closer to the urban proletariat and snatched away from the influence of the rural bourgeoisie and petty property-owning interests. The organisation of poor peasants' committees was one step in this direction; the organisation of Party cells in the villages, the re-election of Soviets to exclude the kulaks, the establishment of special types of trade unions for the proletarians and semi-proletarians of the countryside—all these and similar measures must be effected without fail.

As far as the kulaks, the rural bourgeoisie, are concerned,

the policy of the R.C.P. is one of decisive struggle against their exploiters' intrigues and the suppression of their resistance to Soviet socialist policy.

As far as the middle peasant is concerned, the policy of the R.C.P. is one of a cautious attitude towards him; he must not be confused with the kulak and coercive measures must not be used against him; by their class position the middle peasants can be the allies of the proletarian government during the transition to socialism, or, at least, they can constitute a neutral element. Despite the unavoidable partial failures and waverings of the middle peasant, therefore, we must strive persistently to reach agreement with him, showing a solicitous attitude to all his desires and making concessions in selecting ways of carrying out socialist reforms. In this respect a prominent place must be given to the struggle against the abuses of those representatives of Soviet power who, hypocritically taking advantage of the title of Communist, are carrying out a policy that is not communist but is a policy of the bureaucracy, of officialdom; such people must be ruthlessly banished and a strict control established with the aid of the trade unions and by other means.

Insofar as concerns measures for the transition to communist farming, the R.C.P. will test in practice three principal measures that have already taken shape in practice—state farms, agricultural communes and societies (or co-operatives) for the collective tilling of the soil, care being taken to ensure their more correct application, and on a broader scale, especially in respect of ways of developing the voluntary participation of the peasants in these new forms of co-operative farming and of the organisation of the working peasantry to carry out control from below and ensure comradely discipline.

Published in   *Collected Works*, Vol. 29
Petrogradskaya Pravda No. 43,
February 23, 1919

A GREAT BEGINNING

HEROISM OF THE WORKERS IN THE REAR.
"COMMUNIST SUBBOTNIKS"

(Extract)

I have given the information about the communist subbotniks in the fullest and most detailed manner because in this we undoubtedly observe one of the most important aspects of communist construction, to which our press pays insufficient attention, and which all of us have as yet failed properly to appreciate.

Less political fireworks and more attention to the simplest but living facts of communist construction, taken from and tested by actual life–this is the slogan which all of us, our writers, agitators, propagandists, organisers, etc., should repeat unceasingly.

It was natural and inevitable in the first period after the proletarian revolution that we should be engaged primarily on the main and fundamental task of overcoming the resistance of the bourgeoisie, of vanquishing the exploiters, of crushing their conspiracy (like the "slave-owners' conspiracy" to surrender Petrograd, in which all from the Black Hundreds[101] and Cadets[102] to the Mensheviks[103] and Socialist-Revolutionaries were involved[104]). But simultaneously with this task, another task comes to the forefront just as inevitably and ever more imperatively as time goes on, namely, the more important task of positive communist construction, the creation of new economic relations, of a new society.

As I have had occasion to point out more than once, particularly in the speech I delivered at the meeting of the Petrograd Soviet of Workers', Soldiers' and Peasants' Deputies on March 12, the dictatorship of the proletariat is not only the use of force against the exploiters, and not even mainly the use of force. The economic foundation of this revolutionary coercion, the guarantee of its effectiveness and success is the fact that the proletariat represents and creates a higher type of social organisation of labour compared with capitalism. This is the essence. This is the source of the strength and the guarantee of the inevitable complete triumph of communism.

The feudal organisation of social labour rested on the discipline of the bludgeon, while the working people, robbed and tyrannised by a handful of landowners, were utterly ignorant and downtrodden. The capitalist organisation of social labour rested on the discipline of hunger, and, notwithstanding all the progress of bourgeois culture and bourgeois democracy, the vast mass of the working people in the most advanced, civilised and democratic republics remained an ignorant and downtrodden mass of wage-slaves, or oppressed peasants, robbed and tyrannised by a handful of capitalists. The communist organisation of social labour, the first step towards which is socialism, rests, and will do so more and more as time goes on, on the free and conscious discipline of the working people themselves who have thrown off the yoke both of the landowners and capitalists.

This new discipline does not drop from the skies, nor is it born from pious wishes; it grows out of the material conditions of large-scale capitalist production, and out of them alone. Without them it is impossible. And the repository, or the vehicle, of these material conditions is a definite historical class, created, organised, united, trained, educated and hardened by large-scale capitalism. This class is the proletariat.

If we translate the Latin, scientific, historico-philosophical term "dictatorship of the proletariat" into simpler language, it means just the following:

Only a definite class, namely, the urban workers and the factory, industrial workers in general, is able to lead the whole mass of the working and exploited people in the struggle for the overthrow of the yoke of capital, in the process of this overthrow, in the struggle to maintain and consolidate the victory, in the work of creating the new, socialist system, in the whole struggle for the complete abolition of classes. (Let us observe in parenthesis that the only scientific distinction between socialism and communism is that the first term implies the first stage of the new society arising out of capitalism, while the second implies the next and higher stage.)

The mistake the "Berne" yellow International[105] makes is that its leaders accept the class struggle and the leading role of the proletariat only in word and are afraid to think it out to its logical conclusion. They are afraid of that inevitable conclusion which particularly terrifies the bourgeoisie, and which is absolutely unacceptable to them. They are afraid to admit that the dictatorship of the proletariat is *also* a period of class struggle, which is inevitable as long as classes have not been abolished, and which changes in form, being particularly fierce and particularly peculiar in the period immediately following the overthrow of capital. The proletariat does not cease the class struggle after it has captured political power, but continues it until classes are abolished—of course, under different circumstances, in different form and by different means.

And what does the "abolition of classes" mean? All those who call themselves socialists recognise this as the ultimate goal of socialism, but by no means all ponder over its significance. Classes are large groups of people differing from each other by the place they occupy in a historically determined system of social production, by their relation (in most cases fixed and formulated in law) to the means of production, by their role in the social organisation of labour, and, consequently, by the dimensions and mode of acquiring the share of social wealth of which they dispose. Classes are groups of people one of which can appropriate the labour of another owing to the different places they occupy in a definite system of social economy.

Clearly, in order to abolish classes completely, it is not enough to overthrow the exploiters, the landowners and capitalists, not enough to abolish *their* rights of ownership; it is necessary also to abolish *all* private ownership of the means of production, it is necessary to eliminate the distinction between town and country, as well as the distinction between manual workers and brain workers. This requires a very long period of time. In order to achieve this a gigantic stride forward must be taken in developing the productive forces; it is necessary to overcome the resistance (frequently passive, which is particularly stubborn and particularly dif-

ficult to overcome) of the numerous survivals of small production; it is necessary to overcome the enormous force of
habit and conservatism which are connected with these survivals.

The assumption that all "working people" are equally capable of doing this work would be an empty phrase, or the
illusion of an antediluvian, pre-Marxist socialist; for this
ability does not come of itself, but grows historically, and
grows *only* out of the material conditions of large-scale capitalist production. This ability, at the beginning of the road
from capitalism to socialism, is possessed by the proletariat
alone. It is capable of fulfilling the gigantic task that confronts it, first, because it is the strongest and most advanced
class in civilised societies; secondly, because in the most
developed countries it constitutes the majority of the population, and thirdly, because in backward capitalist countries,
like Russia, the majority of the population consists of semi-
proletarians, i.e., of people who regularly live in a proletarian
way part of the year, who regularly earn a part of their
means of subsistence as wage-workers in capitalist enterprises.

Those who try to solve the problems involved in the transition from capitalism to socialism on the basis of general
talk about liberty, equality, democracy in general, equality
of the labouring democracy, etc. (as Kautsky, Martov and
other heroes of the Berne yellow International do), thereby
only reveal their petty-bourgeois, philistine nature and
ideologically slavishly follow in the wake of the bourgeoisie.
The correct solution of this problem can be found only in a
concrete study of the specific relations between the specific
class which has conquered political power, namely, the proletariat, and the whole non-proletarian, and also semi-proletarian, mass of the working population—relations which do
not take shape in fantastically harmonious, "ideal" conditions, but in the real conditions of the frantic resistance of
the bourgeoisie which assumes diverse forms.

The vast majority of the population—and all the more so
of the working population—of any capitalist country, including Russia, have thousands of times experienced, themselves
and through their kith and kin, the oppression, the robbery
and every sort of tyranny of capitalism. The imperialist war,
i.e., the slaughter of ten million people in order to decide

whether British or German capital was to have supremacy in plundering the whole world, intensified, increased and deepened these ordeals exceedingly, and made the people realise their meaning. Hence the inevitable sympathy displayed by the vast majority of the population, particularly the working people, for the proletariat, because it is with heroic courage and revolutionary ruthlessness overthrowing the yoke of capital, overthrowing the exploiters, suppressing their resistance, and shedding its blood to pave the road for the creation of the new society, in which there will be no room for exploiters.

Great and inevitable as may be their petty-bourgeois waverings and vacillations back to the bourgeois "order", under the "wing" of the bourgeoisie, the non-proletarian and semi-proletarian mass of the working population cannot but recognise the moral and political authority of the proletariat, which is not only overthrowing the exploiters and suppressing their resistance, but is building a new and higher social bond, a social discipline, the discipline of class-conscious and united working people, who know no yoke and no authority except the authority of their own union, of their own, more class-conscious, bold, solid, revolutionary and steadfast vanguard.

In order to achieve victory, in order to build and consolidate socialism, the proletariat must fulfil a twofold or dual task: first, it must, by its supreme heroism in the revolutionary struggle against capital, win over the entire mass of the working and exploited people; it must win them over, organise them and lead them in the struggle to overthrow the bourgeoisie and utterly suppress their resistance. Secondly, it must lead the whole mass of the working and exploited people, as well as all the petty-bourgeois groups, on to the road of new economic construction, on to the road to the creation of new social ties, a new labour discipline, a new organisation of labour which will combine the last word in science and capitalist technology with the mass association of class-conscious workers creating large-scale socialist production.

The second task is more difficult than the first, for it cannot possibly be fulfilled by single acts of heroic fervour; it requires the most prolonged, most persistent and most difficult mass heroism in *plain, everyday* work. But this task is more essential than the first, because, in the last analysis, the deepest source of strength for victories over the bourgeoisie and the sole guarantee of the durability and permanence of this victory can only be a new and higher mode of social production, the substitution of large-scale socialist production for capitalist and petty-bourgeois production.

* * *

"Communist subbotniks" are of such enormous historic significance precisely because they demonstrate the conscious and voluntary initiative of the workers in developing productivity of labour, in adopting a new labour discipline, in creating socialist conditions of economy and life.

J. Jacoby, one of the few, in fact it would be more correct to say one of the exceptionally rare, German bourgeois democrats who, after the lessons of 1870-71, went over not to chauvinism or national-liberalism, but to socialism, once said that the formation of a single trade union was of greater historical importance than the battle of Sadowa.[106] This is true. The battle of Sadowa decided the supremacy of one of two bourgeois monarchies, the Austrian or the Prussian, in creating a German national capitalist state. The formation of one trade union was a small step towards the world victory of the proletariat over the bourgeoisie. And we may similarly say that the first communist subbotnik, organised by the workers of the Moscow-Kazan Railway in Moscow on May 10, 1919, was of greater historical significance than any of the victories of Hindenburg, or of Foch and the British, in the 1914-18 imperialist war. The victories of the imperialists mean the slaughter of millions of workers for the sake of the profits of the Anglo-American and French multi-millionaires, the brutality of doomed capitalism, which is bloated and rotting alive. The communist subbotnik organised by the workers of the Moscow-Kazan Railway is one of the cells of the new, socialist society, which brings to all the peoples of the earth emancipation from the yoke of capital and from wars.

The bourgeois gentlemen and their hangers-on, including the Mensheviks and Socialist-Revolutionaries, who are wont to regard themselves as the representatives of "public opinion", jeer of course at the hopes of the Communists, call

them "a baobab tree in a mignonette pot", sneer at the in-
significance of the number of subbotniks compared with the
vast number of cases of thieving, idleness, decline of productivity, spoilage of raw materials and finished goods, etc.
Our reply to this gentry is: if the bourgeois intellectuals had
dedicated their knowledge to assisting the working people
instead of giving it to the Russian and foreign capitalists in
order to restore their power, the revolution would have proceeded more rapidly and more peacefully. But this is utopian,
for the issue is decided by the class struggle, and the majority of the intellectuals gravitate towards the bourgeoisie. Not
with the assistance of the intellectuals will the proletariat
achieve victory, but in spite of their opposition (at least in
the majority of cases), removing those of them who are in-
corrigibly bourgeois, reforming, re-educating and subordinat-
ing the waverers, and gradually winning ever larger sections
of them to its side. Gloating over the difficulties and setbacks
of the revolution, sowing panic, preaching a return to the past
—these are all weapons and methods of class struggle of the
bourgeois intellectuals. The proletariat will not allow itself
to be deceived by them.

If we take the matter in its essence, however, has it ever
happened in history that a new mode of production took root
immediately, without a long succession of setbacks, blunders
and relapses? Half a century after the abolition of serfdom
there were still quite a number of survivals of serfdom in the
Russian countryside. Half a century after the abolition of
slavery in America the position of the Negroes was still very
often one of semi-slavery. The bourgeois intellectuals, including the Mensheviks and Socialist-Revolutionaries, are true to
themselves in serving capital and in continuing to use utterly
false arguments: before the proletarian revolution they
accused us of being utopian; after the revolution they demand
that we wipe out all traces of the past with fantastic rapidity!

We are not utopians, however, and we know the real value
of bourgeois "arguments"; we also know that for some time
after the revolution traces of the old ethics will inevitably
predominate over the young shoots of the new. When the new
has just been born the old always remains stronger than it
for some time; this is always the case in nature and in social
life. Jeering at the feebleness of the young shoots of the new

order, cheap scepticism of the intellectuals and the like—these are, essentially, methods of class struggle of the bourgeoisie against the proletariat, a defence of capitalism against socialism. We must carefully study the new shoots, we must devote the greatest attention to them, do everything to promote their growth and "nurse" these feeble shoots. Some of them will inevitably perish. We cannot vouch that precisely the "communist subbotniks" will play a particularly important role. But that is not the point. The point is to foster each and every shoot of the new; and life will select the most virile. If the Japanese scientist, in order to help mankind vanquish syphilis, had the patience to test six hundred and five preparations before he developed a six hundred and sixth which met definite requirements, then those who want to solve a more difficult problem, namely, to vanquish capitalism, must have the perseverance to try hundreds and thousands of new ways and means of struggle in order to elaborate the most suitable of them.

The "communist subbotniks" are so important because they were initiated by workers who were by no means placed in exceptionally good conditions, by workers of various specialities, and some with no speciality at all, just unskilled labourers, who are living under *ordinary*, i.e., *exceedingly hard*, conditions. We all know very well the main cause of the decline in the productivity of labour that is to be observed not only in Russia, but all over the world: it is ruin and impoverishment, embitterment and weariness caused by the imperialist war, sickness and malnutrition. The latter is first in importance. Starvation—that is the cause. And in order to do away with starvation, productivity of labour must be raised in agriculture, in transport and in industry. So, we get a sort of vicious circle: in order to raise productivity of labour we must save ourselves from starvation, and in order to save ourselves from starvation we must raise productivity of labour.

We know that in practice such contradictions are solved by breaking the vicious circle, by bringing about a radical change in the people's mood, by the heroic initiative of individual groups which, against the background of such a radical change, often plays a decisive role. The unskilled labourers and railway workers of Moscow (of course, we have in mind the majority of them, and not a handful of profiteers, officials and other whiteguards) are working people who are living in desperately hard conditions. They are constantly underfed, and now, before the new harvest is gathered, with the general worsening of the food situation, they are actually starving. And yet these starving workers, surrounded by the malicious counter-revolutionary agitation of the bourgeoisie, the Mensheviks and the Socialist-Revolutionaries, are organising "communist subbotniks", working overtime *without any pay,* and achieving *an enormous increase in the productivity of labour* in spite of the fact that they are weary, tormented, and exhausted by malnutrition. Is this not supreme heroism? Is this not the beginning of a change of momentous significance?

In the last analysis, productivity of labour is the most important, the principal thing for the victory of the new social system. Capitalism created a productivity of labour unknown under serfdom. Capitalism can be utterly vanquished, and will be utterly vanquished by the fact that socialism creates a new and much higher productivity of labour. This is a very difficult matter and must take a long time; but *it has been started,* and that is the main thing. If in starving Moscow, in the summer of 1919, the starving workers who had gone through four trying years of imperialist war and another year and a half of still more trying civil war could start this great work, how will things develop later when we triumph in the civil war and win peace?

Communism is the higher productivity of labour—compared with that existing under capitalism—of voluntary, class-conscious and united workers employing advanced techniques. Communist subbotniks are extraordinarily valuable as the *actual* beginning of *communism;* and this is a very rare thing, because we are in a stage when "only the *first steps* in the transition from capitalism to communism are being taken" (as our Party Programme quite rightly says[107]).

Communism begins when the *rank-and-file workers* begin to display a self-sacrificing concern, that is undaunted by arduous toil, for increasing the productivity of labour, husbanding *every pood of grain, coal, iron* and other products, which do not accrue to the workers personally or to their "close" kith and kin, but to their "distant" kith and kin, i.e., to society as a whole, to tens and hundreds of millions of people united first in one socialist state, and then in a Union of Soviet Republics.

In *Capital*, Karl Marx ridicules the pompous and grandiloquent bourgeois-democratic great charter of liberty and the rights of man, ridicules all this phrase-mongering about liberty, equality and fraternity *in general*, which dazzles the petty bourgeois and philistines of all countries, including the present despicable heroes of the despicable Berne International. Marx contrasts these pompous declarations of rights to the plain, modest, practical, simple manner in which the question is treated by the proletariat: legislative enactment of a shorter working day is a typical example of such treatment.[108] The aptness and profundity of Marx's observation become the clearer and more obvious to us the more the content of the proletarian revolution unfolds. The "formulas" of genuine communism differ from the pompous, intricate, and solemn phraseology of the Kautskys, the Mensheviks and the Socialist-Revolutionaries and their beloved "brethren" of Berne in that they reduce everything to the *conditions of labour*. Less chatter about "labour democracy", about "liberty, equality and fraternity", about "government by the people", and all such stuff; the class-conscious workers and peasants of our day see the trickery of the bourgeois intellectual through these pompous phrases as easily as a person of ordinary common sense and experience, when glancing at the irreproachably "polished" features and immaculate appearance of the "fain fellow, dontcher know", immediately and unerringly puts him down as "in all probability, a scoundrel".

Fewer pompous phrases, more plain, *everyday* work, concern for the pood of grain and the pood of coal! More concern for supplying this pood of grain and pood of coal needed by the hungry workers and ragged and barefoot peasants, *not* by means of *haggling*, not in a capitalist manner, but by means of the conscious, voluntary, boundlessly heroic labour of plain working men like the unskilled labourers and railwaymen of the Moscow-Kazan line.

We must all admit that traces of the bourgeois-intellectual phrase-mongering approach to questions of the revolution are in evidence at every step, everywhere, even in our own ranks. Our press, for example, does not fight sufficiently against these putrid survivals of the putrid, bourgeois-democratic past; it does not sufficiently foster the simple, modest, commonplace but virile shoots of genuine communism.

Take the position of women. Not a single democratic party in the world, not even in the most advanced bourgeois republic, has done in tens of years a hundredth part of what we did in the very first year we were in power. We literally did not leave a single stone standing of the despicable laws which placed women in a position of inequality, or which restricted divorce and surrounded it with disgusting formalities, or which denied recognition to illegitimate children and enforced a search for their fathers, etc.—laws, numerous survivals of which, to the shame of the bourgeoisie and of capitalism, are to be found in all civilised countries. We have a thousand times the right to be proud of what we have done in this sphere. But the more *thoroughly* we have cleared the ground of the lumber of the old, bourgeois laws and institutions, the clearer it is to us that we have only cleared the ground to build on, but are not yet building.

Notwithstanding all the laws emancipating woman, she continues to be a *domestic slave*, because *petty housework* crushes, strangles, stultifies and degrades her, chains her to the kitchen and to the nursery, and she wastes her labour on barbarously unproductive, petty, nerve-racking, stultifying and crushing drudgery. The real *emancipation of women*, real communism, will begin only where and when a mass struggle begins (led by the proletariat wielding the power of the state) against this petty domestic economy, or rather when its *wholesale transformation* into large-scale socialist economy begins.

Do we in practice pay sufficient attention to this question, which, theoretically, is indisputable for every Communist? Of course not. Are we sufficiently solicitous about the young *shoots* of communism which already exist in this sphere? Again we must say emphatically, No! Public canteens, nurseries, kindergartens—here we have examples of these shoots, here we have the simple, everyday means, involving nothing pompous, grandiloquent or ceremonial, which can *in actual fact emancipate women*, which can in actual fact lessen and abolish their inequality with men as regards their role in social production and public life. These means are not new, they (like all the material prerequisites for socialism) were created by large-scale capitalism; but under capitalism they remained, first, a rarity, and secondly, which is particularly important, either *profit-making* enterprises, with all the worst features of speculation, profiteering, cheating and fraud, or "acrobatics of bourgeois philanthropy", which the best workers quite rightly detested and despised.

There is no doubt that the number of these institutions in our country has increased enormously and that they are *beginning* to change in character. There is no doubt that there is far more *organising talent* among the working women and peasant women than we are aware of, that there are far more people than we think who are capable of organising practical work, with the participation of large numbers of workers and of still larger numbers of consumers, without that abundance of talk, fuss, squabbling and chatter about plans, systems, etc., from which our big-headed "intellectuals" or half-baked "communists" "suffer". But we *do not nurse* these shoots of the new as we should.

Look at the bourgeoisie! How excellently they know how to advertise what *they* need! See how what the capitalists regard as "model" enterprises are lauded in millions of copies of *their* newspapers; see how "model" bourgeois institutions are made an object of national pride! Our press does not take the trouble, or hardly takes the trouble, to describe the best canteens or nurseries, in order, by daily insistence, to get some of them turned into models of their kind. It does not give them enough publicity, does not describe in detail what a saving of human labour, what conveniences for the consumer, what economy of products, what emancipation of women from domestic slavery, what an improvement in sanitary conditions can be achieved with *exemplary communist labour* and extended to the whole of society, to all the working people.

Exemplary production, exemplary communist subbotniks, exemplary care and conscientiousness in procuring and distributing every pood of grain, exemplary canteens, exemplary cleanliness in such-and-such a workers' house, in such-and-such a block—all these should receive ten times more attention and care from our press, as well as from *every* workers' and peasants' organisation, than they receive now. All these are young shoots of communism; and it is our common and primary duty to nurse them. Difficult as our food and production situation is, in the year and a half of Bolshevik rule there has been undoubted progress *along the whole front*: grain procurements have increased from thirty million poods (from August 1, 1917, to August 1, 1918) to one hundred million poods (from August 1, 1918, to May 1, 1919); vegetable gardening has expanded, the margin of unsown land has diminished, railway transport has begun to improve despite the enormous fuel difficulties, and so on. Against this general background, and with the support of the proletarian state power, the young shoots of communism will not wither; they will grow and blossom into complete communism.

* * *

We must ponder very deeply over the significance of the "communist subbotniks", in order that we may draw all the very important practical lessons that follow from this great beginning.

The first and main lesson is that this beginning must have every assistance. The word "commune" is being handled much too freely. Any kind of enterprise started by Communists or with their participation is very often at once declared to be a "commune", it being not infrequently forgotten that this *very honourable title* must be *won* by prolonged and persistent effort, by *practical* achievement in genuine communist construction.

That is why, in my opinion, the decision that has matured in the minds of the majority of the members of the Central Executive Committee to *repeal* the decree of the Council of People's Commissars, as far as it pertains to the *title* "consumers' communes",[100] is quite right. Let the title be simpler —and, incidentally, the defects and shortcomings of the *initial* stages of the new organisational work will not be blamed on the "communes", but (as in all fairness they should be) on *bad* Communists. It would be a good thing to eliminate the word "commune" from *common* use, to prohibit every first-comer from snatching at it, or to *allow this title to be borne only* by genuine communes, which have really demonstrated in practice (and have proved by the unanimous recognition of the whole of the surrounding population) that they are capable of organising their work in a communist manner. First

11*

show that you are capable of working without remuneration
in the interests of society, in the interests of all the working
people, show that you are capable of "working in a revolutionary way", that you are capable of raising productivity of
labour, of organising the work in an exemplary manner, and
then hold out your hand for the honourable title "commune"!

In this respect, the "communist subbotniks" are a most
valuable exception; for the unskilled labourers and railwaymen of the Moscow-Kazan Railway *first* demonstrated *by
deeds* that they are capable of working like *Communists*, and
then adopted the title of "communist subbotniks" for their
undertaking. We must see to it and make sure that in future
anyone who calls his enterprise, institution or undertaking a
commune *without having proved* this by hard work and practical *success in prolonged effort*, by exemplary and truly communist organisation, is mercilessly ridiculed and pilloried as
a charlatan or a windbag.

That great beginning, the "communist subbotniks", must
also be utilised for another purpose, namely, to *purge* the
Party. In the early period following the revolution, when the
mass of "honest" and philistine-minded people was particularly timorous, and when the bourgeois intellectuals to a man,
including, of course, the Mensheviks and Socialist-Revolutionaries, played the lackey to the bourgeoisie and carried on
sabotage, it was absolutely inevitable that adventurers and
other pernicious elements should hitch themselves to the ruling party. There never has been, and there never can be, a
revolution without that. The whole point is that the ruling
party should be able, relying on a sound and strong advanced class, to purge its ranks.

We started this work long ago. It must be continued steadily and untiringly. The mobilisation of Communists for the
war helped us in this respect: the cowards and scoundrels fled
the Party's ranks. Good riddance! *Such* a reduction in the
Party's membership means an *enormous increase* in its
strength and weight. We must continue the purging, and that
new beginning, the "communist subbotniks", must be utilised
for this purpose: members should be accepted into the Party
only after six months', say, "trial", or "probation", at "working in a revolutionary way". A similar test should be demanded of *all* members of the Party who joined after October 25,

1917, and who have not proved by some special work or service that they are absolutely reliable, loyal and capable of being Communists.

The purging of the Party, through the steadily *increasing demands* it makes in regard to working in a genuinely communist way, will improve the state *apparatus*, and will bring ever so much nearer the *final transition* of the peasants to the side of the revolutionary proletariat.

Incidentally, the "communist subbotniks" have thrown a remarkably strong light on the class character of the state apparatus under the dictatorship of the proletariat. The Central Committee of the Party drafts a letter on "working in a revolutionary way". The idea is suggested by the Central Committee of a party from 100,000 to 200,000 members (I assume that that will be the number after a thorough purging; at present the membership is larger).

The idea is taken up by the workers organised in trade unions. In Russia and the Ukraine they number about four million. The overwhelming majority of them are for the state power of the proletariat, for the proletarian dictatorship. Two hundred thousand and four million—such is the ratio of the "cog-wheels", if one may so express it. Then follow the *tens of millions* of peasants, who are divided into three main groups: the most numerous and the one standing closest to the proletariat is that of the semi-proletarians or poor peasants; then come the middle peasants, and lastly the numerically very small group of kulaks or rural bourgeoisie.

As long as it is possible to trade in grain and to make profit out of famine, the peasant will remain (and this will for some time be inevitable under the dictatorship of the proletariat) a semi-working man, a semi-profiteer. As a profiteer he is hostile to us, hostile to the proletarian state; he is inclined to agree with the bourgeoisie and their faithful lackeys, up to and including the Menshevik Sher or the Socialist-Revolutionary B. Chernenkov, who stand for freedom to trade in grain. But *as a working man,* the peasant is a friend of the proletarian state, a most loyal ally of the worker in the struggle against the landowner and against the capitalist. As working men, the peasants, the vast mass of them, the peasant millions, support the state "machine" which is headed by the one or two hundred thousand Communists of the proletarian vanguard, and which consists of millions of organised proletarians.

A state more democratic, in the true sense of the word, one more closely connected with the working and exploited people, has *never yet existed.*

It is precisely proletarian work such as is put into "communist subbotniks" and which is performed at these subbotniks that will win the complete respect and love of peasants for the proletarian state. Such work and such work alone will completely convince the peasant of the justice of our cause and that of communism, and make him our devoted ally, and, hence, will lead to the complete elimination of our food difficulties, to the complete victory of communism over capitalism in the matter of the production and distribution of grain, to the unqualified consolidation of communism.

June 28, 1919

Published as a separate pamphlet   *Collected Works*, Vol. 29
by the State Publishing House,
Moscow, July 1919

Signed: *N. Lenin*

ECONOMICS AND POLITICS
IN THE ERA OF THE DICTATORSHIP
OF THE PROLETARIAT

I had intended to write a short pamphlet on the subject indicated in the title on the occasion of the second anniversary of Soviet power. But owing to the rush of everyday work I have so far been unable to get beyond preliminary preparations for some of the sections. I have therefore decided to essay a brief, summarised exposition of what, in my opinion, are the most essential ideas on the subject. A summarised exposition, of course, possesses many disadvantages and shortcomings. Nevertheless, a short magazine article may perhaps achieve the modest aim in view, which is to present the problem and the groundwork for its discussion by the Communists of various countries.

1

Theoretically, there can be no doubt that between capitalism and communism there lies a definite transition period which must combine the features and properties of both these forms of social economy. This transition period has to be a period of struggle between dying capitalism and nascent communism—or, in other words, between capitalism which has been defeated but not destroyed and communism which has been born but is still very feeble.

The necessity for a whole historical era distinguished by these transitional features should be obvious not only to Marxists, but to any educated person who is in any degree acquainted with the theory of development. Yet all the talk on the subject of the transition to socialism which we hear

from present-day petty-bourgeois democrats (and such, in
spite of their spurious socialist label, are all the leaders of
the Second International, including such individuals as Mac-
Donald, Jean Longuet, Kautsky and Friedrich Adler) is marked
by complete disregard of this obvious truth. Petty-bourgeois democrats are distinguished by an aversion to class
struggle, by their dreams of avoiding it, by their efforts to
smooth over, to reconcile, to remove sharp corners. Such
democrats, therefore, either avoid recognising any necessity for
a whole historical period of transition from capitalism to communism or regard it as their duty to concoct schemes for
reconciling the two contending forces instead of leading the
struggle of one of these forces.

2

In Russia, the dictatorship of the proletariat must inevitably differ in certain particulars from what it would be in the
advanced countries, owing to the very great backwardness
and petty-bourgeois character of our country. But the basic
forces—and the basic forms of social economy—are the same in
Russia as in any capitalist country, so that the peculiarities
can apply only to what is of lesser importance.

The basic forms of social economy are capitalism, petty
commodity production, and communism. The basic forces are
the bourgeoisie, the petty bourgeoisie (the peasantry in particular) and the proletariat.

The economic system of Russia in the era of the dictatorship of the proletariat represents the struggle of labour,
united on communist principles on the scale of a single vast
state and making its first steps—the struggle against petty
commodity production and against the capitalism which still
persists and against that which is newly arising on the basis
of petty commodity production.

In Russia, labour is united communistically insofar as, first,
private ownership of the means of production has been abolished, and, secondly, the proletarian state power is organising large-scale production on state-owned land and in state-
owned enterprises on a national scale, is distributing labour-
power among the various branches of production and the

various enterprises, and is distributing among the working people large quantities of articles of consumption belonging to the state.

We speak of "the first steps" of communism in Russia (it is also put that way in our Party Programme adopted in March 1919), because all these things have been only partially effected in our country, or, to put it differently, their achievement is only in its early stages. We accomplished instantly, at one revolutionary blow, all that can, in general, be accomplished instantly; on the first day of the dictatorship of the proletariat, for instance, on October 26 (November 8), 1917 the private ownership of land was abolished without compensation for the big landowners—the big landowners were expropriated. Within the space of a few months practically all the big capitalists, owners of mills and factories, joint-stock companies, banks, railways, and so forth, were also expropriated without compensation. The state organisation of large-scale production in industry and the transition from "workers' control" to "workers' management" of factories and railways—this has, by and large, already been accomplished; but in relation to agriculture it has only just begun ("state farms", i.e., large farms organised by the workers' state on state-owned land). Similarly, we have only just begun the organisation of various forms of co-operative societies of small farmers as a transition from petty commodity agriculture to communist agriculture.* The same must be said of the state-organised distribution of products in place of private trade, i.e., the state procurement and delivery of grain to the cities and of industrial products to the countryside. Available statistical data on this subject will be given below.

Peasant farming continues to be petty commodity production. Here we have an extremely broad and very sound, deep-rooted basis for capitalism, a basis on which capitalism persists or arises anew in a bitter struggle against communism. The forms of this struggle are private speculation and profi-

---

* The number of "state farms" and "agricultural communes" in Soviet Russia is, as far as is known, 3,536 and 1,961 respectively, and the number of agricultural artels is 3,696. Our Central Statistical Board is at present taking an exact census of all state farms and communes. The results will begin coming in in November 1919.

teering *versus* state procurement of grain (and other products) and state distribution of products in general.

3

To illustrate these abstract theoretical propositions, let us quote actual figures.

According to the figures of the People's Commissariat of Food, state procurements of grain in Russia between August 1, 1917, and August 1, 1918, amounted to about 30,000,000 poods, and in the following year to about 110,000,000 poods. During the first three months of the next campaign (1919-20) procurements will presumably total about 45,000,000 poods, as against 37,000,000 poods for the same period (August-October) in 1918.

These figures speak clearly of a slow but steady improvement in the state of affairs from the point of view of the victory of communism over capitalism. This improvement is being achieved in spite of difficulties without world parallel, difficulties due to the Civil War organised by Russian and foreign capitalists who are harnessing all the forces of the world's strongest powers.

Therefore, in spite of the lies and slanders of the bourgeoisie of all countries and of their open or masked henchmen (the "socialists" of the Second International), one thing remains beyond dispute—as far as the basic economic problem of the dictatorship of the proletariat is concerned, the victory of communism over capitalism in our country is assured. Throughout the world the bourgeoisie is raging and fuming against Bolshevism and is organising military expeditions, plots, etc., against the Bolsheviks, because it realises full well that our success in reconstructing the social economy is inevitable, provided we are not crushed by military force. And its attempts to crush us in this way are not succeeding.

The extent to which we have already vanquished capitalism in the short time we have had at our disposal, and despite the incredible difficulties under which we have had to work, will be seen from the following summarised figures. The Central Statistical Board has just prepared for the press data on the production and consumption of grain—not for the whole of Soviet Russia, but only for twenty-six gubernias.

The results are as follows:

26 gubernias of Soviet Russia	Population in millions	Production of grain (excluding seed and fodder), million poods	Grain delivered, million poods		Total amount of grain at disposal of population, million poods	Grain consumption, poods per capita
			Commissariat of Food	Profiteers		
Producing gubernias	Urban 4 4	—	20.9	20 6	41.5	9.5
	Rural 28.6	625.4	—	—	481.8	16.9
Consuming gubernias	Urban 5.9	—	20.0	20.0	40 0	6.8
	Rural 13.8	114.0	12.1	27.8	151.4	11.0
Total (26 gubernias)	52.7	739.4	53.0	68.4	714.7	13.6

Thus, approximately half the amount of grain supplied to the cities is provided by the Commissariat of Food and the other half by profiteers. This same proportion is revealed by a careful survey, made in 1918, of the food consumed by city workers. It should be borne in mind that for bread supplied by the state the worker pays *one-ninth* of what he pays the profiteer. The profiteering price for bread is *ten times* greater than the state price; this is revealed by a careful study of workers' budgets.

4

A careful study of the figures quoted shows that they present an exact picture of the fundamental features of Russia's present-day economy.

The working people have been emancipated from their age-old oppressors and exploiters, the landowners and capitalists. This step in the direction of real freedom and real equality, a step which for its extent, dimensions and rapidity is without parallel in the world, is ignored by the supporters of the bourgeoisie (including the petty-bourgeois democrats), who, when they talk of freedom and equality, mean parliamentary bourgeois democracy, which they falsely declare to be "democracy" in general, or "pure democracy" (Kautsky).

But the working people are concerned only with real equality and real freedom (freedom from the landowners and capitalists), and that is why they give the Soviet government such solid support.

In this peasant country it was the peasantry as a whole who were the first to gain, who gained most, and gained immediately from the dictatorship of the proletariat. The peasant in Russia starved under the landowners and capitalists. Throughout the long centuries of our history, the peasant never had an opportunity to work for himself: he starved while handing over hundreds of millions of poods of grain to the capitalists, for the cities and for export. Under the dictatorship of the proletariat the peasant *for the first time* has been working for himself and *feeding better than the city dweller*. For the first time the peasant has seen real freedom —freedom to eat his bread, freedom from starvation. In the distribution of the land, as we know, the maximum equality has been established; in the vast majority of cases the peasants are dividing the land according to the number of "mouths to feed".

Socialism means the abolition of classes.

In order to abolish classes it is necessary, first, to overthrow the landowners and capitalists. This part of our task has been accomplished, but it is only a part, and moreover *not* the most difficult part. In order to abolish classes it is necessary, secondly, to abolish the difference between factory worker and peasant, to make *workers of all of them*. This cannot be done all at once. This task is incomparably more difficult and will of necessity take a long time. It is not a problem that can be solved by overthrowing a class. It can be solved only by the organisational reconstruction of the whole social economy, by a transition from individual, disunited, petty commodity production to large-scale social production. This transition must of necessity be extremely protracted. It may only be delayed and complicated by hasty and incautious administrative and legislative measures. It can be accelerated only by affording such assistance to the peasant as will enable him to effect an immense improvement in his whole agricultural technique, to reform it radically.

In order to solve the second and most difficult part of the problem, the proletariat, after having defeated the bourgeoisie, must unswervingly conduct its policy towards the peasantry along the following fundamental lines. The proletariat must separate, demarcate the working peasant from the peasant owner, the peasant worker from the peasant huckster, the peasant who labours from the peasant who profiteers.

In this demarcation lies the *whole essence* of socialism.

And it is not surprising that the socialists who are socialists in word but petty-bourgeois democrats in deed (the Martovs, the Chernovs, the Kautskys and Co.) do not understand this essence of socialism.

The demarcation we here refer to is an extremely difficult one, because in real life all the features of the "peasant", however diverse they may be, however contradictory they may be, are fused into one whole. Nevertheless, demarcation is possible; and not only is it possible, it inevitably follows from the conditions of peasant farming and peasant life. The working peasant has for ages been oppressed by the landowners, the capitalists, the hucksters and profiteers and by *their* state, including even the most democratic bourgeois republics. Throughout the ages, the working peasant has trained himself to hate and loathe these oppressors and exploiters, and this "training", engendered by the conditions of life, *compels* the peasant to seek for an alliance with the worker against the capitalist and against the profiteer and huckster. Yet at the same time, economic conditions, the conditions of commodity production, inevitably turn the peasant (not always, but in the vast majority of cases) into a huckster and profiteer.

The statistics quoted above reveal a striking difference between the working peasant and the peasant profiteer. That peasant who during 1918-19 delivered to the hungry workers of the cities 40,000,000 poods of grain at fixed state prices, who delivered this grain to the state agencies in spite of all the shortcomings of the latter, shortcomings fully realised by the workers' government, but which were unavoidable in the first period of the transition to socialism—that peasant is a working peasant, the comrade and equal of the socialist worker, his most faithful ally, his blood brother in the fight against the yoke of capital. Whereas that peasant who clandestinely sold 40,000,000 poods of grain at ten times the state price, taking advantage of the need and hunger of the city worker, deceiving the state, and everywhere increasing and creating deceit, robbery and fraud—that peasant is a profiteer, an ally of the capitalist, a class enemy of the worker, an exploiter. For whoever possesses surplus grain gathered from land belonging to the whole state with the help of implements in which in one way or another is embodied the labour not only of the peasant but also of the worker and so on—whoever possesses a surplus of grain and profiteers in that grain is an exploiter of the hungry worker.

You are violators of freedom, equality, and democracy—they shout at us on all sides, pointing to the inequality of the worker and the peasant under our Constitution, to the dissolution of the Constituent Assembly,[110] to the forcible confiscation of surplus grain, and so forth. We reply—never in the world has there been a state which has done so much to remove the actual inequality, the actual lack of freedom from which the working peasant has been suffering for centuries. But we shall never recognise equality with the peasant profiteer, just as we do not recognise "equality" between the exploiter and the exploited, between the sated and the hungry, nor the "freedom" for the former to rob the latter. And those educated people who refuse to recognise this difference we shall treat as whiteguards, even though they may call themselves democrats, socialists, internationalists, Kautskys, Chernovs, or Martovs.

5

Socialism means the abolition of classes. The dictatorship of the proletariat has done all it could to abolish classes. But classes cannot be abolished at one stroke.

And classes still *remain* and *will remain* in the era of the dictatorship of the proletariat. The dictatorship will become unnecessary when classes disappear. Without the dictatorship of the proletariat they will not disappear.

Classes have remained, but in the era of the dictatorship of the proletariat *every* class has undergone a change, and the relations between the classes have also changed. The class struggle does not disappear under the dictatorship of the proletariat; it merely assumes different forms.

Under capitalism the proletariat was an oppressed class, a class which had been deprived of the means of production, the only class which stood directly and completely opposed to the bourgeoisie, and therefore the only one capable of being revolutionary to the very end. Having overthrown the bourgeoisie and conquered political power, the proletariat has become the *ruling* class; it wields state power, it exercises control over means of production already socialised; it guides the wavering and intermediary elements and classes; it crushes the increasingly stubborn resistance of the exploiters. All these are specific tasks of the class struggle, tasks which the proletariat formerly did not and could not have set itself.

The class of exploiters, the landowners and capitalists, has not disappeared and cannot disappear all at once under the dictatorship of the proletariat. The exploiters have been smashed, but not destroyed. They still have an international base in the form of international capital, of which they are a branch. They still retain certain means of production in part, they still have money, they still have vast social connections. Because they have been defeated, the energy of their resistance has increased a hundred- and a thousandfold. The "art" of state, military and economic administration gives them a superiority, and a very great superiority, so that their importance is incomparably greater than their numerical proportion of the population. The class struggle waged by the overthrown exploiters against the victorious vanguard of the exploited, i.e., the proletariat, has become incomparably more bitter. And it cannot be otherwise in the case of a revolution, unless this concept is replaced (as it is by all the heroes of the Second International) by reformist illusions.

Lastly, the peasants, like the petty bourgeoisie in general, occupy a half-way, intermediate position *even* under the dictatorship of the proletariat: on the one hand, they are a fairly large (and in backward Russia, a vast) mass of working people, united by the common interest of all working people to emancipate themselves from the landowner and the capitalist; on the other hand, they are disunited small proprietors, property-owners and traders. Such an economic position inevitably causes them to vacillate between the proletariat and the bourgeoisie. In view of the acute form which the struggle between these two classes has assumed, in view of the incredibly severe break-up of all social relations, and in view of the great attachment of the peasants and the petty bourgeoisie generally to the old, the routine, and the unchanging, it is only natural that we should inevitably find them swinging from one side to the other, that we should find them wavering, changeable, uncertain, and so on.

In relation to this class—or to these social elements—the proletariat must strive to establish its influence over it, to guide it. To give leadership to the vacillating and unstable—such is the task of the proletariat.

If we compare all the basic forces or classes and their interrelations, as modified by the dictatorship of the proletariat, we shall realise how unutterably nonsensical and theoretically stupid is the common petty-bourgeois idea shared by all representatives of the Second International, that the transition to socialism is possible "by means of democracy" in general. The fundamental source of this error lies in the prejudice inherited from the bourgeoisie that "democracy" is something absolute and not concerned with classes. As a matter of fact, democracy also passes into an entirely new phase under the dictatorship of the proletariat, and the class struggle rises to a higher level, dominating over each and every form.

General talk about freedom, equality, and democracy is in fact but a blind repetition of concepts shaped by the relations of commodity production. To attempt to solve the concrete problems of the dictatorship of the proletariat by such generalities is tantamount to accepting the theories and principles of the bourgeoisie in their entirety. From the point of view of the proletariat, the question can be put only in the following way: freedom from oppression by which class? equality of which class with which? democracy based on private property, or on a struggle for the abolition of private property?—and so forth.

Long ago Engels in his *Anti-Dühring* explained that the concept "equality" is moulded from the relations of commodity production; equality becomes a prejudice if it is not understood to mean the *abolition of classes*.[111] This elementary truth regarding the distinction between the bourgeois-democratic and the socialist conception of equality is constantly being forgotten. But if it is not forgotten, it becomes obvious that by overthrowing the bourgeoisie the proletariat takes the most decisive step towards the abolition of classes, and that in order to complete the process the proletariat must continue its class struggle, making use of the apparatus of state power and employing various methods of combating, influencing, and bringing pressure to bear on the overthrown bourgeoisie and the vacillating petty bourgeoisie.

(To be continued)[112]

October 30, 1919

Pravda No. 250, and *Izvestia* No. 250, November 7, 1919

Signed: *N. Lenin*

Collected Works, Vol. 30

REPORT ON SUBBOTNIKS DELIVERED TO A MOSCOW CITY CONFERENCE OF THE R.C.P.(B.)[113]

December 20, 1919

Comrades, the organisers of the conference inform me that you have arranged for a report on subbotniks and divided it into two parts so that it would be possible to discuss the main thing in this field in detail; first the organisation of subbotniks in Moscow and the results achieved, and secondly, practical conclusions for their further organisation. I should like to confine myself to general propositions, to the ideas born of the organisation of subbotniks as a new phenomenon in our Party and governmental development. I shall, therefore, dwell only briefly on the practical aspect.

When the first communist subbotniks had just been organised it was difficult to judge to what extent such a phenomenon deserved attention and whether anything big would come of it. I remember that when the first news of them began to appear in the Party press, the appraisals of comrades close to trade union organisational affairs and the Commissariat of Labour were at first extremely restrained, if not pessimistic. They did not think there were any grounds for regarding them as important. Since then subbotniks have become so widespread that their importance to our development cannot be disputed by anyone.

We have actually been using the adjective "communist" very frequently, so frequently that we have even included it in the name of our Party. But when you give this matter some thought, you arrive at the idea that together with the good that has followed from this, a certain danger for us may have been created. Our chief reason for changing the name of the Party was the desire to draw a clear line of distinction between us and the dominant socialism of the Second

International. After the overwhelming majority of the official socialist parties, through their leaders, had gone over to the side of the bourgeoisie of their own countries or of their own governments during the imperialist war, the tremendous crisis, the collapse of the old socialism, became very obvious to us. And in order to stress as sharply as possible that we could not consider socialists those who took sides with their governments during the imperialist war, in order to show that the old socialism had gone rotten, had died—mainly for that reason the idea of changing the Party's name was put forward. This the more so, since the name of "Social-Democratic" has from the theoretical point of view long ceased to be correct. As far back as the forties, when it was first widely used politically in France, it was applied to a party professing petty-bourgeois socialist reformism and not to a party of the revolutionary proletariat. The main reason, the motive for changing the name of our Party which has given its new name to the new International was the desire to cut ourselves off decisively from the old socialism.

If we were to ask ourselves in what way communism differs from socialism, we should have to say that socialism is the society that grows directly out of capitalism, it is the first form of the new society. Communism is a higher form of society, and can only develop when socialism has become firmly established. Socialism implies work without the aid of the capitalists, socialised labour with strict accounting, control and supervision by the organised vanguard, the advanced section of the working people; the measure of labour and remuneration for it must be fixed. It is necessary to fix them because capitalist society has left behind such survivals and such habits as the fragmentation of labour, no confidence in social economy, and the old habits of the petty proprietor that dominate in all peasant countries. All this is contrary to real communist economy. We give the name of communism to the system under which people form the habit of performing their social duties without any special apparatus for coercion, and when unpaid work for the public good becomes a general phenomenon. It stands to reason that the concept of "communism" is a far too distant one for those who are taking the first steps towards complete victory over capitalism. No matter how correct it may have been to change the name

12*

of our Party, no matter how great the benefit the change has brought us, no matter how great what has been done and the scale on which it has developed—Communist Parties now exist throughout the world and although less than a year has passed since the foundation of the Communist International,[114] from the point of view of the labour movement it is incomparably stronger than the old, dying Second International—if the name "Communist Party" were interpreted to mean that the communist system is being introduced immediately, that would be a great distortion and would do practical harm since it would be nothing more than empty boasting.

That is why the word "communist" must be treated with great caution, and that is why communist subbotniks that have begun to enter into our life are of particular value, because it is only in this extremely tiny phenomenon that something communist has begun to make its appearance. The expropriation of the landowners and capitalists enabled us to organise only the most primitive forms of socialism, and there is not yet anything communist in it. If we take our real economy we see that the germs of socialism in it are still very weak and that the old economic forms dominate overwhelmingly; these are expressed either as the domination of petty proprietorship or as wild, uncontrolled profiteering. When our adversaries, the petty-bourgeois democrats, Mensheviks and Socialist-Revolutionaries, assert in their objections to us that we have smashed large-scale capitalism but the worst kind of profiteering, usury capitalism, persists in its place, we tell them that if they imagine that we can go straight from large-scale capitalism to communism they are not revolutionaries but reformists and utopians.

Large-scale capitalism has been seriously undermined everywhere, even in those countries where no steps towards socialism have yet been taken. From this point of view, none of the criticisms or the objections levelled against us by our opponents are serious. Obviously the beginnings of a new, petty, profiteering capitalism began to make their appearance after large-scale capitalism had been crushed. We are living through a savage battle against the survivals of large-scale capitalism that grasps at every kind of petty speculation where it is difficult to catch it and where it takes on the worst and most unorganised form of trading.

The struggle has become much fiercer under war conditions and has led to the most brutal forms of profiteering, especially in places where capitalism was organised on a larger scale, and it would be quite incorrect to imagine that the revolutionary transition could have any other form. That is how matters stand in respect of our present-day economy. If we were to ask ourselves what the present economic system of Soviet Russia is, we should have to say that it consists in laying the foundations of socialism in large-scale industry, the re-organisation of the old capitalist economy with the capitalists putting up a stubborn resistance in millions and millions of different ways. The countries of the West that have emerged from the war as badly off as we are—Austria, for instance—differ from us only in that the disintegration of capitalism and the speculation there are more pronounced than in our country and that there are no germs of socialist organisation there to offer resistance to capitalism. There is, however, not yet anything communist in our economic system. The "communist" begins when subbotniks (i.e., unpaid labour with no quota set by any authority or any state) make their appearance; they constitute the labour of individuals on an extensive scale for the public good. This is not helping one's neighbour in the way that has always been customary in the countryside; it is work done to meet the needs of the country as a whole, and it is organised on a broad scale and is unpaid. It would, therefore, be more correct if the word "communist" were applied not only to the name of the Party but also to those economic manifestations in our reality that are actually implementing communism. If there is anything communist at all in the prevailing system in Russia, it is only the subbotniks, and everything else is nothing but the struggle against capitalism for the consolidation of socialism out of which, after the full victory of socialism, there should grow that communism that we see at subbotniks, not with the aid of a book, but in living reality.

Such is the theoretical significance of subbotniks; they demonstrate that here something quite new is beginning to emerge in the form of unpaid labour, extensively organised to meet the needs of the entire state, something that is contrary to all the old capitalist rules, something that is much more lofty than the socialist society that is conquering capitalism. When the workers on the Moscow-Kazan Railway, people who were living under conditions of the worst famine and the greatest need, first responded to the appeal of the Central Committee of the Party to come to the aid of the country,[115] and when there appeared signs that communist subbotniks were no longer a matter of single cases but were spreading and meeting with the sympathy of the masses, we were able to say that they were a phenomenon of tremendous theoretical importance and that we really should afford them all-round support if we wanted to be communists in more than mere theory, in more than the struggle against capitalism. From the point of view of the practical construction of a socialist society that is not enough. It must be said that the movement can really be developed on a mass scale. I do not undertake to say whether we have proved this since no general summaries of the extent of the movement we call communist subbotniks have yet been prepared. I have only fragmentary information and have read in the Party press that these subbotniks are developing more and more widely in a number of towns. Petrograd comrades say that subbotniks are far more widespread in their city than in Moscow. As far as the provinces are concerned many of the comrades who have a practical knowledge of this movement have told me that they are collecting a huge amount of material on this new form of social labour. However, we shall only be able to obtain summarised data after the question has been discussed many times in the press and at Party conferences of different cities, and on the basis of those data we shall be able to say whether the subbotniks have really become a mass phenomenon, and whether we have really achieved important successes in this sphere.

Whatever may be the case, whether or not we shall soon obtain that sort of complete and verified data, we should have no doubt that from the theoretical point of view we have no manifestation other than subbotniks to show that we do not only call ourselves communists, and not only want to be communists, but are actually doing something that is communist and not merely socialist. Every communist, therefore, everyone who wants to be true to the principles of communism should devote all his attention and all his efforts to the explanation of this phenomenon and to its practical implementation. That is the theoretical significance of the subbotniks. At every Party conference, therefore, we must persistently raise this question and discuss both its theoretical and its practical aspect. We must not limit this phenomenon to its theoretical significance. Communist subbotniks are of tremendous importance to us not only because they are the practical implementation of communism. Apart from this, subbotniks have a double significance—from the standpoint of the state they are purely practical aid to the state, and from the standpoint of the Party—and for us, members of the Party, this must not remain in the shade—they have the significance of purging the Party of undesirable elements and are of importance in the struggle against the influences experienced by the Party at a time when capitalism is decaying. From the economic standpoint the subbotniks are needed to save the Soviet Republic from economic dislocation and launch upon socialism. I should like to deal with the second aspect of this question in somewhat greater detail . . . .*

Brief report published in
Izvestia No. 287,
December 21, 1919

First published in full
in *Pravda* No. 245,
October 26, 1927

Collected Works, Vol. 30

---

* The verbatim report stops here.—*Ed.*

"LEFT-WING" COMMUNISM,
AN INFANTILE DISORDER

VI

SHOULD REVOLUTIONARIES WORK IN REACTIONARY TRADE UNIONS?

(Extract)

Capitalism inevitably leaves socialism the legacy, on the one hand, of old trade and craft distinctions among the workers, distinctions evolved in the course of centuries; and, on the other hand, trade unions, which only very slowly, in the course of years and years, can and will develop into broader industrial unions with less of the craft union about them (embracing whole industries, and not only crafts, trades and occupations), and later proceed, through these industrial unions, to eliminate the division of labour among people, to educate and school people, give them *all-round development and an all-round* training, so that they *know how to do everything*. Communism is advancing and must advance towards this goal, and *will reach* it, but only after very many years. To attempt in practice today to anticipate this future result of a fully developed, fully stabilised and formed, fully expanded and mature communism would be like trying to teach higher mathematics to a four-year-old child.

We can (and must) begin to build socialism, not with abstract human material, not with human material specially prepared by us, but with the human material bequeathed to us by capitalism. True, that is very "difficult", but no other approach to this task is serious enough to warrant discussion....

X

CERTAIN CONCLUSIONS

(Extract)

As long as national and state differences exist among peoples and countries—and these differences will continue to exist for a very long time even after the dictatorship of the proletariat has been established on a world scale—the unity of international tactics of the communist working-class movement of all countries demands, not the elimination of variety, not the abolition of national differences (that is a foolish dream at the present moment), but an application of the *fundamental* principles of communism (Soviet power and the dictatorship of the proletariat) such as will *correctly modify* these principles in certain *particulars*, correctly adapt and apply them to national and national-state differences. The main task of the historical period through which all the advanced (and not only the advanced) countries are now passing is to investigate, study, seek, divine, grasp that which is peculiarly national, specifically national, in the *concrete* manner in which each country is to approach the fulfilment of the tasks *common* to all—the victory over opportunism and Left doctrinairism within the working-class movement, the overthrow of the bourgeoisie, and the establishment of a Soviet republic and a proletarian dictatorship. The main thing—not everything by a very long way, of course, but the main thing—has already been achieved: the vanguard of the working class has been won over, it has ranged itself on the side of Soviet government against parliamentarism, on the side of the dictatorship of the proletariat against bourgeois democracy. Now all efforts, all attention must be concentrated on the *next* step, namely, seeking the forms of *transi-*

tion or *approach* to the proletarian revolution, which seems—and from a certain standpoint really is—less fundamental, but which, on the other hand, is actually closer to the practical carrying out of the task.

The proletarian vanguard has been won over ideologically. That is the main thing. Without this not even the first step towards victory can be made. But it is still a fairly long way from victory. Victory cannot be won with the vanguard alone. To throw the vanguard alone into the decisive battle, before the whole class, before the broad masses have taken up a position either of direct support of the vanguard, or at least of sympathetic neutrality towards it, and one in which they cannot possibly support the enemy, would be not merely folly but a crime. And in order that really the whole class, that really the broad masses of the working people, those oppressed by capital, may take up such a position, propaganda and agitation alone are not enough. For this the masses must have their own political experience. Such is the fundamental law of all great revolutions, now confirmed with astonishing force and vividness not only in Russia but also in Germany. In order to turn resolutely toward communism, not only the uncultured, often illiterate masses of Russia, but the highly cultured masses of Germany, who are all literate, had to realise through their own painful experience the absolute impotence and spinelessness, the absolute helplessness and servility to the bourgeoisie, the utter vileness of the government of the knights of the Second International, to realise that a dictatorship of the extreme reactionaries (Kornilov[116] in Russia, Kapp and Co.[117] in Germany) is inevitably the only alternative to a dictatorship of the proletariat.

The immediate task that confronts the class-conscious vanguard of the international working-class movement, i.e., the Communist parties, groups and trends, is to be able *to lead* the broad masses (now, for the most part, slumbering, apathetic, bound by routine, inert and dormant) to their new position, or, rather, to be able to lead *not only* their own party, but also these masses in their approach, their transition to the new position. While the first historic task (that of winning over the class-conscious vanguard of the proletariat to Soviet power and the dictatorship of the working class) could not be accomplished without a complete ideological and political victory over opportunism and social-chauvinism, the second task, which now becomes the immediate task, and which consists in being able to lead the *masses* to the new position that can ensure the victory of the vanguard in the revolution—this immediate task cannot be accomplished without eliminating Left doctrinairism, without completely overcoming and eliminating its mistakes.

Propaganda was in the forefront so long as and to the extent that the question was (and insofar as it still is) one of winning over the vanguard of the proletariat to communism; even propaganda circles, with all the defects of the circle spirit, are useful under these conditions and produce fruitful results. But when it is a question of practical action by the masses, of the disposition, if one may so express it, of vast armies, of the alignment of *all* the class forces of the given society *for the final and decisive battle*, then propaganda habits alone, the mere repetition of the truths of "pure" communism, are of no avail. In these circumstances one must not count in thousands, as the propagandist does who belongs to a small group that has not yet given leadership to the masses; in these circumstances one must count in millions and tens of millions. In these circumstances we must not only ask ourselves whether we have convinced the vanguard of the revolutionary class, but also whether the historically effective forces of *all* classes—positively of all the classes of the given society without exception—are aligned in such a way that everything has fully matured for the decisive battle; in such a way that (1) all the class forces hostile to us have become sufficiently entangled, are sufficiently at loggerheads with each other, have sufficiently weakened themselves in a struggle which is beyond their strength; (2) all the vacillating, wavering, unstable, intermediate elements— the petty bourgeoisie and the petty-bourgeois democrats as distinct from the bourgeoisie—have sufficiently exposed themselves in the eyes of the people, have sufficiently disgraced themselves through their practical bankruptcy; and (3) among the proletariat a mass sentiment in favour of supporting the most determined, supremely bold, revolutionary action against the bourgeoisie has emerged and begun to grow vigorously. Then revolution is indeed ripe; then, indeed, if we have correctly gauged all the conditions indicated and briefly outlined above, and if we have chosen the moment rightly, our victory is assured.

Written April-May 1920

Published in pamphlet form
by the State Publishing House,
Petrograd, June 1920   *Collected Works*, Vol. 31

THE TASKS OF THE YOUTH LEAGUES

SPEECH DELIVERED AT THE THIRD ALL-RUSSIA CONGRESS
OF THE RUSSIAN YOUNG COMMUNIST LEAGUE
OCTOBER 2, 1920[118]

(The Congress greeted Lenin with a tremendous ovation.)
Comrades, I would like to discuss today the fundamental
tasks of the Young Communist League and, in this connection, what the youth organisations in a socialist republic should
be like in general.

It is all the more necessary to deal with this question because in a certain sense it may be said that it is the youth
that will be faced with the real task of creating a communist
society. For it is clear that the generation of workers brought
up in capitalist society can, at best, accomplish the task of
destroying the foundations of the old, capitalist social life,
which was built on exploitation. At best it can accomplish the
task of creating a social system that would help the proletariat and the working classes to retain power and to lay a
firm foundation, on which only the generation that is starting
to work under the new conditions, in a situation in which
exploiting relations between men no longer exist, can build.

And so, in approaching the tasks of the youth from this
angle, I must say that the tasks of the youth in general, and
of the Young Communist Leagues and all other organisations in particular, may be summed up in one word: learn.

Of course, this is only "one word". It does not answer the
principal and most essential questions: what to learn, and
how to learn? And the whole point here is that with the
transformation of the old, capitalist society, the teaching,
training and education of the new generations that will
create the communist society cannot be conducted on the old
lines. The teaching, training and education of the youth must
proceed from the material that has been left to us by the

old society. We can build communism only on the basis of the totality of knowledge, organisations and institutions, only by using the stock of human forces and means that have been left to us by the old society. Only by radically remoulding the teaching, organisation and training of the youth shall we be able to ensure that the efforts of the younger generation will result in the creation of a society that will be unlike the old society, i.e., in the creation of a communist society. That is why we must deal in detail with the question of what we should teach the youth and how the youth should learn if it really wants to justify the name of communist youth, and how it should be trained so as to be able to complete and consummate what we have started.

I must say that the first and most natural reply would seem to be that the Youth League, and the youth in general that wants to advance to communism, should learn communism.

But this reply—"learn communism"—is too general. What do we need in order to learn communism? What must be singled out from the sum of general knowledge to acquire a knowledge of communism? Here a number of dangers arise, which often manifest themselves whenever the task of learning communism is presented incorrectly, or when it is interpreted too one-sidedly.

Naturally, the first thought that enters one's mind is that learning communism means imbibing the sum of knowledge that is contained in communist manuals, pamphlets and books. But such a definition of the study of communism would be too crude and inadequate. If the study of communism consisted solely in imbibing what is contained in communist books and pamphlets, we might all too easily obtain communist text-jugglers or braggarts, and this would very often cause us harm and damage, because such people, having learned by rote what is contained in communist books and pamphlets, would prove incapable of combining all branches of knowledge, and would be unable to act in the way communism really demands.

One of the greatest evils and misfortunes left to us by the old, capitalist society is the complete alienation of books from practical life; for we have had books in which everything was described in the best possible manner, yet in the majority of cases these were books containing the most disgusting and hypocritical lies that described capitalist society falsely.

That is why it would be extremely wrong merely to absorb what is written in books about communism. In our speeches and articles we do not now merely repeat what was formerly said about communism, because our speeches and articles are connected with our daily work in every branch. Without work, without struggle, an abstract knowledge of communism obtained from communist pamphlets and books would be absolutely worthless, for it would continue the old separation of theory and practice, that old separation which constituted the most disgusting feature of the old, bourgeois society.

It would be still more dangerous to start imbibing only communist slogans. Had we not realised this danger in time, and had we not directed all our efforts to avert this danger, the half million or million young men and women who would have called themselves Communists after studying communism in this way would only occasion great damage to the cause of communism.

Here the question arises: how should we combine all this for the study of communism? What must we take from the old school, from the old science? The old school declared that its aim was to produce men with an all-round education, to teach the sciences in general. We know that this was utterly false, for the whole of society was based and maintained on the division of men into classes, into exploiters and oppressed. Naturally, the whole of the old school, being thoroughly imbued with the class spirit, imparted knowledge only to the children of the bourgeoisie. Every word was falsified in the interests of the bourgeoisie. In these schools the younger generation of workers and peasants were not so much educated as drilled in the interests of this bourgeoisie. They were trained in such a way as to be useful servants of the bourgeoisie, able to create profits for it without disturbing its peace and leisure. That is why, while rejecting the old school, we have made it our task to take from it only what we require for real communist education.

This brings me to the reproaches and accusations which we constantly hear levelled at the old school, and which often lead to totally wrong conclusions. It is said that the old school was a school of cramming, grinding, learning by rote. That is true, but we must distinguish between what was bad in the old school and what is useful for us, and we must be able to choose from it what is necessary for communism.

The old school was a school of cramming; it compelled pupils to imbibe a mass of useless, superfluous, barren knowledge, which clogged the brain and transformed the younger generation into bureaucrats regimented according to one single pattern. But you would be committing a great mistake if you attempted to draw the conclusion that one can become a Communist without acquiring what has been accumulated by human knowledge. It would be a mistake to think that it is enough to learn communist slogans, the conclusions of communist science, without acquiring the sum of knowledge of which communism itself is a result. Marxism is an example of how communism arose out of the sum of human knowledge.

You have read and heard that communist theory, the science of communism mainly created by Marx, this doctrine of Marxism, has ceased to be the product of a single socialist of the nineteenth century, even though he was a genius, and that it has become the doctrine of millions and tens of millions of proletarians all over the world, who are applying it in their struggle against capitalism. And if you were to ask why the teachings of Marx were able to capture the hearts of millions and tens of millions of the most revolutionary class, you would receive only one answer: it was because Marx based his work on the firm foundation of the human knowledge acquired under capitalism. Marx studied the laws of development of human society and realised the inevitability of the development of capitalism towards communism. And the principal thing is that he proved this precisely on the basis of the most exact, most detailed and most profound study of this capitalist society, by fully assimilating all that earlier science had produced. He critically reshaped everything that had been created by human society, not ignoring a single point. Everything that had been created by human thought he reshaped, criticised, tested on the working-class movement, and drew conclusions which people restricted by bourgeois limits or bound by bourgeois prejudices could not draw.

We must bear this in mind when, for example, we talk about proletarian culture. Unless we clearly understand that only by an exact knowledge of the culture created by the whole development of mankind and only by reshaping this culture can we build proletarian culture—unless we understand that, we shall not be able to solve this problem. Proletarian culture is not something that has sprung nobody knows whence, it is not an invention of people who call themselves experts in proletarian culture. That is all nonsense. Proletarian culture must be the result of the natural development of the stores of knowledge which mankind has accumulated under the yoke of capitalist society, landowner society, bureaucratic society. All these roads and paths have led, are leading, and will continue to lead to proletarian culture, in the same way as political economy, reshaped by Marx, showed us what human society must come to, showed us the transition to the class struggle, to the beginning of the proletarian revolution.

When we so often hear representatives of the youth and certain advocates of a new system of education attacking the old school and saying that it was a school of cramming, we say to them that we must take what was good from the old school. We must not take from the old school the system of loading young people's minds with an immense amount of knowledge, nine-tenths of which was useless and one-tenth distorted. But this does not mean that we can confine ourselves to communist conclusions and learn only communist slogans. You will not create communism that way. You can become a Communist only when you enrich your mind with the knowledge of all the treasures created by mankind.

We do not need cramming; but we do need to develop and perfect the mind of every student by knowledge of fundamental facts. For communism would become a void, a mere signboard, and a Communist a mere braggart, if all the knowledge he has obtained were not digested in his mind. You must not only assimilate this knowledge, you must assimilate it critically, so as not to cram your mind with useless lumber, but enrich it with all those facts that are indispensable to the modern man of education. If a Communist took it into his head to boast about his communism because of the ready-made conclusions he had acquired, without putting in a great deal of serious and hard work, without understanding the facts which he must examine critically, he would be a very deplorable Communist. Such superficiality would be decidedly fatal. If I know that I know little, I shall strive to learn more; but if a man says that he is a Communist and that he need know nothing thoroughly, he will never be anything like a Communist.

The old school turned out servants needed by the capitalists; the old school transformed men of science into men who had to write and say what pleased the capitalists. Therefore, we must abolish it. But does the fact that we must abolish it, destroy it, mean that we must not take from it all that mankind has accumulated and that is essential to man? Does it mean that we do not have to distinguish between what was necessary for capitalism and what is necessary for communism?

We are replacing the old drill-sergeant methods that were employed in bourgeois society in opposition to the will of the majority by the class-conscious discipline of the workers and peasants, who combine hatred of the old society with determination, ability and readiness to unite and organise their forces for this fight, in order to transform the wills of millions and hundreds of millions of people, disunited, dispersed and scattered over the territory of a huge country, into a single will; for without this single will defeat is inevitable. Without this solidarity, without this conscious discipline of the workers and peasants, our cause will be hopeless. Without this we shall not be able to beat the capitalists and landowners of the whole world. We shall not even consolidate the foundation, let alone build a new, communist society on that foundation. Similarly, while rejecting the old school, while cherishing an absolutely legitimate and essential hatred for the old school, while prizing the readiness to destroy the old school, we must realise that we must replace the old system of tuition, the old cramming, the old drill by the ability to acquire the totality of human knowledge, and to acquire it in such a way that communism shall not be something learned by rote, but something that you yourselves have thought over, that it shall embody the conclusions which are inevitable from the standpoint of modern education.

That is the way we must present the main tasks when speaking of the aim—learn communism.

In order to explain this to you, and as an approach to the question of how to learn, I shall take a practical example. You all know that following immediately on the military tasks, the tasks of defending the republic, we are now being confronted with economic tasks. We know that communist society cannot be built unless we regenerate industry and agriculture, and they must not be regenerated in the old way. They must be regenerated on a modern basis, in accordance with the last word in science. You know that this basis is electricity, and that only when the whole country, all branches of industry and agriculture have been electrified, only when you have achieved this aim, will you be able to build for yourselves the communist society which the older generation cannot build. Confronting you is the task of economically reviving the whole country, of reorganising and restoring both agriculture and industry on modern technical lines, based on modern science and technology, on electricity. You realise perfectly well that illiterate people cannot tackle electrification, and that mere literacy is not enough either. It is not enough to understand what electricity is; it is necessary to know how to apply it technically to industry and to agriculture, and to the various branches of industry and agriculture. We must learn this ourselves, and must teach it to the whole of the growing generation of working people. This is the task that confronts every class-conscious Communist, every young person who regards himself a Communist and who clearly understands that by joining the Young Communist League he has pledged himself to help the Party build communism and to help the whole younger generation create a communist society. He must realise that he can create it only on the basis of modern education; and if he does not acquire this education communism will remain only a pious wish.

The task of the older generation was to overthrow the bourgeoisie. The main task then was to criticise the bourgeoisie, to arouse hatred of the bourgeoisie among the masses, to develop class-consciousness and the ability to unite their forces. The new generation is confronted with a much more complicated task. Not only have you to combine all

13*

your forces to uphold the power of the workers and peasants against the attacks of the capitalists. That you must do.
That you have clearly understood; that the Communist dis-
tinctly perceives. But it is not enough. You must build a
communist society. In many respects half of the work has
been done. The older order has been destroyed, as it deserved
to be, it has been transformed into a heap of ruins, as it
deserved to be. The ground has been cleared, and on this
ground the younger communist generation must build a communist society. You are faced with the task of construction,
and you can cope with it only by mastering all modern
knowledge, only if you are able to transform communism
from ready-made, memorised formulas, counsels, recipes,
prescriptions and programmes into that living thing which
unites your immediate work, and only if you are able to
transform communism into a guide for your practical work.

This is the task by which you should be guided in educating, training and rousing the whole of the younger generation. You must be the foremost among the millions of builders of communist society, which every young man and young
woman should be. Unless you enlist the whole mass of young
workers and peasants in the work of building communism,
you will not build a communist society.

This naturally brings me to the question how we should
teach communism and what the specific features of our
methods should be.

Here, first of all, I shall deal with the question of communist ethics.

You must train yourselves to be Communists. The task of
the Youth League is to organise its practical activities in
such a way that, by learning, organising, uniting and fighting, its members should train themselves and all who look
to it as a leader; they should train Communists. The whole
object of training, educating and teaching the youth of today
should be to imbue them with communist ethics.

But is there such a thing as communist ethics? Is there
such a thing as communist morality? Of course, there is. It
is often made to appear that we have no ethics of our own;
and very often the bourgeoisie accuse us Communists of re-
pudiating all ethics. This is a method of shuffling concepts,
of throwing dust in the eyes of the workers and peasants.

In what sense do we repudiate ethics and morality?

In the sense in which it was preached by the bourgeoisie, who derived ethics from God's commandments. We, of course, say that we do not believe in God, and that we know perfectly well that the clergy, the landowners and the bourgeoisie spoke in the name of God in pursuit of their own interests as exploiters. Or instead of deriving ethics from the commandments of morality, from the commandments of God, they derived it from idealist or semi-idealist phrases, which always amounted to something very similar to God's commandments.

We repudiate all morality drawn from outside human society and classes. We say that it is a deception, a fraud, a befogging of the minds of the workers and peasants in the interests of the landowners and capitalists.

We say that our morality is entirely subordinated to the interests of the class struggle of the proletariat. Our morality is derived from the interests of the class struggle of the proletariat.

The old society was based on the oppression of all the workers and peasants by the landowners and capitalists. We had to destroy this, we had to overthrow them; but for this we had to create unity. God would not create such unity.

This unity could be provided only by factories, only by the proletariat, trained and roused from its long slumber. Only when that class was formed did the mass movement begin which has led to what we see now—the victory of the proletarian revolution in one of the weakest of countries, which for three years has been repelling the onslaught of the bourgeoisie of the whole world. And we see how the proletarian revolution is growing all over the world. We now say, on the basis of experience, that only the proletariat could have created that solid force which the disunited and scattered peasantry are following and which has withstood all the onslaughts of the exploiters. Only this class can help the working masses to unite, rally their ranks and finally defend, finally consolidate and finally build up communist society.

That is why we say that for us there is no such thing as morality outside human society; it is a fraud. Morality for us is subordinated to the interests of the class struggle of the proletariat.

What does this class struggle mean? It means overthrowing the tsar, overthrowing the capitalists, abolishing the capitalist class.

And what are classes in general? Classes are what permits one section of society to appropriate the labour of the other section. If one section of society appropriates all the land, we have a landowner class and a peasant class. If one section of society possesses the factories, shares and capital, while another section works in these factories, we have a capitalist class and a proletarian class.

It was not difficult to drive out the tsar—that required only a few days. It was not very difficult to drive out the landowners—that was done in a few months. Nor was it very difficult to drive out the capitalists. But it is incomparably more difficult to abolish classes; we still have the division into workers and peasants. If the peasant is settled on his separate plot of land and appropriates superfluous grain, that is, grain that he does not need for himself or for his cattle, while the rest of the people have to go without bread, then the peasant becomes an exploiter. The more grain he clings to, the more profitable he finds it; as for the rest, let them starve: "The more they starve, the dearer I can sell this grain." Everybody must work according to a single common plan, on common land, in common factories and in accordance with a common system. Is it easy to attain this? You see that it is not as easy as driving out the tsar, the landowners and the capitalists. What is required is that the proletariat re-educate, re-train a section of the peasantry; it must win over those who are working peasants in order to crush the resistance of those peasants who are rich and are profiting by the poverty and want of the rest. Hence the task of the proletarian struggle is not completed by the fact that we have overthrown the tsar and have driven out the landowners and capitalists, and to complete it is the task of the system we call the dictatorship of the proletariat.

The class struggle is still continuing; it has merely changed its forms. It is the class struggle of the proletariat to prevent the return of the old exploiters, to unite the scattered masses of unenlightened peasants into one union. The class struggle is continuing and it is our task to subordinate all interests to this struggle. And we subordinate our communist morality to this task. We say: morality is what serves to destroy the old exploiting society and to unite all the working people around the proletariat, which is building up a new, communist society.

Communist morality is the morality which serves this struggle, which unites the working people against all exploitation, against all small property; for small property puts into the hands of one person what has been created by the labour of the whole of society. In our country the land is common property.

But suppose I take a piece of this common property and grow on it twice as much grain as I need and profiteer in the surplus? Suppose I argue that the more starving people there are the more they will pay? Would I then be behaving like a Communist? No, I would be behaving like an exploiter, like a proprietor. This must be combated. If this is allowed to go on things will slide back to the rule of the capitalists, to the rule of the bourgeoisie, as has more than once happened in previous revolutions. And in order to prevent the restoration of the rule of the capitalists and the bourgeoisie we must not allow profiteering, we must not allow individuals to enrich themselves at the expense of the rest, and the working people must unite with the proletariat and form a communist society. This is the principal feature of the fundamental task of the League and of the organisation of the communist youth.

The old society was based on the principle: rob or be robbed, work for others or make others work for you, be a slave-owner or a slave. Naturally, people brought up in such a society imbibe with their mother's milk, so to speak, the psychology, the habit, the concept: you are either a slave-owner or a slave, or else, a small owner, a small employee, a small official, an intellectual—in short, a man who thinks only of himself, and doesn't give a hang for anybody else.

If I work this plot of land, I don't give a hang for anybody else; if others starve, all the better, the more I will get for my grain. If I have a job as a doctor, engineer, teacher, or clerk, I don't give a hang for anybody else. Perhaps if I toady to and please the powers that be I shall keep my job, and even get on in life and become a bourgeois. A Communist cannot have such a psychology and such sentiments. When the workers and peasants proved that they are able by their own efforts to defend themselves and create a new society—that was the beginning of the new, communist training, training in the struggle against the exploiters, training in alliance with the proletariat against the self-seekers and small owners, against the psychology and habits which say: I seek my own profit and I don't give a hang for anything else.

This is the reply to the question of how the young and rising generation should learn communism.

It can learn communism only by linking up every step in its studies, training and education with the continuous struggle the proletarians and the working people are waging against the old exploiting society. When people talk to us about morality, we say: for the Communist, all morality is in this solid, united discipline and conscious mass struggle against the exploiters. We do not believe in an eternal morality, and we expose the deceit of all the fables about morality. Morality serves the purpose of helping human society to rise to a higher level and to get rid of the exploitation of labour.

To achieve this we need that younger generation which began to awaken to conscious life in the midst of the disciplined and desperate struggle against the bourgeoisie. In this struggle that generation is training genuine Communists, it must subordinate to this struggle and link with it every step in its studies, education and training. The training of the communist youth must consist not in giving them sentimental speeches and moral precepts. This is not what training consists in. When people saw how their fathers and mothers lived under the yoke of the landowners and capitalists, when they themselves experienced the sufferings that befell those who started the struggle against the exploiters, when they saw what sacrifices the continuation of this struggle entailed in order to defend what had been won, and when they saw what frenzied foes the landowners and capitalists are—they were trained in this environment to become Communists. The basis of communist morality is the struggle for the consolidation and completion of communism. That too is the basis of communist training, education, and teaching.

That is the reply to the question of how communism should be learnt.

We would not believe in teaching, training and education if they were confined only to the school and were divorced from the storm of life. As long as the workers and peasants continue to be oppressed by the landowners and capitalists, and as long as the schools remain in the hands of the landowners and capitalists, the rising generation will remain blind and ignorant. But our school must impart to the youth the fundamentals of knowledge, the ability to work out communist views independently; it must make educated people of them. In the time during which people attend school, it must train them to be participants in the struggle for emancipation from the exploiters. The Young Communist League will justify its name as the League of the rising communist generation only when it links up every step of its teaching, training and education with participation in the general struggle of all the working people against the exploiters. For you know perfectly well that as long as Russia remains the only workers' republic, while the old, bourgeois system exists in the rest of the world, we shall be weaker than they, we shall be under the constant menace of a new attack; and that only if we learn to be solid and united shall we win in the further struggle and—having gained strength—become really invincible. Thus, to be a Communist means that you must organise and unite the whole rising generation and set an example of training and discipline in this struggle. Then you will be able to start building the edifice of communist society and bring it to completion.

In order to make this clearer to you I will quote an example. We call ourselves Communists. What is a Communist? Communist is a Latin word. "Communis" is the Latin for "common". Communist society is a society in which all things—the land, the factories—are owned in common and the people work in common. That is communism.

Is it possible to work in common if each one works separately on his own plot of land? Work in common cannot be brought about all at once. That is impossible. It does not drop from the skies. It comes by toil and suffering, it is created in the course of struggle. Old books are of no use here; no one will believe them. One's own living experience

is required. When Kolchak and Denikin advanced from
Siberia and the South the peasants were on their side. They
did not like Bolshevism because the Bolsheviks took their
grain at a fixed price. But when the peasants in Siberia and
the Ukraine experienced the rule of Kolchak and Denikin,
they realised that they had only one alternative: either to
go to the capitalist, and he would at once hand them over
into slavery to the landowner; or to follow the worker, who,
it is true, did not promise a land flowing with milk and
honey, who demanded iron discipline and firmness in an
arduous struggle, but who would lead them out of enslavement to the capitalists and landowners. When even the
ignorant peasants realised and saw this from their own experience they became conscious adherents of communism,
who had passed through a stern school. It is such experience
that must form the basis of all the activities of the Young
Communist League.

I have replied to the questions what we must learn, what
we must take from the old school and from the old science.
I shall now try to answer the question how this must be
learnt. The answer is: only by inseparably linking every
step in the activities of the school, every step in training,
education and teaching with the struggle of all the working
people against the exploiters.

I shall quote a few examples from the experience of the
work of some of the youth organisations to illustrate how this
training in communism should proceed. Everybody is talk-
ing about abolishing illiteracy. You know that a communist
society cannot be built in an illiterate country. It is not
enough for the Soviet government to issue an order, or for
the Party to issue a particular slogan, or to assign a certain
number of the best workers to this task. The younger generation itself must take up this work. Communism means that
the youth, the young men and women who belong to the
Youth League, would say: this is our job; we shall unite and
go into the rural districts to abolish illiteracy, so that there
shall be no illiterates among our rising generation. We are
trying to get the rising generation to devote its activities to
this work. You know that we cannot quickly transform ignorant, illiterate Russia into a literate country. But if the Youth
League sets to work on this job, if all the young people work

for the benefit of all, the League, which unites 400,000 young men and women, will be entitled to call itself a Young Communist League. It is also a task of the League, not only to acquire knowledge itself, but to help those young people who are unable to extricate themselves from the darkness of illiteracy by their own efforts. Being a member of the Youth League means devoting one's labour and efforts to the common cause. That is what communist training means. Only in the course of such work does a young man or woman become a real Communist. Only if they achieve practical results in this work will they become Communists.

Take, for example, work on the suburban vegetable gardens. Isn't this a task? This is one of the tasks of the Young Communist League. The people are starving; there is hunger in the factories. In order to save ourselves from starvation, vegetable gardens must be developed. But agriculture is being carried on in the old way. Therefore, more class-conscious elements must undertake this work, and you would then find that the number of vegetable gardens would increase, their area grow, and the results improve. The Young Communist League must take an active part in this work. Every League and every branch of a League should regard this as its job.

The Young Communist League must be a shock group, helping in every job and displaying initiative and enterprise. The League should be such that any worker may see that it consists of people whose teachings he may not understand, whose teachings he perhaps may not immediately believe, but from whose practical work and activity he could see that they are really the people who are showing him the right road.

If the Young Communist League fails to organise its work in this way in all fields, it will mean that it is slipping into the old, bourgeois path. We must combine our training with the struggle of the working people against the exploiters in order to help the former to perform the tasks that follow from the teachings of communism.

The members of the League should use every spare hour to improve the vegetable gardens, or to organise the education of young people in some factory, and so forth. We want to transform Russia from a poverty-stricken and

wretched country into a wealthy country. And the Young
Communist League must combine its education, teaching and
training with the labour of the workers and peasants, so as
not to shut itself up in its schools and not to confine itself
to reading communist books and pamphlets. Only by working side by side with the workers and peasants can one
become a genuine Communist. And everyone must be made
to realise that all those who belong to the Youth League
are literate and at the same time know how to work. When
everyone sees that we have driven the old drill methods
from the old school and have replaced them by conscious
discipline, that all young men and women are taking part in
subbotniks, that they are utilising every suburban farm to
help the population—the people will cease to look upon
labour as they looked upon it before.

It is the task of the Young Communist League to organise
assistance in the village or in the city block in such a matter
as—I take a small example—cleanliness or the distribution of
food. How was this done in the old, capitalist society? Everybody worked for himself alone, and nobody cared whether
there were aged or sick, or whether all the housework fell
on the shoulders of the women, who, as a result, were in a
state of oppression and slavery. Whose business is it to combat this? It is the business of the Youth Leagues, which must
say: we shall change all this; we shall organise detachments
of young people who will help to maintain cleanliness or to
distribute food, who will make systematic house-to-house
inspections, who will work in an organised way for the
benefit of the whole of society, properly distributing their
forces and demonstrating that labour must be organised
labour.

The generation which is now about fifty years old cannot
expect to see communist society. This generation will die out
before then. But the generation which is now fifteen years
old will see communist society, and will itself build this
society. And this generation must know that the whole purpose of its life is to build communist society. In the old
society work was carried on by separate families, and labour
was not united by anybody except the landowners and capitalists, who oppressed the masses of the people. We must
organise all labour, no matter how dirty and arduous it may

be, in such a way that every worker and peasant may say: I am part of the great army of free labour, and I shall be able to build my life without the landowners and capitalists, I shall be able to establish the communist system. The Young Communist League must train everybody to conscious and disciplined labour from an early age. In this way we shall be sure that the problems that now confront us will be solved. We must assume that no less than ten years will be required for the electrification of the country, so that our impoverished land may be served by the latest achievements of technology. And so, the generation which is now fifteen years old, and which in ten or twenty years' time will be living in communist society, must approach all its tasks in education in such a way that every day, in every village and in every town, the young people engage in the practical solution of some problem of common labour, even though the smallest, even though the simplest. To the extent that this is done in every village, to the extent that communist emulation develops, to the extent that the youth prove that they can unite their labour, to that extent will the success of communist construction be ensured. Only by regarding every step from the standpoint of the success of this construction, only by asking ourselves whether we have done all we can to be united, politically conscious working people, will the Young Communist League succeed in uniting its half a million members into a single army of labour and win universal respect. (*A thunder of applause.*)

Pravda Nos. 221, 222 and 223,   *Collected Works*, Vol. 31
October 5. 6 and 7. 1920

EIGHTH ALL-RUSSIA CONGRESS
OF SOVIETS

December 22-29, 1920

1

REPORT ON THE WORK
OF THE COUNCIL OF PEOPLE'S COMMISSARS
DECEMBER 22

(Extract)

You will hear the report of the State Electrification Commission that was set up in conformity with the decision of the All-Russia Central Executive Committee of February 7, 1920. On February 21 the Presidium of the Supreme Economic Council signed the final ordinance determining the composition of the commission, and a number of the finest experts and workers, mainly from the Supreme Economic Council, over a hundred of them, and also from the People's Commissariat of Railways and the People's Commissariat of Agriculture, are devoting their entire energy to this work. We have before us the results of the work of the State Commission for the Electrification of Russia in the shape of this small volume which will be distributed to you today or tomorrow. I trust you will not be scared by this little volume. I think I shall have no difficulty in convincing you of the particular importance of this book. In my opinion it is a second programme of our Party. We have a Party programme which has been excellently explained by Comrades Preobrazhensky and Bukharin in the form of a book not quite as big, but extremely valuable. That is the political programme; it is an enumeration of our objects, it is an explanation of the relations between classes and masses. But it must also be realised that it is time to take this road in actual fact and to measure the practical results. Our Party Programme must not remain merely a programme of the Party. It must be converted into the programme of our economic development, otherwise it will be valueless even as a programme of the Party. It must be supplemented by a second Party programme, a plan of work for restoring our entire economy and raising it to the level of modern technical development. Without a plan for electrification, we cannot undertake any real constructive work. When we discuss the restoration of agriculture, industry and transport, and their harmonious co-ordination, we are obliged to discuss a broad economic plan. We must adopt a definite plan. Of course, it will be a tentative, approximate plan. This Party programme will not be as unchangeable as our real Party programme, which can be changed only by Party congresses. No, this programme will be improved, elaborated, perfected and modified every day, in every workshop and in every volost. We need it as a first draft, which will be submitted to the whole of Russia as a great economic plan designed for a period of not less than ten years and indicating how Russia is to be placed on the real economic basis which is required by communism. When we fought and won on the war front, what was one of the most powerful impulses that served to multiply our strength and our energies to a tremendous degree? It was the realisation of danger. Everybody asked: can the landowners and capitalists return to Russia? And the reply was that they could. We therefore multiplied our efforts a hundredfold, and we were victorious.

Take the economic front and ask whether capitalism can be restored economically in Russia. We fought the "Sukharevka".[119] The other day, just prior to the opening of All-Russia Congress of Soviets, this not very pleasant institution was closed by the Moscow Soviet of Workers' and Red Army Deputies. (*Applause.*) The "Sukharevka" has been closed, but it is not it that is so sinister. The old "Sukharevka" on Sukharevskaya Square has been closed, and it was not difficult to do that. The sinister thing is the "Sukharevka" that is in the heart and actions of every petty proprietor. That is the "Sukharevka" that must be eliminated for it is the basis of capitalism. As long as it exists, the capitalists may return to Russia and may grow stronger than we are. This must be clearly realised. This must serve as the mainspring of our work and the condition and criterion of our actual success. As long as we live in a small-peasant country, there is a surer economic basis for capitalism in Russia than for communism. This must be borne in mind. Anyone who has carefully observed life in the countryside, as compared with life in the towns, knows that we have not torn up the roots of capitalism and have not undermined the foundation, the basis of the internal enemy. The latter depends on small-scale production, and there is only one way of undermining it, namely, to place the economy of the country, including agriculture, on a new technical basis, the technical basis of modern large-scale production. And it is only in electricity that we have such a basis.

Communism is Soviet power plus the electrification of the whole country. Otherwise the country will remain a small-peasant country, and that we must clearly understand. We are weaker than capitalism, not only on the world scale, but also within the country. Everybody knows that. We have realised it, and we shall see to it that the economic basis is transformed from a small-peasant basis into a large-scale industrial basis. Only when the country has been electrified, when industry, agriculture and transport have been placed on the technical basis of modern large-scale industry, only then shall we be fully victorious.

We have already drawn up a preliminary plan for the electrification of the country; two hundred of our best scientific and technical men have worked on it. We have a plan which gives us estimates of materials and finance covering a long period of years, not less than ten years. This plan indicates how many million barrels of cement and how many million bricks we shall require for the purpose of electrification. From the financial point of view, in order to accomplish the task of electrification it is estimated that 1,000 to 1,200 million gold rubles will be required. You know that we are a long way from being able to cover this sum with our gold reserve. Our food fund is also not very large. We must therefore cover the expenditure indicated in these estimates by concessions, in accordance with the plan I have mentioned. You will see the calculation showing how the restoration of our industry and transport is being planned on this basis.

Not long ago I had occasion to be present at a peasant festival in a remote part of Moscow Gubernia, Volokolamsk Uyezd, where the peasants have electric light.[120] A meeting was arranged in the street, and one of the peasants came forward and began to make a speech in which he welcomed this new event in the lives of the peasants. "We peasants were unenlightened," he said, "and now light has appeared among us, unnatural light, which will light up our peasant darkness." I personally was not astonished at these words. Of course, to the non-Party peasant masses electric light is an "unnatural" light; but what is unnatural to us is that the peasants and workers could have lived for hundreds and thousands of years in such darkness, poverty and oppression by the landowners and capitalists. We cannot emerge from this darkness very quickly. But what we must strive for at the present moment is that every electric power station we build should actually become a stronghold of enlightenment and is used to make the masses electricity conscious, so to speak. It is important for everyone to know why these small electric power stations—of which we already have a few dozen—are connected with the rehabilitation of industry. We have a worked-out plan of electrification, but the fulfilment of this plan is designed to cover a number of years. We must fulfil this plan at all costs, and the period of its fulfilment must be reduced. Here we must have the same thing as we had in the case of one of our first economic plans, the plan for the restoration of transport—Order No. 1042—which was designed to cover a period of five years, but which has now been reduced to three and a half years because we are ahead of schedule. We shall need something like ten or twenty years to implement our electrification plan and work the changes that will eradicate the possibility of a return to capitalism. This will be social development at a pace unheard of in the world. We must be sure to carry out this plan and reduce the time it takes us to do it.

This is the first time we have an integrated long-range plan for economic development besides the separate plans which were drawn up in the various industries, say, transport, and were applied to other industries. This is no easy task but it is designed to secure the victory of communism.

But it must be realised and remembered that we cannot go in for electrification when we have illiterate people. Our commission will endeavour to put an end to illiteracy—but that is not enough. It has done a good deal compared with what existed before, but it has done little compared with what has to be done. In addition to literacy, we need cultured, enlightened and educated working people; the majority of the peasants must definitely realise the tasks confronting us. This programme of the Party must be a standard book, which must be used in every school. You will find in it, in addition to the general plan of electrification, separate plans for every district of Russia. And every comrade, when he goes to the provinces, will have a definitely worked-out scheme of electrification for his district, a scheme for transition from darkness to a normal existence. And, comrades, you can and must compare the propositions given you, elaborate and check them on the spot; and you must see to it that in every school and in every study circle, when the question "What is communism?" is replied to, the answer should not only contain what is written in the Party programme but should also state how we can emerge from the state of darkness.

Our best men, our business experts, have accomplished the task we set them of drawing up a plan for the electrification of Russia and the restoration of her economy. We must now see to it that the workers and peasants should realise how great and difficult this task is, how it must be approached, how it must be tackled.

We must see to it that every factory and every electric power station becomes a centre of enlightenment. And if Russia is covered by a dense network of electric power stations and powerful technical installations, our communist economic development will become a model for a future socialist Europe and Asia. (*Long and stormy applause.*)

First published in 1921
in *Eighth All-Russia
Congress of Soviets.
Verbatim Report*

Collected Works, Vol. 31

ON CO-OPERATION[121]

I

It seems to me that not enough attention is being paid to the co-operative movement in our country. Not everyone understands that now, since the time of the October Revolution and quite apart from NEP[122] (on the contrary, in this connection we must say—because of NEP), our co-operative movement has become one of great significance. There is a lot of fantasy in the dreams of the old co-operators. Often they are ridiculously fantastic. But why are they fantastic? Because people do not understand the fundamental, the rock-bottom significance of the working-class political struggle for the overthrow of the rule of the exploiters. We have overthrown the rule of the exploiters, and much that was fantastic, even romantic, even banal in the dreams of the old co-operators is now becoming unvarnished reality.

Indeed, since political power is in the hands of the working class, since this political power owns all the means of production, the only task, indeed, that remains for us is to organise the population in co-operative societies. With most of the population organised in co-operatives, the socialism which in the past was legitimately treated with ridicule, scorn and contempt by those who were rightly convinced that it was necessary to wage the class struggle, the struggle for political power, etc., will achieve its aim automatically. But not all comrades realise how vastly, how infinitely important it is now to organise the population of Russia in co-operative societies. By adopting NEP we made a concession to the peasant as a trader, to the principle of private trade; it is precisely for this reason (contrary to what some people think) that the co-operative movement is of such immense importance.

14*

All we actually need under NEP is to organise the population of Russia in co-operative societies on a sufficiently large scale, for we have now found that degree of combination of private interest, private commercial interest, with state super-vision and control of this interest, that degree of its subordina-tion to the common interests which was formerly the stumbl-ing-block for very many socialists. Indeed, the power of the state over all large-scale means of production, political power in the hands of the proletariat, the alliance of this proletariat with the many millions of small and very small peasants, the assured proletarian leadership of the peasantry, etc.—is this not all that is necessary to build a complete socialist society out of co-operatives, out of co-operatives alone, which we formerly ridiculed as huckstering and which from a certain aspect we have the right to treat as such now, under NEP? It is still not the building of socialist society, but it is all that is necessary and sufficient for it.

It is this very circumstance that is underestimated by many of our practical workers. They look down upon our co-oper-ative societies and do not appreciate their exceptional impor-tance, first, from the standpoint of principle (the means of production are owned by the state), and, secondly, from the standpoint of transition to the new order by means that are the *simplest, easiest, and most acceptable to the peasant.*

But this again is of fundamental importance. It is one thing to draw up fantastic plans for building socialism through all sorts of workers' associations, and quite another thing to learn to build socialism in practice in such a way that *every* small peasant may take part in it. That is the stage we have now reached. And there is no doubt that, having reached it, we are taking too little advantage of it.

We went too far when we introduced NEP, but not because we attached too much importance to the principle of free industry and trade—we went too far because we lost sight of the co-operatives, because we now underrate the co-oper-atives, because we are already beginning to forget the vast importance of the co-operatives from the above two points of view.

I now propose to discuss with the reader what can and must at once be done practically on the basis of this "co-operative" principle. By what means can we, and must we, start at once to develop this "co-operative" principle so that its socialist meaning may be clear to all?

Co-operation must be politically so organised that it will not only generally and always enjoy certain privileges, but that these privileges should be of a purely material nature (a favourable bank-rate, etc.). The co-operatives must be granted state loans that are greater, if only by a little, than the loans we grant to private enterprises, even to heavy industry, etc.

Every social system arises only if it has the financial backing of a definite class. There is no need to mention the hundreds of millions of rubles that the birth of "free" capitalism cost. At present we must realise that the social system we must now give more than ordinary assistance to is the co-operative system, and we must actually give that assistance. But it must be assisted in the real sense of the word, i.e., it will not be enough to interpret it to mean assistance for any kind of co-operative trade; by assistance we must mean aid to the co-operative trade in which *really large masses of the population really take part*. It is certainly a correct form of assistance to give a bonus to peasants who take part in co-operative trade; but the whole point is to verify the nature of this participation, to verify the awareness behind it, and to verify its quality. Strictly speaking, when a co-operator goes to a village and opens a co-operative store, the people take no part in this whatever; but at the same time, guided by their own interests, the people will hasten to try to take part in it.

There is another aspect to this question. From the point of view of the "civilised" (primarily, literate) European there is not much left for us to do to induce absolutely everyone to take not a passive, but an active part in co-operative operations. Strictly speaking, there is *"only"* one thing left for us to do, and that is, to make our people so "civilised" that they understand all the advantages of everybody participating in the work of the co-operatives, and organise this participation. *"Only"* that. There are now no other devices needed to advance to socialism. But to achieve this "only", there must be a veritable revolution—the entire people must go through a period of cultural development. Therefore, our rule must be: as little philosophising and as few acrobatics as possible. In this respect NEP is an advance, because it is adjustable to the level of the most ordinary peasant and does not demand anything higher of him. But it will take a whole historical epoch to get the entire population into the work of the co-operatives through NEP. At best we can achieve this in one or two decades. Nevertheless it will be a distinct historical epoch, and without this historical epoch, without universal literacy, without a proper degree of efficiency, without training the population sufficiently to acquire the habit of book-reading, and without the material basis for this, without certain safeguards against, say, bad harvests, famine, etc.—without this we shall not achieve our object. The thing now is to learn to combine the wide revolutionary range of action, the revolutionary enthusiasm which we have displayed, and displayed sufficiently, and crowned with complete success—to learn to combine this with (I am almost inclined to say) the ability to be an efficient and capable trader, which is fully sufficient to be a good co-operator. By ability to be a trader I mean the ability to be a cultured trader. Let those Russians, or plain peasants, who imagine that since they trade they are good traders, get that well into their heads. This does not follow at all. They do trade, but that is far from being cultured traders. They now trade in an Asiatic manner, but to be a trader one must trade in the European manner. They are a whole epoch behind in that.

In conclusion: a number of economic, financial and banking privileges must be granted to the co-operatives—this is the way our socialist state must promote the new principle on which the population must be organised. But this is only the general outline of the task; it does not define and depict in detail the entire content of the practical task, i.e., we must find what form of "bonus" to give for joining the co-operatives (and the terms on which we should give it), the form of bonus by which we shall assist the co-operatives sufficiently, the form of bonus that will produce the civilised co-operator. And given social ownership of the means of production, given the class victory of the proletariat over the bourgeoisie, the system of civilised co-operators is the system of socialism.

January 4, 1923

II

Whenever I wrote about the New Economic Policy I always quoted the article on state capitalism which I wrote in 1918.* This has more than once aroused doubts in the minds of certain young comrades. But their doubts were mainly on abstract political points.

It seemed to them that the term state capitalism could not be applied to a system under which the means of production were owned by the working class, a working class that held political power. They did not notice, however, that I used the term "state capitalism", *firstly*, to connect historically our present position with the position adopted in my controversy with the so-called Left Communists[123]; also, I argued at that time that state capitalism would be superior to our existing economy. It was important for me to show the continuity between ordinary state capitalism and the unusual, even very unusual, state capitalism to which I referred in introducing the reader to the New Economic Policy. *Secondly*, the practical purpose was always important to me. And the practical purpose of our New Economic Policy was to lease out concessions. In the prevailing circumstances, concessions in our country would unquestionably have been a pure type of state capitalism. That is how I argued about state capitalism.

But there is another aspect of the matter for which we may need state capitalism, or at least a comparison with it. That is the question of co-operatives.

In the capitalist state, co-operatives are no doubt collective capitalist institutions. Nor is there any doubt that under

---

* See V. I. Lenin, *Collected Works*, Vol. 27, pp. 323-54.—*Ed.*

our present economic conditions, when we combine private
capitalist enterprises—but in no other way than on nationalised
land and in no other way than under the control of the working-class state—with enterprises of a consistently socialist
type (the means of production, the land on which the enterprises are situated, and the enterprises as a whole belonging
to the state), the question arises about a third type of enterprise, the co-operatives, which were not formerly regarded as
an independent type differing in principle from the others.
Under private capitalism, co-operative enterprises differ from
capitalist enterprises as collective enterprises differ from
private enterprises. Under state capitalism, co-operative
enterprises differ from state-capitalist enterprises, firstly, because they are private enterprises, and, secondly, because
they are collective enterprises. Under our present system, co-operative enterprises differ from private capitalist
enterprises because they are collective enterprises but do not
differ from socialist enterprises if the land on which they are
situated and the means of production belong to the state, i.e.,
the working class.

This circumstance is not considered sufficiently when co-
operatives are discussed. It is forgotten that owing to the special features of our political system, our co-operatives acquire
an altogether exceptional significance. If we exclude concessions, which, incidentally, have not developed on any considerable scale, co-operation under our conditions nearly always
coincides fully with socialism.

Let me explain what I mean. Why were the plans of the
old co-operators, from Robert Owen onwards, fantastic? Because they dreamed of peacefully remodelling contemporary
society into socialism without taking account of such fundamental questions as the class struggle, the capture of political
power by the working class, the overthrow of the rule of the
exploiting class. That is why we are right in regarding as
entirely fantastic this "co-operative" socialism, and as romantic,
and even banal, the dream of transforming class enemies into
class collaborators and class war into class peace (so-called
civil peace) by merely organising the population in co-operative societies.

Undoubtedly we were right from the point of view of the
fundamental task of the present day, for socialism cannot be

established without a class struggle for political power in the state.

But see how things have changed now that political power is in the hands of the working class, now that the political power of the exploiters is overthrown and all the means of production (except those which the workers' state voluntarily abandons conditionally and for a certain time to the exploiters in the form of concessions) are owned by the working class.

Now we are entitled to say that for us the mere growth of co-operation (with the "slight" exception mentioned above) is identical with the growth of socialism, and at the same time we have to admit that there has been a radical modification in our whole outlook on socialism. The radical modification is this: formerly we placed, and had to place, the main emphasis on the political struggle, on revolution, on winning power, etc. Now the emphasis is changing, and shifting to peaceful, organisational, "cultural" work. I should say that emphasis was shifting to educational work, were it not for our international relations, were it not for the fact that we have to fight for our position on a world scale. If we leave that aside, however, and confine ourselves to internal economic relations, the emphasis in our work is certainly shifting to education.

Two main tasks confront us, which constitute the epoch—to reorganise our machinery of state, which is utterly useless, and which we took over in its entirety from the preceding epoch; during the past five years of struggle we did not, and could not, drastically reorganise it. Our second task is educational work among the peasants. And the economic object of this educational work among the peasants is to organise the latter in co-operative societies. If the whole of the peasantry had been organised in co-operatives, we would by now have been standing with both feet on the soil of socialism. But the organisation of the entire peasantry in co-operative societies presupposes a standard of culture among the peasants (precisely among the peasants as the overwhelming mass) that cannot, in fact, be achieved without a cultural revolution.

Our opponents told us repeatedly that we were rash in undertaking to implant socialism in an insufficiently cultured country. But they were misled by our having started from the end opposite to that prescribed by theory (the theory of pedants of all kinds), because in our country the political and social revolution preceded the cultural revolution, that very cultural revolution which nevertheless now confronts us.

This cultural revolution would now suffice to make our country a completely socialist country; but it presents immense difficulties of a purely cultural (for we are illiterate) and material character (for to be cultured we must achieve a certain development of the material means of production, must have a certain material base).

January 6, 1923

First published in *Pravda*   *Collected Works*, Vol. 33
Nos. 115 and 116,
May 26 and 27, 1923
Signed: *N. Lenin*

OUR REVOLUTION

APROPOS OF N. SUKHANOV'S NOTES[124]

I

I have lately been glancing through Sukhanov's notes on the revolution. What strikes one most is the pedantry of all our petty-bourgeois democrats, and of all the heroes of the Second International. Apart from the fact that they are all extremely faint-hearted, that when it comes to the minutest deviation from the German model even the best of them fortify themselves with reservations—apart from this characteristic which is common to all petty-bourgeois democrats and has been abundantly manifested by them throughout the revolution, what strikes one is their slavish imitation of the past.

They all call themselves Marxists, but their conception of Marxism is impossibly pedantic. They have completely failed to understand what is decisive in Marxism, namely, its revolutionary dialectics. They have even absolutely failed to understand Marx's plain statements that in times of revolution the utmost flexibility[125] is demanded, and have even failed to notice, for instance, the statement Marx made in his letters—I think it was in 1856—expressing the hope of combining a peasant war in Germany, which might create a revolutionary situation, with the working-class movement[126]—they avoid even this plain statement and walk round and about it like a cat around a bowl of hot porridge.

Their conduct betrays them as cowardly reformists who are afraid to deviate from the bourgeoisie, let alone break with them, and at the same time they disguise their cowardice with the wildest rhetoric and braggartry. But what strikes one in all of them even from the purely theoretical point of view is their utter inability to grasp the following Marxist considerations. Up to now they have seen capitalism and bourgeois democracy in Western Europe follow a definite path of development, and cannot conceive that this path can be taken as a model only *mutatis mutandis*, only with certain amendments (quite insignificant from the standpoint of the general development of world history).

First—the revolution connected with the first imperialist world war. Such a revolution was bound to reveal new features, or variations, resulting from the war itself, for the world has never seen such a war in such a situation. We find that since the war the bourgeoisie of the wealthiest countries have to this day been unable to restore "normal" bourgeois relations. Yet our reformists—petty bourgeois who make a show of being revolutionaries—believed, and still believe, that normal bourgeois relations are the limit (thus far shalt thou go and no farther). And even their conception of "normal" is extremely stereotyped and narrow.

Secondly, they are complete strangers to the idea that, while the development of world history as a whole follows general laws, it is by no means precluded, but, on the contrary, presumed, that certain periods of development may display peculiarities in either the form or the sequence of this development. For instance, it does not even occur to them that because Russia stands on the border-line between the civilised countries and the countries which this war has for the first time definitely brought into the orbit of civilisation, that is, all the Oriental, non-European countries, she could, and was, indeed, bound to reveal certain distinctive features; although these, of course, are in keeping with the general line of world development, they distinguish her revolution from those which took place in the West-European countries and introduce certain partial innovations as the revolution moves on to the countries of the East.

Infinitely stereotyped, for instance, is the argument they learned by rote during the development of West-European Social-Democracy, namely, that we are not yet ripe for socialism, that, as certain "learned" gentlemen among them put it, the objective economic premises for socialism do not exist in our country. It does not occur to any of them to ask themselves, but what about a people that found itself in a revolutionary situation such as that created during the first imperialist war? Might it not, influenced by the hopelessness of its situation, fling itself into a struggle that would offer it at least some chance of securing conditions for the further development of civilisation that were somewhat unusual?

"The development of the productive forces of Russia has not attained the level that makes socialism possible." All the heroes of the Second International, including, of course, Sukhanov, beat the drums about this proposition. They keep harping on this incontrovertible proposition in a thousand different keys, and think that it is the decisive criterion of our revolution.

But what if, first, at the time of the imperialist world war that involved every more or less influential West-European country, peculiar circumstances put Russia and Russia's development on the eve of the revolutions maturing or partly already begun in the East in a situation which enabled us to achieve precisely that combination of a "peasant war" with the working-class movement suggested in 1856 by no less a "Marxist" than Marx himself as a possible prospect for Prussia?

What if the complete hopelessness of the situation, by stimulating the efforts of the workers and peasants tenfold, offered us the opportunity to create the fundamental prerequisites of civilisation in a different way from that of the West-European countries? Has that altered the general line of development of world history? Has that altered the basic relations between the basic classes of all the countries that are being, or have been, drawn into the general course of world history?

If a definite level of culture is required for the building of socialism (although nobody can say just what that definite "level of culture" is, for it differs in every European country), why cannot we begin by first achieving the prerequisites for that definite level of culture in a revolutionary way, and *then*, with the aid of the workers' and peasants' government and the Soviet system, proceed to overtake the other nations?

January 16, 1923

II

You say that civilisation is necessary for the building of socialism. Very good. But why could we not first create such prerequisites of civilisation in our country as the expulsion of the landowners and the Russian capitalists, and then start moving towards socialism? Where, in what books, have you read that such variations of the customary historical order of events are impermissible or impossible?

Napoleon, I think, wrote: *"On s'engage et puis ... on voit."* Rendered freely this means: "First engage in a serious battle and then see what happens." Well, we did first engage in a serious battle in October 1917, and then saw such details of development (from the standpoint of world history they were certainly details) as the Brest Peace,[127] the New Economic Policy,[128] and so forth. And now there can be no doubt that in the main we have been victorious.

Our Sukhanovs, not to speak of Social-Democrats still farther to the right, never even dream that revolutions could be made otherwise. Our European philistines never even dream that the subsequent revolutions in Oriental countries, which possess much vaster populations and a much vaster diversity of social conditions, will undoubtedly display even greater peculiarities than the Russian revolution.

It need hardly be said that a textbook written on Kautskian lines was a very useful thing in its day. But it is time, for all that, to abandon the idea that it foresaw all the forms of development of subsequent world history. It would be timely to say that those who think so are simply fools.

January 17, 1923

Published in *Pravda* No. 117,   *Collected Works*, Vol. 33
May 30, 1923

Signed: *Lenin*

NOTES

1 *Contrat social*—one of the chief works of Jean Jacques Rousseau. Its full title is *Du Contrat social; ou, Principes du droit politique (The Social Contract, or the Principles of Political Law)*. Its main idea is that every social system should be the result of a free agreement, or contract between men. While being fundamentally idealistic, the "social contract" theory had a revolutionary role to play in the eighteenth century, on the eve of the French bourgeois revolution, for it expressed the bourgeois demand for equality, the abolition of feudal privileges and the establishment of a bourgeois republic. p. 7

2 The reference is to Plekhanov's article "Bernstein and Materialism", which was published in *Die Neue Zeit* No. 44 (1897-98).

Die Neue Zeit—theoretical journal of the German Social-Democratic Party, published in Stuttgart from 1883 to 1923. It was edited by Karl Kautsky until October 1917 and after that by Heinrich Cunow. p. 12

3 The *Hannover Congress* of the German Social-Democratic Party was held October 9-14, 1899. August Bebel gave a report on the main item of the agenda, "The Attack on the Fundamental Views and Tactics of the Party". Lenin wrote that his speech would long remain "an example of how to uphold Marxist views and struggle for a genuinely socialist working-class party". The Congress voted down Bernstein's revisionist views, but failed to subject them to extensive criticism. p. 12

4 The reference is to *Rabochaya Gazeta* (Workers' Gazette) which was adopted as the Party's official organ at the First Congress of the R.S.D.L.P., held illegally in Minsk from March 1 to 3 (13-15), 1898. Its third issue, prepared for the press, did not appear after the Congress, because the members of the Central Committee and the editors were arrested and the print-shop destroyed by the police. An attempt to renew publication was made in 1899, the editorial group inviting Lenin to edit the paper and later to contribute. Lenin sent the editorial group his article "Our Programme" together with other articles and a letter but efforts to resume publication failed and the articles were never printed. p. 13

[5] *Rabochaya Mysl* (Workers' Thought)–the newspaper of the Economists, published from October 1897 to December 1902. Of its 16 issues Nos. 1 and 2 were published in St. Petersburg, 3 to 11 in Berlin, 12 to 15 in Warsaw; No. 16 was also issued abroad.   p. 13

[6] The reference is to the strikes in St. Petersburg, chiefly of textile workers, in 1895 and 1896. These strikes stimulated the growth of the working-class movement in Moscow and other Russian cities; they forced an early government revision of the factory laws and the adoption of the June 2 (14), 1897 law, reducing the working day at industrial enterprises to eleven and a half hours.   p. 14

[7] *Narodism*–a petty-bourgeois trend in the Russian revolutionary movement which arose in the late 1860s. The Narodniks asserted that capitalism in Russia was a freak, which was why no Russian proletariat could be expected to grow. They considered the peasantry to be the main revolutionary force and regarded the village commune as the embryo of socialism. Their socialism was not scientific because it was not based on the objective laws of social development. The Narodniks proceeded from an erroneous view of the role of the class struggle in history, maintaining that history was made by heroes, outstanding personalities, who led the "crowd", the passive masses. The Narodniks used terrorist tactics against the tsarist autocracy. In the 1880s and 1890s, they made their peace with tsarism, promoted the interests of the kulaks (the rich peasants who exploited the poor) and fought Marxism tooth and claw.   p. 16

[8] *Osvobozhdeniye* (Emancipation)–a fortnightly published abroad from June 18 (July 1), 1902 to October 5 (18), 1905, under the editorship of P. B. Struve. A vehicle of Russian liberal bourgeoisie, it expressed the ideas of moderate monarchist liberalism. In 1903, it served as a rallying point for the Osvobozhdeniye League, which took shape in January 1904, and kept going until October 1905.   p. 16

[9] *Revolutsionnaya Rossiya* (Revolutionary Russia)–illegal Socialist-Revolutionary newspaper, published by the League of Socialist-Revolutionaries in Russia from the end of 1900. From January 1902 to December 1905, it was published abroad (in Geneva) as the official organ of the Socialist-Revolutionary Party.   p. 16

[10] *Socialist-Revolutionaries* (S.R.s)–a petty-bourgeois party formed at the end of 1901 and the beginning of 1902 as a result of the amalgamation of various Narodnik groups and circles. The Socialist-Revolutionaries called themselves socialists, but theirs was a petty-bourgeois equalitarian socialism which was not scientific. The main plank of their programme was a demand for equalitarian individual land tenure on the basis of a labour standard, which would have actually created the most favourable conditions for the development of capitalism.

The S.R.s did not see the proletariat and the peasantry as

different classes and covered up the class distinctions and antagon·
isms within the peasantry (between the kulaks and the toiling
farmers); they denied the proletariat's leading role in the revolution. Terrorist acts were their basic tactics in fighting the autocracy.

After the bourgeois-democratic revolution in February 1917, the
S.R.s, together with the Mensheviks, constituted the mainstay of the
counter-revolutionary Provisional Government, while their leaders
were in it. The S.R.s refused to support the peasants' demand for
the abolition of landed estates, and their ministers in the Provisional
Government sent punitive expeditions against peasants who seized
landed estates.

After the October Socialist Revolution, the S.R.s fought on the
side of the bourgeoisie, the landowners and foreign interventionists against the Soviet power.

At the end of November 1917 the Left wing of the S.R.s founded
an independent party. To retain their influence among the peasant
masses, they recognised the Soviet power formally and entered into
an agreement with the Bolsheviks, but soon turned against the
Soviet power.   p. 16

[11] The *Second Congress of the R.S.D.L.P.* was held from July 17 (30) to
August 10 (23), 1903. It held its first thirteen sittings in Brussels,
but owing to police harassment it had to move to London.

Preparations for the Congress were made by *Iskra,* the first
illegal All-Russia Marxist newspaper founded by Lenin in 1900.
Under Lenin's guidance, it carried out the tremendous work
involved in uniting the Russian Social-Democrats under the banner
of revolutionary Marxism.

The most important items on the agenda were the Party Programme and Party Rules, and election of the leading Party bodies.
Lenin and his followers carried on a determined struggle against
the opportunists.

The Bolshevik-Menshevik split occurred at this congress. The
firm supporters of Lenin and *Iskra* won a majority and were elected
to the Party bodies—hence their name, Bolsheviks (Russ. *bolshe*
—more); Martov's supporters, the opportunists, were left in the
minority, and were called Mensheviks (Russ. *menshe*—less).

The Congress was of great importance for the development of
the working-class movement in Russia. It took the Social-Democratic
movement out of its early amateurish circle stage and laid the
cornerstone of a revolutionary Marxist party in Russia, the Bolshevik Party. Lenin wrote, "As a trend of political thought and
as a political party, Bolshevism has existed since 1903" (see
V. I. Lenin, *Selected Works* in 3 volumes, Vol. 3, Moscow, p. 378).

The Congress marked a turning point in the international working-class movement for it created a new type of proletarian party
which became the model for revolutionary Marxists throughout
the world.   p. 16

[12] See Marx and Engels, *Selected Works,* Vol. I, Moscow, 1962,
pp. 54-64.   p. 17

[13] The reference is to the Peasant Reform of 1861, which abolished serfdom in Russia.   p. 21

[14] The reference is to the first Russian bourgeois-democratic revolution of 1905-07.   p. 23

[15] "Two nations" is the subtitle of the novel *Sybil* by Benjamin Disraeli.   p. 23

[16] *Polish Socialist Party (Polska Partia Socjalistyczna)*—a reformist nationalist party founded in 1892. Its programme was based on the struggle for Poland's national liberation; it carried on separatist nationalist propaganda among the Polish workers and tried to distract them from the common struggle with the Russian workers against the autocracy and capitalism.

Leftist groups were formed within the party throughout its history on the initiative of its rank-and-file worker-members, and some of them subsequently joined the revolutionary wing of the Polish working-class movement.

In 1906, the P.S.P. split into the *Lewica* (Left-wing) P.S.P. and the Right-wing, chauvinist P.S.P. known as the "Revolutionary Faction".

Under the influence of the Bolshevik Party, and of the Social-Democracy of the Kingdom of Poland and Lithuania the *Lewica* P.S.P. gradually adopted a consistently revolutionary stand.   p. 26

[17] *Przedświt* (Dawn)—political journal, founded in 1881 by a group of Polish socialists; in 1884 it became the organ of the first Polish workers' party, the Proletariat Party; in 1892, it was controlled by Right-wing socialist and nationalist elements; between 1893 and 1899, it was the organ of the Union of Polish Socialists Abroad (the foreign organisation of the P.S.P.); and from 1900 to 1905, the theoretical and propagandist organ of the P.S.P. The Draft Agrarian Programme of the Polish Socialist Party was published in its issue Nos. 6-8, 1905.   p. 26

[18] *Szarwark*—statute labour and carriage service in the repair and construction of roads, bridges and other military and public structures, imposed on the peasants in Poland.   p. 27

[19] *Moskovskiye Vedomosti* (Moscow Recorder)—a newspaper, originally issued (from 1756) as a small sheet by Moscow University. In 1863, it became a monarchist nationalist organ, reflecting the views of the most reactionary sections of the landowners and the clergy. The newspaper continued to appear until the October Revolution in 1917.   p. 27

[20] The reference is to the congress of Zemstvo functionaries held in September 1905.

Zemstvo—the name given to local government bodies formed in the central provinces of Russia in 1864. They were dominated by the nobility and their powers were limited to purely local economic problems (hospital and road building, statistics, insurance). Their activities were controlled by the Provincial Governors and the

Ministry of the Interior, which could rescind any decisions of which the government disapproved.

The Zemstvo movement, a liberal-bourgeois oppositional movement, started in Russia at the beginning of the 1860s. From the outset it proved incapable of waging an active struggle against the autocracy. It strove to get some constitutional concessions through a deal with the tsarist autocracy behind the people's backs. p. 30

21 "Cut-off" lands—lands cut off from peasant holdings by the landowners when serfdom was abolished in Russia in 1861.   p. 30

22 *Proudhonism*—the teaching of Pierre Joseph Proudhon, French pettybourgeois socialist and anarchist.

Proudhon criticised big capitalist property and hoped to perpetuate small property; he proposed the foundation of a people's and an "exchange" banks to help the workers acquire means of production, become handicraftsmen and have "fair" marketing outlets for their wares. Proudhon believed capitalism could be healed and improved by reforms.

Marx took Proudhonism to pieces in his book, *Poverty of Philosophy*, where he exposed the reactionary nature of the idea of "improving" capitalism; Marx showed that Proudhon's chief mistake was his failure to understand that poverty, inequality, exploitation, crises and unemployment all sprang from the capitalist mode of production, and could be abolished only with capitalist relations, through the socialisation of the means of production and the establishment of socialism.   p. 32

23 *Blanquism*—a trend in the French socialist movement named after the prominent French revolutionary and outstanding utopian communist—Louis August Blanqui (1805-1881).

The Blanquists expected mankind to be "emancipated from wage slavery, not by the proletarian class struggle, but through a conspiracy hatched by a small minority of intellectuals" (V. I. Lenin, *Collected Works*, Vol. 10, p. 392). They did not take account of the concrete situation requisite for the victory of an uprising and neglected to establish contact with the masses, substituting the actions of a secret group of conspirators for the activity of a revolutionary party.   p. 32

24 A reference is to the peasant movement in Poltava and Kharkov Gubernias at the end of March and the beginning of April 1902. It was the first mass revolutionary movement of the peasantry in Russia in the early twentieth century. It was sparked off by the peasants' desperate economic condition in these gubernias, which worsened in the spring of 1902 after the 1901 crop failure. The peasants demanded a re-allotment of land and seized food and forage supplies in the landed estates. The peasant movement was brutally suppressed, and the peasants were forced to make good the damage caused.   p. 33

25 *Bernsteinism*—an anti-Marxist opportunist trend in the international Social-Democratic movement which arose in Germany at the end

of the nineteenth century. It got its name from the German Social-Democrat Eduard Bernstein, the ideologist of blatant revisionism. He and his followers denied "the possibility of putting socialism on a scientific basis and of demonstrating its necessity and inevitability from the point of view of the materialist conception of history. Denied was the fact of growing impoverishment, the process of proletarisation, and the intensification of capitalist contradictions; the very concept, *ultimate aim*, was declared to be unsound and the idea of the dictatorship of the proletariat was completely rejected. Denied was the antithesis in principle between liberalism and socialism. Denied was *the theory of the class struggle....*" (V. I. Lenin, *Collected Works*, Vol. 5, p. 353.)

Bernstein's revisionism of Marxism was aimed at converting the Social-Democratic parties of social revolution into parties of social reform. In Russia, it was supported by the "legal Marxists" and the Economists.

The Russian revolutionary Marxists, the Bolsheviks, who were led by Lenin, fought Bernsteinism on every point. Lenin hit out at Bernstein in his pamphlet *A Protest by Russian Social-Democrats*; he gave an extensive critique of Bernsteinism in his book *What Is To Be Done?* and the articles "Marxism and Revisionism", and "Differences in the European Labour Movement" (see V. I. Lenin, *Collected Works*, Vol. 4, pp. 167-82; Vol. 5, pp. 347-529; Vol. 15, pp. 29-39; Vol. 16, pp. 347-52).   p. 33

[26] *Labour service*—a system surviving from feudal days under which peasants with their draught animals and implements were hired by landowners and kulaks, on hard terms.   p. 38

[27] *Corvée system*—a form of labour service, unpaid compulsory work performed by serfs for their masters.   p. 38

[28] See Karl Marx, *Capital*, Vol. III, Moscow, 1959, pp. 763-93.

p. 38

[29] V. A. Karpinsky's article "The Peasant Congress", over the signature of V. Kalinin, was published in *Proletary* No. 25 on November 3 (16), 1905. Lenin made the insert when editing the article.

Proletary—an illegal Bolshevik weekly, the Central Organ of the R.S.D.L.P., founded by a decision of the Third Party Congress and published in Geneva from May 14 (27) to November 12 (25), 1905.
p. 41

[30] *General Redistribution (Chorny Peredel)* was a popular slogan among the peasants of tsarist Russia which expressed their desire for the abolition of landed estates and a general redistribution of land.

In his *The Agrarian Programme of Russian Social-Democracy* Lenin pointed out that the demand for "a general redistribution" contained the reactionary utopian idea of perpetuating small-scale peasant production, but it also had its revolutionary side, namely, "the desire to sweep away by means of a peasant revolt all the remnants of the serf-owning system" (V. I. Lenin, *Collected Works*, Vol. 6, p. 139).   p. 41

[31] *All-Russia Peasant Union*–a revolutionary-democratic organisation founded in 1905. The Union demanded political liberty, immediate convocation of a constituent assembly, abolition of the landed estates, and confiscation and transfer of monastery, crown and state lands to the peasants, but it pursued a vacillating middle-of-the-road policy. Under police persecution it broke up at the beginning of 1907.   p. 42

[32] The *Emancipation of Labour Group*–the first Russian Marxist group formed by G. V. Plekhanov in Switzerland in 1883. The other members of the group were P. B. Axelrod, L. G. Deutsch, V. I. Zasulich and V. N. Ignatov.

The group spread Marxism in Russia. At the Second Congress of the R.S.D.L.P., the group announced its dissolution.   p. 42

[33] *The Third Congress of the R.S.D.L.P.* was held in London between April 12 and 27 (April 25 and May 10), 1905. It was organised and held by the Bolsheviks under the direction of Lenin.

It discussed the basic issues of the revolution that had started in Russia and outlined the tasks of the proletariat and its party.

Lenin wrote the draft resolutions on all the fundamental items before it.

The Congress condemned the activity of the Mensheviks, their opportunism on the questions of organisation and tactics. The Congress instructed the C.C. to found the new Party Central Organ, the newspaper *Proletary*. The plenary meeting of the Central Committee held April 27 (May 10), 1905, appointed V. I. Lenin its editor.

The Third Congress was of great historical importance. It was the first Congress of the Bolsheviks. For details see Lenin's article "The Third Congress" (V. I. Lenin, *Collected Works*, Vol. 8, pp. 442-49) and his book *Two Tactics of Social-Democracy in the Democratic Revolution* (*ibid.*, Vol. 9, pp. 15-140).   p. 43

[34] *Fabian Society*–a British reformist organisation, founded by a group of bourgeois intellectuals in 1884. It took its name from the Roman general, Fabius Maximus Cunctator (the Delayer), famed for his procrastinating tactics and his avoidance of a decisive battle against Hannibal.

The Fabians denied the necessity of the class struggle of the proletariat and of the socialist revolution and asserted that the transition from capitalism to socialism could be effected by way of small reforms and the gradual transformation of society. In 1900, the Fabian Society joined the Labour Party.   p. 46

[35] See Engels's letter to F. A. Sorge of January 18, 1893 (Marx and Engels, *Selected Correspondence*, Moscow, 1955, p. 537).   p. 46

[36] *Manilov*–a character from Nikolai Gogol's novel, *Dead Souls*, a complacent sentimental landowner, idle dreamer and chatterbox.
                                                                       p. 52

[37] *Men of December 14 (The Decembrists)*—revolutionaries who came
from the ranks of the Russian nobility; they opposed serfdom and
the autocracy, and staged the uprising of December 14, 1825.

p. 52

[38] Quoted from Alexander Herzen's *Ends and Beginnings*.   p. 52

[39] Lenin quotes from Herzen's *Letters to an Old Comrade* (letters four
and two).   p. 54

[40] *Trudoviks (Trudovik Group)*—a group of petty-bourgeois democrats,
consisting of peasant deputies to the First Duma. The group was
formed in April 1906.

Their programme was a reflection of the democratic aspirations
of the peasantry. They demanded the transfer to the peasants of
all monastery, crown and state land and of all landed estates,
the abolition of all social and national inequalities and universal
suffrage in the elections to the Duma.

Their agrarian programme was based on the Narodnik principle
of equalised land tenure; only those who tilled the land themselves
were to have the right to use it.

Because the peasants, as a class, were petty proprietors, the
Trudoviks vacillated in the Duma between the Cadets and the
Social-Democrats.

After the bourgeois-democratic revolution in February 1917, the
Trudoviks supported the bourgeois Provisional Government and
defended the interests of the kulaks, who exploited the poor peasants. After the October Socialist Revolution they sided with the
counter-revolutionary bourgeoisie.   p. 55

[41] See Note 31.   p. 55

[42] *Kolokol* (The Bell)—a political journal published under the motto
of *Vivos voco!* (I call on the living!) by A. I. Herzen and N. P. Ogaryov, in London from July 1, 1857 to April 1865, and in Geneva
from May 1865 to July 1867. The journal was printed by the Free
Russian Press founded by Herzen. It appeared monthly, and for a
short time, fortnightly. There were a total of 245 issues. In 1868,
15 issues of the journal were published in French with Russian
supplements for some of them. *Kolokol* had a printing of 2,500
copies and was circulated throughout Russia. It exposed the tyranny
of the autocracy, the corruption in the civil service and the landowners' ruthless exploitation of the peasants. Its revolutionary
appeals played an important part in awakening the popular masses
to the struggle against the autocracy and the ruling classes.   p. 55

[43] *Polyarnaya Zvezda* (The Pole Star)—a collection of literary and
political articles printed between 1855 and 1862 by the Free Russian Press in London. Its first three issues were published by Herzen, and the rest by Herzen and Ogaryov. The last issue, the eighth,
appeared in Geneva in 1868.

The title itself and the picture of the five executed Decembrists
on the cover served to underline the idea of continuity with the
revolutionary cause of the Decembrists. Herzen described *Polyar-*

naya Zvezda as a "Russian periodical, free from censorship and devoted exclusively to the question of Russian emancipation and dissemination of free ideas in Russia".   p. 55

44 *Narodnaya Volya* (The People's Will)—a secret political organisation of Russian revolutionary intellectuals; it came into being in August 1879, following the split in the Narodnik organisation *Zemlya i Volya* (Land and Freedom). Its members the Narodovoltsi, while still subscribing to the ideas of Narodnik utopian socialism, adopted a policy of political struggle. Their main aim was to overthrow the tsarist autocracy and win political freedom. Their programme provided for the establishment of a "permanent popular representative body" elected on the basis of universal suffrage, proclamation of democratic liberties, transfer of land to the people, and elaboration of measures for transferring the factories into the hands of the workers.

Narodnaya Volya conducted a heroic struggle against the autocracy but it worked on the wrong theory of "active" heroes and the "passive" crowd; they expected to transform society without the participation of the people, using only their own forces, by means of terroristic acts and by intimidating and disorganising the government.

After March 1, 1881 (the assassination of Alexander II) the government crushed the organisation by savage persecution, acts of provocation and executions.

Lenin criticised Narodnaya Volya's mistaken utopian programme and terrorist tactics but had respect for the dedicated struggle of its members against tsarism. He had a high opinion of their underground organisation and strict centralisation.   p. 58

45 A revolution broke out in China in the spring of 1911. It overthrew the Manchu dynasty and proclaimed China a republic. Dr. Sun Yat-sen, who led the revolutionary movement, was elected provisional President. However, under counter-revolutionary pressure he was compelled to withdraw in favour of the adventurist Yüan Shih-kai, who established a military dictatorship.   p. 59

46 *The Duma*—a representative body which the tsarist government was compelled to convene as a result of the 1905-07 revolution. Nominally the Duma was a legislative body, but it had no actual power. Elections to the Duma were non-direct, unequal and non-universal. In the case of the working classes and the non-Russian nationalities inhabiting Russia, the suffrage was greatly curtailed, a considerable section of the workers and peasants having no voting rights whatsoever.

The First Duma (April-July 1906) and the Second Duma (February-June 1907) were dissolved by the tsarist government. The Third (1907-12) and the Fourth Duma (1912-17) were dominated by the reactionary monarchist bloc of landowners and big capitalists. (For Trudoviks see Note 40.)   p. 60

47 The reference is to the leaders of the Great French Revolution of 1789-94.   p. 61

[48] See Marx, *The Poverty of Philosophy. Answer to the "Philosophy of Poverty" by M. Proudhon*, Moscow; Karl Marx, *Capital*, Vol. III, Moscow, 1959, pp. 634-57; Karl Marx, *Theorien über den Mehrwert*, Teil 2, Dietz Verlag Berlin, 1959, S. 139-51.   p. 64

[49] The expression is taken from Marx's letter to L. Kugelmann on the Paris Commune dated April 12, 1871 (Marx and Engels, *Selected Works*, Vol. II, Moscow, 1962, p. 463).   p. 67

[50] See Engels's preface to the first German edition of Marx's *The Poverty of Philosophy*, Moscow, pp. 12-13.   p. 68

[51] *Russkoye Bogatstvo* (Russian Wealth)—a monthly magazine published in St. Petersburg from 1876 to 1918. In the early 1890s it became an organ of the Liberal Narodniks with N. K. Mikhailovsky at the head. It called for collaboration with the tsarist government and bitterly fought Marxism and the Russian Marxists. In 1906, it became the organ of the semi-Cadet Popular Socialist Party.   p. 73

[52] *Stoikaya Mysl* (Staunch Thought)—one of the names of the Left-Narodnik (Socialist-Revolutionary) legal newspaper *Zhivaya Mysl* (Living Thought) published in St. Petersburg from August 1913 to July 1914.   p. 73

[53] *Put Pravdy* (The Path of Truth)—one of the names of the Bolshevik legal daily *Pravda* (Truth) founded by Lenin in May 1912.

Pravda was subjected to constant police harassment. It was banned eight times, but always reappeared under other names, until it was closed down on July 8 (21), 1914.

It resumed publication after the bourgeois-democratic revolution in February 1917. From March 5 (18) it was the organ of the Central and Petrograd Committees of the R.S.D.L.P.

Pravda was the first legal mass working-class newspaper, and marked a new stage in the development of the working-class press in Russia and the world.

It played a great part in enlightening the working people of Russia and preparing them for the Great October Socialist Revolution and the construction of socialism.

It first appeared on May 5, and since 1914 the date has been observed as the Day of the Working-Class Press.   p. 74

[54] See Marx, *Capital*, Vol. I, Moscow, 1959, pp. 484, 489-90.
                                                                         p. 77

[55] See Marx and Engels, *Selected Work*, Vol. I, Moscow, 1962, p. 51.
                                                                         p. 78

[56] See Marx and Engels, *Selected Works*, Vol. II, Moscow, 1962, p. 320.
                                                                         p. 78

[57] See Engels, *Anti-Dühring*, Moscow, 1954, p. 389.   p. 79

[58] See Marx and Engels, *Selected Works*, Vol. II, Moscow, 1962, p. 322.
                                                                         p. 79

[59] See Marx and Engels, *Selected Works*, Vol. II, Moscow, 1962, p. 433.
                                                                  p. 79

[60] See Marx's letter to Engels of April 9, 1863. (Marx and Engels, *Selected Correspondence*, Moscow, 1955, p. 172.)   p. 80

[61] See Marx, *The Poverty of Philosophy*, Moscow, pp. 194-95.   p. 81

[62] See Engels's letter to Marx of February 5, 1851.   p. 81

[63] See Engels's letter to Marx of December 18, 1857 and October 7, 1858. (Marx and Engels, *Selected Correspondence*, Moscow, 1955, pp. 132-33.)   p. 81

[64] *Chartism*—the first mass working-class movement which developed in Britain in the 1830s and 1840s. Its members published the People's Charter which demanded universal suffrage, abolition of land and property qualifications in elections to Parliament, etc. Millions of workers and handicraftsmen took part in meetings and demonstrations across the country over a period of many years.

In April 1848, they sent a petition to Parliament which was signed by over five million people.

But the British Parliament was packed with aristocrats and big capitalists and they refused to grant the People's Charter and rejected all petitions. The government carried out brutal reprisals against the Chartists—their leaders were arrested and the movement was crushed. However, Chartism had a great influence on the development of the international working-class movement.   p. 81

[05] See Engels's letter to Marx of April 8, 1863 and Marx's letters to Engels of April 9, 1863 (Marx and Engels, *Selected Correspondence*, Moscow, 1955, p. 172) and April 2, 1866.   p. 81

[66] See Engels's letters to Marx of November 19, 1869 and August 11, 1881.   p. 81

[67] See Marx and Engels, *Selected Works*, Vol. I, Moscow, 1962, p. 64.
                                                                  p. 82

[68] The reference is to the uprising for national liberation and democratic changes in the Cracow Republic, which from 1815 was under the joint control of Prussia, Austria and Russia. The rebels set up a National Government which issued a manifesto abolishing all feudal duties and promising to transfer the land to the peasants without compensation. Its other appeals proclaimed the establishment of national industrial shops, higher wages for their workers, and equal rights for all citizens. But the uprising was soon crushed.

"The Cracow revolution," Said Marx, "set a brilliant example to the whole of Europe in combining the national cause with the cause of democracy and the emancipation of the oppressed class." (Marx/Engels, *Gesamtausgabe*, Erste Abteilung, Bd. 6, S. 411.)
                                                                  p. 82

[69] See Marx and Engels, *Selected Works*, Vol. I, Moscow, 1962, p. 69.
                                                                  p. 82

70 See Marx's letter to Engels of April 16, 1856. (Marx and Engels, *Selected Works*, Vol. II, Moscow, 1962, p. 454.)   p. 82

71 See Engels's letters to Marx of January 27, 1865 and February 5, 1865.   p. 83

72 See Engels's letters to Marx of June 11, 1863 (*Selected Correspondence*, Moscow, 1955, p. 173), November 24, 1863, September 4, 1864, January 27, 1865, October 22, 1867 and December 6, 1867 and Marx's letters to Engels of June 12, 1863, December 10, 1864, February 3, 1865 (*Selected Correspondence*, Moscow, 1955, pp. 193-96) and December 14, 1867.   p. 83

73 See Marx and Engels, *Selected Works*, Vol. II, Moscow, 1962, p. 463.
                                                                                                     p. 83

74 The *Anti-Socialist Law* was promulgated in Germany in 1878 by Bismarck to fight the working-class and the socialist movement. Under it all organisations of the Social-Democratic Party, all workers' mass organisations and the working-class press were prohibited, socialist literature was confiscated, the Social-Democrats were subjected to persecution and some of them deported. Under the pressure of the mass working-class movement the law was annulled in 1890.
                                                                                                     p. 84

75 See Marx's letters to Engels of July 23, 1877, August 1, 1877 and September 10, 1879 and Engels's letters to Marx of August 20, 1879 and September 9, 1879.   p. 84

76 It was in this article that Lenin first spoke of the various forms of proletarian dictatorship.
    He subsequently stressed again and again that this variety was the result of different ways by which the proletariat assumes power and of the specific socio-economic and political conditions in different countries.   p. 85

77 *Suzdal daubing*–crude, primitive work. The expression originally referred to the cheap, gaudy icons made in Suzdal Uyezd before the revolution.   p. 85

78 See Marx and Engels, *Selected Works*, Vol. II, Moscow, 1962, pp. 15-17.   p. 91

79 See Marx and Engels, *Selected Works*, Vol. II, Moscow, 1962, pp. 38-44.   p. 91

80 The reference is to the Paris Commune, the 72-day revolutionary government set up as a result of the workers' uprising in Paris on March 18, 1871. It lasted from March 18 to May 28, 1871, and was the first attempt in history to establish a proletarian dictatorship.
                                                                                                     p. 91

81 See Marx and Engels, *Selected Works*, Vol. II, Moscow, 1962, p. 32.
                                                                                                     p. 93

[82] See Marx and Engels, *Selected Works*, Vol. II, Moscow, 1962, pp. 32-33.   p. 94

[83] See Marx and Engels, *Selected Works*, Vol. I, Moscow, 1962, p. 53.
                                                    p. 94

[84] See Marx and Engels, *Selected Works*, Vol. I, Moscow, 1962, p. 520.
                                                    p. 95

[85] See Engels's letter to August Bebel of March 18-28, 1875. (Marx and Engels, *Selected Works*, Vol. II, Moscow, 1962, p. 42.)   p. 96

[86] See Marx and Engels, *Selected Works*, Vol. II, Moscow, 1962, p. 23.
                                                    p. 99

[87] See Marx and Engels, *Selected Works*, Vol. II, Moscow, 1962, p. 24.
                                                    p. 100

[88] See Marx and Engels, *Selected Works*, Vol. II, Moscow, 1962, p. 24.
                                                    p. 101

[89] See Marx and Engels, *Selected Works*, Vol. II, Moscow, 1962, p. 24.
                                                    p. 102

[90] The reference is to N. G. Pomyalovsky's *Sketches of Seminary Life.* The seminarians were notorious for their extreme ignorance and barbarous customs.   p. 104

[91] The *Second All-Russia Congress of Soviets of Workers' and Soldiers' Deputies* was held in Petrograd on October 25-26 (November 7-8), 1917. It was also attended by delegates from a number of gubernia and uyezd Soviets of Peasants' Deputies. Of the 649 delegates present at the moment of its opening 390 were Bolsheviks, 160 Socialist-Revolutionaries, 72 Mensheviks and 14 internationalist Mensheviks. Delegates continued to arrive after the Congress opened.

It opened at the Smolny Institute at 10.40 p.m. while Red Guard detachments, sailors and revolutionary regiments of the Petrograd garrison were still attacking the Winter Palace, which was being defended by officer cadets and shock battalions. The Provisional Government was inside. Lenin directed the operations and was not present at the first sitting of the Congress.

At the second sitting on October 26 (November 8), Lenin gave his reports on peace and land. The Congress approved the Decree on Peace and the Decree on Land, which were drafted by Lenin, and formed the Soviet Workers' and Peasants' Government, the Council of People's Commissars with Lenin as Chairman. Only Bolsheviks were in it, because the Left-Revolutionaries had refused to participate. The Congress elected the 101-man All-Russia Central Executive Committee, of whom 62 were Bolsheviks, 29 were Left S.R.s, 6 internationalist Social-Democrats, 3 representatives from the Ukrainian Socialist Party and one representative of the Socialist-Revolutionary Maximalist League. The Congress also passed a decision to enlarge the All-Russia C.E.C. by the inclusion of members of the Peasants' Soviets, army organisations and the groups that had left the Congress.   p. 110

[92] See Note 110.   p. 113

[93] *Novaya Zhizn group*–a group of Social-Democrats known as Internationalists, whose members were Menshevik adherents of Martov
and non-aligned intellectuals of a semi-Menshevik trend. The
group took its name from its organ, the newspaper *Novaya Zhizn*
(New Life), published in St. Petersburg from April 1917.

In October 1917, the Novaya Zhizn group together with the Mensheviks came out against an armed uprising. After the October
Revolution, the group, with the exception of a few members who
joined the Bolsheviks, adopted a hostile stand towards the Soviet
government. The newspaper was closed down in July 1918 with
all the other counter-revolutionary papers.   p. 116

[94] The reference is to Gogol's characters.   p. 117

[95] See Marx and Engels, *Selected Works*, Vol. II, Moscow, 1962, p. 16.
                                                                     p. 122

[96] A quotation from Goethe's *Faust*, Part I, Scene 4–"Faust's Study".
                                                                     p. 122

[97] The reference is to the Peace Treaty signed by Soviet Russia and
Germany at Brest-Litovsk in March 1918. Its terms were extremely
harsh: Poland, Latvia and Estonia went to the Germans and the
Ukraine was made a separate state dependent on Germany. Russia
had to pay Germany a heavy indemnity.

Despite the onerous terms of the treaty, it had to be signed,
because the old tsarist army had disintegrated and the Red Army
was embryonic. The Brest-Litovsk Peace gave the Soviet Republic
a breathing space, enabled it to withdraw from the war and to
muster the forces for the struggle against the internal counter-
revolution and foreign armed intervention. The Brest-Litovsk Treaty
was annulled after the November 1918 revolution in Germany.
                                                                     p. 125

[98] After the October Revolution, almost all piece rates were replaced
by time rates, which had a bad effect on productivity and labour
discipline. Accordingly, the Soviet Labour Code published in December 1918 established a system of piece rates.   p. 127

[99] Quoted from Engels's *Anti-Dühring*, Moscow, p. 393.
                                                                     p. 129

[100] *The Man in a Muffler*–a character in Chekhov's story personifying
a narrow-minded philistine who is afraid of everything novel.
                                                                     p. 134

[101] *Black Hundreds*–gangs of monarchists organised by the tsarist
police to fight the revolutionary movement. They assassinated revolutionaries, attacked progressive intellectuals and staged pogroms.
                                                                     p. 151

[102] *Cadets*–members of the Constitutional-Democratic Party, the chief
party of the liberal-monarchist bourgeoisie in Russia. Founded in

October 1905, its membership was made up of representatives of the bourgeoisie, landowners and bourgeois intellectuals.

The Cadets came out against the slogan of a republic, sought to preserve the landed estates and tsarism in the form of a constitutional monarchy. They approved of the tsar's drive against the revolutionary movement. During the First World War, they supported the imperialist annexationist policy of the tsarist government.

After the October Socialist Revolution, the Cadets became the sworn enemies of the Soviet power and took part in all the counter-revolutionary acts and campaigns of the interventionists.   p. 151

103 *Mensheviks*–representatives of a petty-bourgeois, opportunist trend in the Russian Social-Democratic movement that carried bourgeois influences to the working class. (See Note 11.)

The Mensheviks pursued an opportunist line in the working-class movement, and strove to achieve an agreement between the proletariat and the bourgeoisie.

After the February 1917 Revolution they joined the Socialist-Revolutionaries in taking part in the bourgeois Provisional Government, supported its imperialist policy and fought against the mounting proletarian revolution. After the October Socialist Revolution, they became a counter-revolutionary party that organised and took part in conspiracies and revolts against the Soviet power.
                                                           p. 151

104 The reference is to the plot to surrender Petrograd, led by a counter-revolutionary organisation which co-ordinated the anti-Soviet and espionage activities of a number of groups. It was headed by a "national centre". On the night of June 12, 1919, the plotters raised a revolt at the Krasnaya Gorka fort, one of the most important fortified approaches to Petrograd. Coastal Red Army units, volunteer detachments and ships and planes of the Baltic fleet were sent against the counter-revolutionary insurrectionists. The revolt was put down on the night of June 15; the counter-revolutionary organisation which master-minded the plot was exposed and broken up.   p. 151

105 *Berne International*–an alliance of social-chauvinist and Centrist parties formed at a conference in Berne in February 1919 with the object of re-establishing the Second International.   p. 153

106 The *Battle of Sadowa* (a village in Bohemia, near the town of Hradec Králové (Königgrätz) took place on July 3, 1866. Austria was routed and this decided the outcome of the Austro-Prussian war.   p. 156

107 The reference is to the Party Programme adopted at the Eighth Congress of the R.C.P.(B.), which was held in March 1919.   p. 159

108 See Marx, *Capital*, Vol. I, p. 302.   p. 160

109 By a decree of March 16, 1919, the Council of People's Commissars amalgamated and reorganised the consumers' co-operatives under

the name of "Consumers' Communes". In some parts of the country this name was misinterpreted, and so the All-Russia Central Executive Committee, in its decision of June 30, 1919, which approved the decree, adopted the more familiar name of "Consumers' Co-operative Society".   p. 163

[110] *The Constituent Assembly* was convened by the Soviet government on January 5, 1918. The elections had been held, in the main, before the October Revolution, so that the Assembly was a reflection of the period when power had been in the hands of the Mensheviks, the Socialist-Revolutionaries and the Cadets. The policy of the Menshevik Socialist-Revolutionary and Cadet majority of the Assembly, which spoke for the bourgeoisie and the kulaks, was in sharp contrast to the will of the vast majority of the population, which had found expression in the establishment of the Soviet power and in the various Soviet decrees.

The Constituent Assembly refused to discuss the Bolshevik Declaration on the Rights of the Toiling and Exploited People nor to endorse the decrees of the Second Congress of Soviets on peace, land and the transfer of power to the Soviets.

After reading out the Declaration the Bolshevik members left the Assembly, which had fully revealed its hostility to the interests of the working people. On January 7, 1918, the Constituent Assembly was dissolved by a decree of the All-Russia Central Executive Committee.   p. 174

[111] See Engels, *Anti-Dühring*, Moscow, pp. 148-49.   p. 177

[112] The article remained unfinished.   p. 177

[113] The *Moscow City Conference of the R.P.C.(B.)* was held on December 20-21, 1919. Its agenda included the convocation of an All-Russia Party Conference, the fuel problem, subbotniks, measures of combating the typhus epidemic, the food situation in Moscow, universal military training, and special detachments.   p. 178

[114] *The Third, Communist International*—an international revolutionary proletarian organisation, an alliance of Communist parties of various countries, founded in March 1919.

It played a great part in exposing the opportunists in the labour movement, restoring contacts between the working people of different countries and founding and strengthening the Communist parties.   p. 180

[115] The reference is to the "Theses of the Central Committee of the Russian Communist Party (Bolsheviks) on the Situation of the Eastern Front", written April 11, 1919. It was an appeal to all Party organisations and all trade unions "to set to work in a revolutionary way".   p. 182

[116] The reference is to the counter-revolutionary revolt staged in August 1917 by the bourgeoisie and the landowners and led by the Army Supreme Commander-in-Chief General Kornilov. Their object was to seize Petrograd, crush the Bolshevik Party, disband the Soviets,

establish a military dictatorship and prepare the restoration of the autocracy.

The Kornilov revolt was suppressed by the workers and peasants, who were led by the Bolshevik Party.   p. 186

[117] The reference is to the military-monarchist putsch in Germany organised under the leadership of the landowner W. Kapp and Generals Ludendorff, Seeckt and Luttwitz which became known as the "Kapp Putsch". On March 13, 1920, army units under the Kappists advanced on Berlin and, meeting with no resistance from the Social-Democratic government, they declared it dissolved and set up a military junta. The German workers responded with a general strike and on March 17, under pressure from the working class, Kapp's government fell and state power reverted to the Social-Democrats.   p. 186

[118] *The Third All-Russia Congress of the Russian Young Communist League* was held in Moscow, October 2-10, 1920. Lenin spoke at the first sitting of the Congress on the evening of October 2.

Proceeding from Lenin's instructions, the Congress laid particular stress on the following programme demand:

"The main task of the Russian Young Communist League is communist education of the working young people, which should combine academic studies with active participation in the nation's life, work, struggle and creative activities. The activity of the R.Y.C.L. in all spheres should be subordinated to this task of communist upbringing of the youth, of training energetic and capable organisers of the socialist economy, defenders of the Soviet Republic and builders of a new society."   p. 189

[119] *Sukharevka*—a market at Sukharevskaya Square (now Kolkhoznaya Square) in Moscow. In 1917-20 it was the chief "black market" and was closed by a decision of the Presidium of the Moscow Soviet on December 13, 1920.   p. 207

[120] On November 14, 1920, at the invitation of peasants, Lenin and N. K. Krupskaya attended the opening of the electric power station in Kashino Village, Volokolamsk Uyezd, Moscow Gubernia.   p. 209

[121] Lenin's ideas on co-operation in the countryside served as the guiding principles for the Thirteenth Party Congress resolutions on "Co-operation" and on "Work in the Countryside". The fundamental Party line on this question, it was pointed out, has been outlined in Lenin's last article "On Co-operation".

Lenin elaborated in it a programme of organising the peasants into co-operatives, as the main means of achieving socialism in a peasant country. The present situation in the country shows with striking clarity the correctness of the path indicated by Lenin and calls on the Party to concentrate its main attention first of all on organising co-operatives of small producers, which will play a gigantic part in building socialism.   p. 211

[122] *The New Economic Policy* (NEP)—the economic policy of the proletarian state in the period of transition from capitalism to socialism. Called new in contrast to "War Communism", the economic policy,

which the Soviet government had to pursue in the period of the foreign military intervention and the Civil War (1918-20), was based on extreme centralisation of industry and distribution, prohibition of free marketing, and the system of requisitioning under which the peasants were obliged to deliver to the state all surplus products.

Under the New Economic Policy trade became the basic form of contact between socialist industry and small peasant farming. With the abolition of requisitioning in favour of a tax in kind, the peasants were able to dispose of their surplus products at will, sell them on the market and purchase the manufactured goods they needed.

The New Economic Policy gave a certain margin to capitalist enterprise, but the basic economic positions were retained by the proletarian state. NEP envisaged a struggle between the socialist and capitalist elements, with the restriction, ousting, and eventual elimination of the capitalist elements and reorganisation of the small peasant and handicraft economy along socialist lines.   p. 211

[123] "*Left Communists*"–an opportunist group within the R.C.P.(B.) led by Bukharin; it was formed early in 1918 in connection with the Brest Peace issue. Behind a screen of Leftist phraseology and appeals for a "revolutionary war", the group advocated an adventuristic policy that would have drawn the unarmed Soviet republic into a war with imperialist Germany and would have jeopardised the very existence of Soviet power. The "Left Communists" also opposed one-man management, labour discipline and employment of bourgeois experts in industry. Led by Lenin, the Party defeated the policy of the "Left Communists".   p. 215

[124] Written by Lenin in response to the third and fourth books of *Notes about the Revolution* by the prominent Menshevik N. Sukhanov.   p. 219

[125] The reference here seems to be to Marx's characterisation of the Paris Commune as "a highly flexible political form" in his work *The Civil War in France* (see Marx and Engels, *Selected Works*, Vol. I, Moscow, 1962, p. 552) and his high appraisal of "the flexibility of the Parisians" given in his letter to Kugelmann dated April 12, 1871 (*ibid.*, Vol. II, p. 463).   p. 219

[126] The reference is to Marx's letter to Engels of April 16, 1856, in which he says, "the whole thing in Germany will depend on the possibility of backing the proletarian revolution by some second edition of the Peasant War. Then the affair will be splendid." (See Marx and Engels, *Selected Correspondence*, Moscow, 1955, p. 111.)   p. 219

[127] See Note 97.   p. 222

[128] See Note 122.   p. 222

NAME INDEX

A

Adler, Friedrich (1879-1960) – Austrian Social-Democratic leader, a theoretician of Austro-Marxism, which covered its renunciation of revolutionary Marxism and the class struggle of the proletariat by a screen of Marxist phraseology – 168

Alexander II (Romanov) (1818-1881) – Russian emperor (1855-1881) – 55, 56

Arakcheyev, Alexei Andreyevich (1769-1834) – arch-reactionary tsarist statesman, Minister of War in the reign of Alexander I. His name is associated with a long period of police tyranny, brutal militarism, spying, bribery, corruption and soulless petty formalism – known as the "Arakcheyev regime" – 52

B

Bakunin, Mikhail Alexandrovich (1814-1876) – Russian revolutionary leader, who preached anarchism – 54

Bebel, August (1840-1913) – outstanding leader of the German Social-Democratic Party and of the international working-class movement; vigorously opposed revisionism and reformism in the German labour movement – 91-92, 96

Belinsky, Vissarion Grigoryevich (1811-1848) – Russian revolutionary democrat, outstanding literary critic, publicist and materialist philosopher – 117

Bernstein, Eduard (1850-1932) – leader of the extreme opportunist wing of the German Social-Democratic Party and of the Second International, ideologist of revisionism and reformism. In his writings he opposed the basic tenets of revolutionary Marxism: the theory of the socialist revolution, the dictatorship of the proletariat and the inevitability of transition from capitalism to socialism – 12, 33

Biron, Ernst Johann (1690-1772) – a favourite of the Russian Empress Anna Ioannovna. He established a regime of terror in Russia; he Prussianised the Russian state apparatus and abused his position by dipping his hands into the state treasury, taking bribes and engaging in speculation – 52

Bismarck, Otto Eduard Leopold (1815-1898) – Prussian statesman and diplomat; first Chancellor of the German Empire (1871-1890). He forcibly united Germany under Prussian domination; author of the Anti-Socialist Law (1878-1890) −83

Bracke, Wilhelm (1842-1880)− German Social-Democrat, one of the founders and leaders of the Social-Democratic Workers' Party of Germany (Eisenachers) (1869). Played an important part in publishing and circulating Party literature−91

Bukharin, Nikolai Ivanovich (1888-1938)−joined the R.C.P.(B.) in 1906; worked as a Party propagandist in various districts in Moscow. After the October Revolution he held responsible posts in the Party; repeatedly opposed the Party Leninist line, for which he was expelled from the Party in 1937−206

C

Chernenkov, B. N. (b. 1883)− Socialist-Revolutionary, a statistician−165

Chernov, Viktor Mikhailovich (1876-1952)−a leader of the Socialist-Revolutionary Party; Minister of Agriculture in the bourgeois Provisional Government. After the Socialist Revolution of October 1917 helped to organise the counter-revolution. Emigrated in 1920 and continued anti-Soviet activities abroad−73, 89, 104, 173, 174

Chernyshevsky, Nikolai Gavrilovich (1828-1889)−outstanding Russian revolutionary democrat, utopian socialist, writer and literary critic, leader of the revolutionary-democratic movement of the 1850-60s in Russia, a forerunner of Russian Social-Democrats−55, 56, 58, 130

Cornelissen, Christian−Dutch anarchist; during the First World War (1914-18) adopted a social-chauvinist stand−104

D

Dan, Fyodor Ivanovich (1871-1947)−a Menshevik leader− 88-89

Danielson, Nikolai Frantsevich (Nik −on, Nikolai −on) (1844-1918)−Russian economist writer, ideologist of Liberal Narodism of the 1880-90s− 18, 38

Darwin, Charles Robert (1809-1882)−great English naturalist, founder of scientific biology based on the theory of evolution−9-10

David, Eduard (1863-1930)− Right-wing leader of the German Social-Democrats, revisionist, economist by profession. In 1894 took part in drafting the Party's agrarian programme. He advocated revision of Marxist teachings on the agrarian question, sought to prove the stability of small-scale peasant farming under capitalism. In 1903 he published Socialism and Agriculture, which Lenin called "the main revisionist work on the agrarian question"−18, 27

Denikin, Anton Ivanovich (1872-1947)−tsarist general. During the Civil War commanded the whiteguard army in the south of Russia. In the summer of 1919 he launched an offensive on Moscow, but was defeated by the Red Army by the beginning of 1920−201

Dobrolyubov, Nikolai Alexandrovich (1836-1861)−outstanding Russian revolutionary democrat, literary critic and materialist philosopher, a close friend and associate of Chernyshevsky's−55, 130

E

Engels, Frederick (1820-1895)—
11, 12, 46, 47, 68-69, 78, 79,
80, 81, 82, 83, 91-92, 96, 104,
107, 129, 176-77

F

Feuerbach, Ludwig Andreas
(1804-1872)—a leading German
materialist philosopher of the
pre-Marxian period—53

Feofilaktov, A. Y.—Left Socialist-
Revolutionary, delegate to the
Extraordinary Congress of
Peasants' Deputies in Novem-
ber 1917—113

Foch, Ferdinand (1851-1929)—
French Marshal. During the
First World War was Chief of
the General Staff (from May
1917) and Supreme Commander-in-Chief of the Allied forces
(from April 1918); one of the
organisers of the military intervention against Soviet Russia in 1918-20—156

G

George, Henry (1839-1897)—
American bourgeois economist
and publicist; advocated the
nationalisation of land by the
bourgeois state as a means of
overcoming all the social
antagonisms existing under
capitalism; tried to lead the
American workers' movement
towards bourgeois reformism
—63

Ghe, Alexander (d. 1919)—
Russian anarchist; after the
October Socialist Revolution
supported the Soviet government—105

Grave, Jean (1854-1939)—French
petty-bourgeois socialist, theoretician of anarchism; during

the First World War adopted
a social-chauvinist stand—104

H

Hegel, Georg Wilhelm Friedrich
(1770-1831)—classical German
philosopher, objective idealist,
an ideologist of the German
bourgeoisie. Hegel elaborated
idealist dialectics, which
served as a theoretical source
of dialectical materialism—52

Hertz, Friedrich Otto (b. 1878)
—Austrian Social-Democrat,
revisionist; opposed Marxist
teachings on the agrarian
question in his book *Die
Agrarischen Fragen im Ver-
hältnis zum Sozialismus*
(*Agrarian Questions from the
Viewpoint of Socialism*).
Translated into Russian, this
book was used by Chernov
and other bourgeois apolo-
gists in their struggle against
Marxism—18

Herzen, Alexander Ivanovich
(1812-1870)—Russian revolu-
tionary-democrat, materialist
philosopher, writer and publicist. Lenin describes Herzen's
role in the emancipation
movement in Russia in the
article "In Memory of Herzen"—52-58, 60

Hindenburg, Paul von (1847-
1934)—German statesman.
Commander-in-Chief of the
German Army, represented
the reactionary and chauvin-
ist-minded circles of the German imperialist bourgeoisie—
156

Holyoak, George Jacob (1817-
1906)—a leader of the co-
operative movement in Britain,
reformist—81

J

Jacoby, Johann (1805-1877) – German publicist and politician, a physician by profession. Marx and Engels thought highly of him as a democrat who had joined the proletarian movement, though they disagreed with him on many points – 156

K

Kapp, Wolfgang (1858-1922) – German Junker; fled to Sweden in March 1920 after the abortive military-monarchist putsch, led by him, in Germany – 186

Karpinsky, V. A. (V. Kalinin) (b. 1880) – one of the oldest active members of the C.P.S.U.; a Party writer and propagandist – 41

Kautsky, Karl (1854-1938) – a leader of the German Social-Democratic Party and of the Second International; ideologist of Centrism, i.e., of the most dangerous and harmful brand of opportunism; subsequently became a renegade from Marxism – 113, 154, 160, 168, 172, 173, 174, 222

Kavelin, Konstantin Dmitrievich (1818-1885) – Russian bourgeois-liberal historian and lawyer. In the period of preparation for and during the Peasant Reform of 1861 opposed the revolutionary-democratic movement and supported the reactionary policy of the tsarist autocracy – 56

Kerensky, Alexander Fyodorovich (b. 1881) – Socialist-Revolutionary. After the February 1917 bourgeois-democratic revolution entered the bourgeois Provisional Government as Minister of Justice, later as Minister for War and finally Prime Minister and Supreme Commander-in-Chief. After the October Socialist Revolution fought against the Soviet Government; fled the country in 1918–89, 110, 125, 126

Kolchak, Alexander Vasilyevich (1873-1920) – tsarist admiral, monarchist. After the October Socialist Revolution proclaimed himself supreme ruler of Russia, heading the military bourgeois-landowner dictatorship, which he established in Siberia, in the Far East and the Urals. His troops were defeated by the Red Army early in 1920 – 201

Kornilov, Lavr Georgiyevich (1870-1918) – tsarist general, monarchist; supreme commander-in-chief of the counter-revolutionary forces in Russia in 1917-18; following the October Socialist Revolution headed the whiteguard Volunteer Army – 89, 125, 126, 186

Kostrov (Jordania, Noi Nikolayevich) (1870-1953) – Social-Democrat, leader of Georgian Mensheviks – 46

Kropotkin, Pyotr Alexeyevich (1842-1921) – a leader of the revolutionary movement in Russia and chief theoretician of anarchism. During the First World War (1914-18) adopted a social-chauvinist stand – 104

Kugelmann, Ludwig (1830-1902) – German Social-Democrat, a friend of Marx; participated in the 1848-49 Revolution in Germany; member of the First International. Between 1862 and 1874 corresponded with Karl Marx, who lived in London, informing him of the state of affairs in Germany—83

L

Larin, Y. (1882-1932)—Russian Social-Democrat, Menshevik, in 1917 joined the R.S.D.L.P.(B.)—46, 47, 48

Lassalle, Ferdinand (1825-1864)—German petty-bourgeois socialist, a founder of the General German Workers' Union, which played a significant role in the labour movement. However, Lassalle, who was elected President, made it veer towards opportunism. His theoretical and political views were sharply criticised by Marx and Engels—83, 91, 98, 99, 100

Lenin (Ulyanov), V. I. (1870-1924)—38, 110, 189

Lensch, Paul (1873-1926)—German Social-Democrat, during the First World War (1914-1918) adopted a social-chauvinist stand; after the war was editor of *Deutsche Allgemeine Zeitung*, mouthpiece of the Ruhr industrial magnates —88

Liebknecht, Wilhelm (1826-1900)—outstanding leader of the German and international working-class movement; one of the founders and leaders of the German Social-Democratic Party—83

Longuet, Jean (1876-1938)—a leader of the French Socialist Party and of the Second International; publicist—168

M

MacDonald, James Ramsay (1866-1937)—British politician, one of the founders and leaders of the Labour Party; pursued an extremely opportunist policy in the Party and in the Second International; advocated a reactionary theory of class collaboration and of the gradual growing of capitalism into socialism—168

Martov, L. (Tsederbaum, Yuly Osipovich) (1873-1923)—a Menshevik leader. After the October Revolution became an enemy of the Soviet government. In 1920 emigrated to Germany—130, 154, 173, 174

Marx, Karl (1818-1883)—9, 10, 11, 12, 33, 37, 38, 54, 63, 67, 71, 72, 74, 76, 77, 78, 79, 80, 81, 82, 83, 91, 92, 95, 98, 99, 100, 101, 102, 105, 122, 160, 192, 193, 219, 221

Mikhailovsky, Nikolai Konstantinovich (1842-1904)—Russian sociologist, publicist and literary critic, outstanding theoretician of Liberal Narodism. From 1892 edited the magazine *Russkoye Bogatstvo*; in its columns waged a bitter struggle against Marxism—10

Milyukov, Pavel Nikolayevich (1859-1943)—one of the leaders of the liberal-monarchist party of Constitutional-Democrats, prominent ideologist of the Russian imperialist bourgeoisie, historian and publicist—89

Most, Johann Joseph (1846-1906)—German Social-Democrat, subsequently an anarchist—84

N

Napoleon I (1769-1821)—Emperor of France (1804-1814 and 1815)—222

Napoleon III (Louis Bonaparte) (1808-1873)—Emperor of France

(1852-70), nephew of Napoleon I–53

Nik –on, Nikolai –on–see Danielson, N. F.–18, 38

O

Owen, Robert (1771-1858)–English utopian socialist; sharply criticised the fundamental principles of the capitalist system but failed to reveal the true causes of the antagonisms existing under capitalism. He regarded the main cause of social inequality to be the lack of universal education and not the capitalist mode of production, and held that it could be eliminated by spreading knowledge and carrying out social reforms. He drew up an extensive programme of social reforms. However, he failed to put his ideas into effect–216

P

Peshekhonov, A. V. (1867-1933) –Russian bourgeois civic leader and publicist–75

Plekhanov, Georgy Valentinovich (1856-1918)–outstanding leader of the Russian and international working-class movement, the first propagandist of Marxism in Russia. However, following the Second Congress of the R.S.D.L.P. in 1903 he advocated conciliation with the opportunists and subsequently joined the Mensheviks. His attitude towards the October Socialist Revolution was negative, but he did not actively oppose the Soviet Government–12, 35, 88, 89

Pomyalovsky, Nikolai Gerasimovich (1935-1863)–Russian democratic writer of the latter half

of the 19th century, author of Sketches of Seminary Life –104

Preobrazhensky, Y. A. (1886-1937)–member of the C.P.S.U. from 1903. After the 1917 February bourgeois-democratic revolution worked in the Urals–206

Purishkevich, Vladimir Mitrofanovich (1870-1920)–wealthy landowner, monarchist, rabid reactionary; was well known in Russia for his anti-Semitic, pogromist speeches in the Duma–66, 67

R

Rakitnikov, N. I. (b. 1864)– Narodnik, subsequently a Socialist-Revolutionary, journalist–74, 75

Reitern (d. 1861)–colonel of the tsarist army; shot himself in 1861, not wishing to take part in suppressing the demonstration organised in Warsaw at the time–57

Rodbertus-Jagetzow, Johann Karl (1805-1875)–German vulgar economist and political figure–63

Rocquigny, Robert de (b. 1845) –French bourgeois economist, author of works on agricultural insurance and co-operation. In his book Les Syndicats Agricoles et leur Oeuvre (Syndicates in Agriculture and Their Activities) he preached the organisation of agricultural co-operatives, which he regarded as a means of uniting the workers with the bourgeoisie–29

Romanovs–dynasty of Russian tsars and emperors that ruled between 1613 and 1917–57

S

Schapper, Karl (1812-1870) – prominent figure in the German and international labour movement, member of the Central Committee of the Communist League; when the League split in 1850 he became one of the leaders of the sectarian ultra-"Left" group – 82

Scheidemann, Philipp (1865-1939) – leader of the extreme Right, opportunist, wing of the German Social-Democratic Party; was at the head of the German bourgeois government in February-June 1919; brutally suppressed the working-class movement in Germany in 1918-21 – 130

Serno-Solovyevich, Alexander Alexandrovich (1838-1869) – prominent figure in the revolutionary-democratic movement of the 1860s; author of the pamphlet *Our Home Affairs*, which sharply criticised Herzen's vacillations towards Liberalism – 55

Sher, V. V. (1884-1940) – Russian Social-Democrat, Menshevik – 165

Sorge, Friedrich Albert (1828-1906) – German socialist, prominent figure in the international working-class and socialist movement, personal friend and associate of Karl Marx and Frederick Engels – 46, 84

Struve, Pyotr Berngardovich (1870-1944) – bourgeois economist and publicist; outstanding representative of "legal Marxism" in the 1890s; came out with "criticism" and "revision" of Marx's economic and philosophical teachings; sought to adapt Marxism and the working-class movement to the interests of the bourgeoisie; afterwards a Cadet Party leader – 87

Sukhanov, N. (Gimmer, Nikolai Nikolayevich) (b. 1882) – Russian economist and publicist, Narodnik; afterwards joined the Mensheviks, tried to combine Narodism with Marxism. After the October Socialist Revolution worked in Soviet economic institutions – 219, 221, 222

Sun Yat-sen (1866-1925) – outstanding Chinese revolutionary democrat, leader of the Chinese revolution of 1911-13; Provisional President of the Chinese Republic in 1911-12, friend of Soviet Russia – 59, 60, 61, 62, 63

T

Taylor, Frederick Winslow (1856-1915) – American engineer, founder of a system of labour organisation, aimed at saving as much working-time as possible and making the most rational use of tools and means of production. Under capitalism this system is being used to intensify the exploitation of the working people – 127

Tsereteli, Irakly Georgiyevich (1882-1959) – a Menshevik leader; in 1917 Minister of the Interior in the bourgeois Provisional Government. After the October Socialist Revolution was one of the leaders of the counter-revolutionary Menshevik government in Georgia. When Soviet power was established in Georgia (1921), he became a counter-revolutionary émigré – 89, 104

Tugan-Baranovsky, Mikhail Ivanovich (1865-1919) – Russian

bourgeois economist, outstanding representative of "legal Marxism" in the 1890s; later joined the Cadet Party —100

Turgenev, Ivan Sergeyevich (1818-1883)—Russian liberal writer—56-57, 130

V

Vikhlyaev, P. A. (1869-1928)— Liberal Narodnik, statistician and agronomist; wrote several statistical surveys of peasant farming in tsarist Russia, in which he denied that there was class differentiation among the peasantry and extolled the peasant commune— 73

Vorontsov, Vasily Pavlovich (V. V.). (1847-1918)—economist and publicist, ideologist of Liberal Narodism of the 1880-1890s; wrote a number of books in which he maintained that there was no prospect of development of capitalism in Russia, extolled petty commodity production and idealised the peasant commune. Lenin sharply criticised his views in many of his writings —18, 21, 38

W

Willich, August (1810-1878)— Prussian officer, took part in the revolutionary movement in Germany in 1849, one of the leaders of the adventurist, sectarian ultra-"Left" group, which broke away from the Communist League in 1850-82

Y

Yüan Shih-kai (1859-1916)— Chinese general and reactionary statesman. After the defeat of the Chinese revolution of 1911-13 became President of China, establishing a military dictatorship—61, 64